Life★Time
Astrology

A.T. Mann

Harper & Row, Publishers, San Francisco

Cambridge, Hagerstown, New York, Philadelphia, Washington
London, Mexico City, São Paulo, Singapore, Sydney

FIRST U.S. EDITION PUBLISHED 1988.

This work was originally published in Great Britain by George Allen &
Unwin, Ltd. It is here reprinted by arrangement with Unwin Hyman, Ltd.

Library of Congress Cataloging-in-Publication Data

Mann, A. T., 1943-
    Life time astrology.

    Includes index.
    1. Astrology. I. Title.
BF1708.1.M366 1988   133.5   87-46217
ISBN 0-06-250586-6

88 89 90 91 92 MCN 10 9 8 7 6 5 4 3 2 1

★ *Acknowledgements* ★

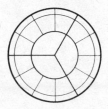

To the American Federation of Astrologers, Inc, PO Box 22040, Tempe, Arizona 85282, USA, for kind permission to reproduce pages from Reinhold Ebertin's *Combination of Stellar Influences*, and to Dr Baldur Ebertin for his kind permission to reproduce this reflection of the great work of Cosmobiology.

To Arthur Balaskas for early contacts and encouragement. Caradoc King of A P Watt Ltd has assisted throughout the writing of the book in his capacity as my literary agent and advisor. To Marion Nicholls and Diedre Stonebridge for their secretarial assistance.

For support in developing the computer programs integral to Life★Time Astrology, I thank Michael Erlewine and Doug Pierce of Matrix Software in Big Rapids, Michigan, for their calculation routines and for the use of their superb M65 Chart and Research System; Wim Van Dam of Holland for the first Log Time Scale program; and Ad Strack van Schijndel of Holland for very helpful routines. All further development on the Log Time Scale programs was done in close collaboration with John Astrop, who cannot be thanked enough: credit also to him for the drawing on p. 65.

I would especially like to acknowledge Margo Russell for her essential and valuable editing of the text and for her insistence that this book be clear and explicit in all ways.

To the more than 1000 people for whom I have done readings using the principles of Life★Time Astrology over the last twelve years, a great credit is due. I owe them my sincere support for their trust, verification and criticism of the noble art and science of astrology.

★ Symbol Keys ★

		Sign	Symbol	Dates
♈	AR	Aries	Ram	21 Mar to 21 Apr
♉	TA	Taurus	Bull	21 Apr to 22 May
♊	GE	Gemini	Twins	22 May to 22 Jun
♋	CN	Cancer	Crab	22 Jun to 23 Jul
♌	LE	Leo	Lion	23 Jul to 24 Aug
♍	VI	Virgo	Virgin	24 Aug to 23 Sep
♎	LI	Libra	Scales	23 Sep to 23 Oct
♏	SC	Scorpio	Scorpion	23 Oct to 23 Nov
♐	SG	Sagittarius	Centaur	23 Nov to 22 Dec
♑	CP	Capricorn	Goat	22 Dec to 21 Jan
♒	AQ	Aquarius	Waterbearer	21 Jan to 19 Feb
♓	PI	Pisces	Fishes	19 Feb to 21 Mar

		Planet	Principle	Cycle
☉	SU	Sun	Spirit	1 year
☾	MO	Moon	Soul	29½ days
☿	ME	Mercury	Mind	88 days
♀	VE	Venus	Harmony	225 days
♂	MA	Mars	Conflict	687 days
♃	JU	Jupiter	Expansion	12 years
♄	SA	Saturn	Contraction	29½ years
♅	UR	Uranus	Rhythm	84 years
♆	NE	Neptune	Sensitivity	165 years
♇	PL	Pluto	Regeneration	270 years
☊	NO	Node	Association	19 years
	AS	Ascendant	Personality	1 day
	MC	Midheaven	Ego	1 day

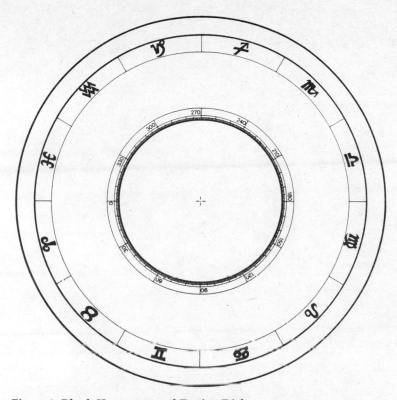

Figure 1: Blank Horoscope and Dating Disk
This blank is for your horoscope. Photocopy this page for additional blanks and cut the disk out for dating planets. Superimpose this disk over the horoscope with 0 on the ASC to read the correct dates in life directly from the wheel. On page 56 you will find a smaller disk which may be used with all the example horoscopes in this book.

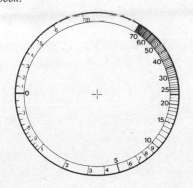

★ *Table of Contents* ★

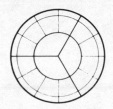

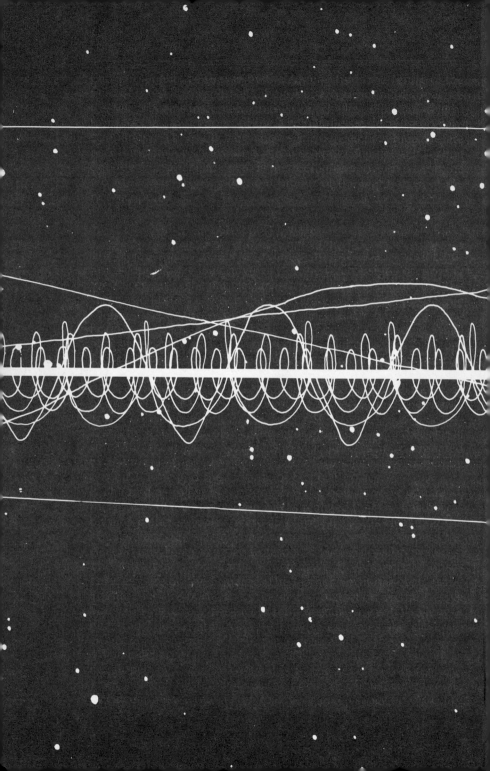

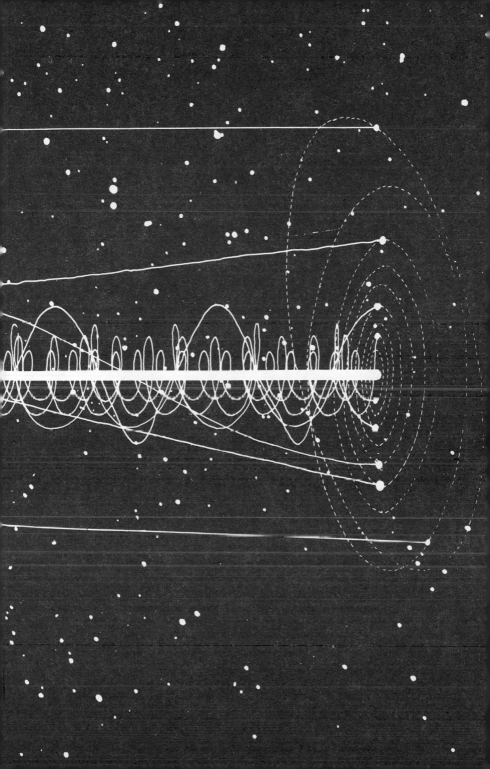

'. . .the journey through the planetary houses boils down to becoming conscious of the good and bad qualities in our character, and the apotheosis means no more than maximum consciousness; which amounts to maximum freedom of will.'

Carl Gustav Jung, 'Mysterium Coniunctionis'

Figure 2: The Spiral Solar System
The central filament is the Sun travelling through space, round which the planetary paths spiral in their order from the Sun. Earth is the third planet out, and as we can see twelve complete cycles, the diagram shows twelve earth years of time.

★ Introduction ★

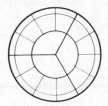

Our world is in crisis. Familiar structures and systems are breaking down, and chaos and destruction seem to be approaching at an accelerating pace. Political, ecological, financial, marital or health crises affect virtually every person alive today. If we are to survive, we must transform our mechanistic world view into an ecological one; the mania for analysis into creative synthesis; the rigidity of masculine hierarchy into feminine circularity; and the reduction of parts into a dynamic wholism. Although we align ourselves on either side of the major outer issues of our time, the primary battleground is within each of us. The current holistic/transpersonal movement embodies a desire for individual unity as the first step to healing our world. We must start the unification process within ourselves and in our lives. As recognized in the New Physics, mind and matter are interdependent. The world is a dynamic web of relations and we are the world in our lives and actions.

Life★Time Astrology presents a new and revolutionary way for understanding ourself and the world. The astrological pattern is a key to a *'knowledge of time'* and the ultimate tool for guiding us toward our natural condition of wholeness.

Although it is commonly believed that the planets orbit around the sun, our entire solar system moves through space at about two million kilometres per day, so that the planets appear to spiral around the central bright path of the sun as filaments enwrapping a live wire, like a cosmic step-down transformer of energy and light. Through time our solar system traces out a complex cylinder, as shown in Figure 2. Each complete revolution of our earth, the third planet out from the sun, is one year. The illustration shows twelve years of time.

The astrological horoscope is a slice through the cylinder at an angle reflecting an exact time and place of birth. Every being born on earth has its own relative slice through the identical spiralling circus, which provides us with a cosmic unity of origin. We all see the same earth and solar system from a multitude of different but relative and successive vantage points.

The spiral of our solar system through time is similar in form to models of the double helix of the genetic code DNA, which is also a pattern in time: both encode the entire process of life. If the spiralling solar system were drawn with the earth's path as a straight line, it would trace out a double helix. A cross-section of DNA describes an encoded biological instruction just as an astrological horoscope describes a moment in life. The movements of the planets in space mirror the structure of the genetic code in the cell. Humankind is exactly halfway between these two reciprocal systems, and astrology is the medium through which this connection can be made. This concept gives credence to the ancient axioms, *'as above, so below'* and *'the microcosm is the macrocosm'*.

By superimposing a time scale over the horoscope (Figure 3), Life★Time Astrology allows us to reconstruct our life from conception to the present, and from the present into the future. The system enables us to date, describe and understand the events of our life, the individuals who affect us and the interrelationship between events and people which is our life. The inclusion of a specific date for each planetary event makes astrological interpretation more accurate and relevant. Although they are inherent at conception, our life characteristics unfold as our life develops. The unfoldment of life as a process in time is the only way to understand the inherent unity of our own lives, and is a necessity before we can achieve unity with others.

We all live in accordance with an identical sequence of developmental stages. We are conceived, carried within our mother's body, born into the world, experience childhood and live out our various possibilities during maturity. The events which define life occupy moments from conception to death, except those which transcend time and space altogether. Life★Time Astrology is unique because its time scale reflects the relative, changing perceptions of time as we age, and

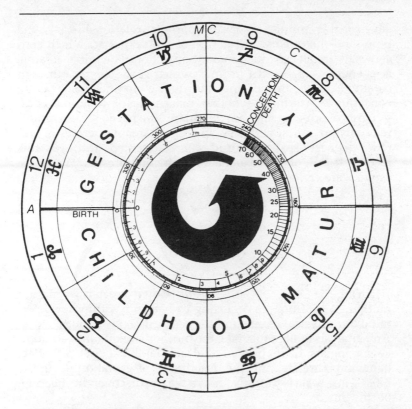

Figure 3: Life★Time Astrology Houses
Life★Time Astrology grades the houses from conception at the beginning of the 9th House round to the archetypal death moment, also at the 9th House cusp. The average dates for each house developmental time are shown in the central ring.

describes both our inner and outer realities.

Due to biological time and the nature of memory, time passes slowly when we are young, and more quickly as we age. Due to our subjective time sense or inner clock, the earlier events in our life carry more importance than later events. The Life★Time scale allows the relative importance of all life events and perceptions to be determined, because it is mathematically based upon the rate at which our perceptions change – the first astrological system to do so.

The process of life begins before conception when our parents first have the impulse to conceive us. Which parent is responsible for this impulse, what our parents' relationship is at the time, and the quality and nature of the sexual act which conceives us are all described in our horoscope. The initial creative act generates a 'pattern in time' which is the key to our own creativity; past, present and future. The circumstances before conception determine whether masculine or feminine components of our character are dominant, the nature of their interrelationship and how this creative mechanism operates in life. Our deepest sexual attitudes are clarified through this reconstruction of the sexual act which generates us. We create as we were created!

During the *Octave of Gestation* our body is created within our mother. All influences occurring to her and within her determine our physical reality and the deepest levels of our psyche. Any analysis of life must take the mother's reality into account. Psychologists have proven that prenatal experiences affect behaviour directly, and the description of gestation using the Life★Time scale is the only known way to discover the meaning of this time.

The moment of birth signals our transition to the *Octave of Childhood*. As the body is created during gestation, the personality is determined by the circumstances of birth and develops in childhood within the home and family. An easy birth allows the personality to express itself easily; a long arduous labour means difficulty in self expression; surgery leads to others intervening in our personality; and delivery by a team of doctors, nurses and anaesthetists makes for a dependency upon group situations throughout life. Everyone present at our birth and those affecting us from afar show up as planets near or in aspect to our rising sign and become components of our personality. The first seven years are described in reference to the family system of parents and siblings within the home.

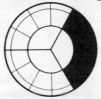

At about seven years old begins the developmental *Octave of Maturity*, when body integrates with personality and the resultant combination is projected into the world to work out the various possibilities. Critical events of both outer and inner meaning appear as planets during these three octaves of life. When all the possibilities are exhausted, life ends.

If we are able to extend our reality beyond the confines of our own personal world view, an *Octave of Transcendence* is available, which describes the higher implications of the circumstances of our gestation. This overlap on a higher level completes the circle like the ouroburos snake of eternity which bites its tail. Transcendence is the key to true creativity and wholeness.

When the sequence of twelve developmental stages, the *houses* of astrology, is superimposed upon our horoscope, we can see life as a process in time. Early events condition later events; later events become more and more complex. The causes of all our ways of being lie within our horoscope, waiting to be decoded. Life★Time Astrology makes the quest for discovery become reality.

The uses of such an interpretive technique are many. A mother can experience pregnancy and childbirth with a greater comprehension of those influences which are likely to affect her newborn child. Parents can understand the capabilities and potential of their children from birth onwards, in order to facilitate and enlighten childrearing. The psychologist can

identify at a glance those times at which the traumas at the root
of psychic disorders were formed: who was responsible for
them, and what may be done to rectify their equivalent
psychological states. Doctors and healers may discover the
causes of physical and psychosomatic afflictions undetected by
conventional diagnostics. For all those aspiring to self-
discovery, the potential for exploration and realization of our
entire life from conception to the grave is unlimited.

The only proof of any scientific, psychological or astrological
theory is its relevance for us. In the chapter *Your Story* the
analysis of the horoscope is presented so that we can follow
along with our own horoscope and reconstruct our own life.
Please note that John Lennon's horoscope is used throughout
Life★Time Astrology to illustrate structural techniques and is
analysed in depth in the chapter on *Complete Interpretation*.

The computation of a horoscope, while not a difficult process,
entails many calculations and reference books. Life★Time
Astrology is intended to introduce the operation and practice of
the time scale and does not include information regarding
horoscope construction. It is suggested that you use one of the
many astrological computer services, (including *Life★Time
Service* designed specifically for the time scale) to have your own
birth horoscope constructed (See Appendix C). If you wish to
learn how to calculate the horoscope yourself, source books including my book, *The Round Art*, are listed in Sourcebooks.
General interpretation tables are included in Chapter Six, but
should you require more detail other sources are also listed.
Once you understand the theory and application of Life★Time
Astrology, more specialized texts will allow interpretation in
greater depth from the German schools of Ebertin or Witte;
from the psychological orientation of Jung and others; from a
Theosophical viewpoint; from esoteric revelation; and from a
seemingly endless range of alternative viewpoints. The rec-
ommended interpretive text is Ebertin's *The Combination of
Stellar Influences*, two pages of which are reproduced on page
100-101.

Life★Time Astrology is a valuable guide as we seek to decode
the pattern of our unfoldment through time – the process of
conception, gestation, birth, childhood and maturity – and the
prediction of future opportunities for the realization of our
potential. To know ourselves is the first condition of enlighten-
ment and the transformation of the quality of our life and all life.

★ Chapter One ★
The Zodiac

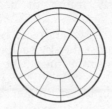

Early humans were aware of the Sun, Moon, planets and stars as a necessity of survival. The Sun rises, moves across the sky creating heat and light, and sets in the evening, and it was worshipped as the source of life. The Moon wanders across the sky and changes her shape continually. On nights when the Moon was out, men could hunt and travel, but when it was hidden they were forced to remain where they were. The tidal rhythm of the Moon was integral to everyone because men were forced to comply outwardly, and the monthly menstrual cycle bound women to the Moon inwardly. We all retain instinctive links to the luminaries in the sky.

The Sun and Moon also measured time. The position of the Sun measured time during the day and year, while the Moon measured time during the month. Longer periods of time were measured by moons (months) or by suns (years). The two were combined in the year subdivided into months.

It was inevitable that early humankind would observe correspondences between repetitive heavenly motions and earthly events, and the study of such correspondences became astrology. We still date significant events of our culture by day, month and year, but the astrological correlations have been ignored. Modern man remembers and celebrates yearly anniversaries, as well as tenth, twenty-fifth, fiftieth and century returns of the dates of significant past events, but has lost the meaning of natural cycles.

The stars are apparently fixed positions against which the Sun, Moon and other planets move. As the seasons change during the year, the Sun rises and sets accompanied by dif-

ferent groups of stars in sequence. The band of fixed stars along
which the planets move is the *Zodiac*. Individual groupings of
stars along the zodiac are named after the animals which
represented the yearly round of activities and seasonal
qualities.

The band of zodiac constellations is circular and appears to
repeat its movement across the sky each day due to the rotation
of the Earth. Against this movement, the Moon moves through
the entire zodiac every month and the Sun every year. The
other planets take longer to circumnavigate the zodiac: Saturn,
for example, takes thirty years to pass through the twelve signs.
Each heavenly body passes through the round of signs and
returns to its starting point to begin another cycle. Time is circular and repetitive.

Throughout thousands of years basic observations were
made by people living outside. Herdsmen, wanderers, explorers, navigators, farmers, hunters and warriors all benefited
from knowing that when the moon was new it was going to be
dark throughout the night; when it would get colder in the
year; when to plant and when to harvest; and when to act and
when to remain passive. Priestly castes based much of their
power upon knowledge of the times of eclipses, of comets and
of the appearances of the stellar bodies. Those who did not attempt to attain and use this information often paid with their
lives. Those who tried to understand Time created the early
civilizations.

The Babylonians transformed the zodiac from irregularly
spaced constellations to a measuring circle of 360 degrees,
divided into twelve equal 30 degree signs which are correspon-
dent to the solstices and equinoxes. The adjustment was made
because of the *Precession of the Equinoxes*. The earth has an eccentric movement around its polar axis, like an erratic top (Figure
4), and as a result of this wobble, the zodiac constellations do
not align with their original equivalent yearly times. The
Babylonians altered the 360 degree sequence of signs so that
they stayed in alignment with the beginnings of the four
seasons. The beginning of the astrological and astronomical
year is the Spring Equinox (March 21), when day is equal to
night and the days are getting longer. This is equivalent to zero
degrees of the first sign, Aries. The beginning (cusp) of Cancer
coincides with the longest day in the year, the Summer Solstice
(June 21). In Libra day again balances night, but the days
shorten after the Autumn Equinox (September 21). At the

Figure 4: Earth's Axial Wobble
The Earth spins like an eccentric top around its axis, which is angular to the plane of the solar system. The axis itself revolves in the opposite direction, passing through the twelve signs in reverse order every 25,000 years.

Winter Solstice (December 21) day is shortest in the year, and the sign Capricorn marks the return towards Spring. At present the zodiac signs correspond to their seasonal times but do not match the constellations of the same name.

Due to the irregular solar year length of 365.24 days, it is necessary to add one day every four years (the Leap Year) to keep our calendar synchronized to the seasonal equinoxes and solstices. As a result of this correction factor, the starting days of the twelve signs vary slightly from year to year. To know our Sun sign accurately, it is necessary to have our exact horoscope calculated for the time and year of our birth. When our birthday falls near any of the dates when the signs change we are affected by both conjoining signs.

The signs and their qualities are derived from their equivalent times in the yearly cycle of nature and the characteristics associated with these times. Table 1: The Zodiac Signs, shows the signs, their approximate dates, their positions in the 360 degree measuring wheel of the zodiac, their equivalences and their traditional meanings.

The qualities of each sign, derived from its yearly time and position relative to the other signs, are imparted to a 30-degree zone in our horoscope. There are eight planets in addition to the Sun and Moon, so we cover at least four or five of the zodiac signs ourself, and possibly as many as ten. This belies the popular Sun sign astrology of newspapers and magazines, as everyone is a blend of many zodiacal qualities.

Table 1: The Zodiac Signs

♈ *Aries the Ram*   Cardinal   Masculine Fire Sign   00° – 30°
21 March to 20 April   Germinating time; unfolding energy. Self assertion; initiatory energy; adventure; daring; impatience; the personality.

♉ *Taurus the Bull*   Fixed   Feminine Earth Sign   30° – 60°
20 April to 21 May   Invigoration and strengthening; form creation; preservation. Physical world; matter; fertility; security; finances; stewardship; form; endurance.

♊ *Gemini the Twins*   Mutable   Masculine Air Sign   60° – 90°
21 May to 22 June   Diversity; multiplication; vitality; adaptability. Instinctive mind; imitation; communication; duality; versatility; mobility; facility.

♋ *Cancer the Crab*   Cardinal   Feminine Water Sign   90° – 120°
22 June to 23 July   Mothering; fecundation; fertilization. Feeling; emotions; mother; home and family; the unconscious; dreams; protective urge.

♌ *Leo the Lion*   Fixed   Masculine Fire Sign   120° – 150°
23 July to 24 August   Ripening; summer heat; full energy; extraversion; harvest. Self expression; personal love; games; pleasure; ruling; vanity; arrogance.

♍ *Virgo the Virgin*   Mutable   Feminine Earth Sign   150° – 180°
24 August to 23 September   Ripe fruit; orderly storage and collection; selection. Discrimination; work; perfectionism; health & hygiene; analysis; prudence; diet.

♎ *Libra the Balance*   Cardinal   Masculine Air Sign   180° – 210°
23 September to 24 October   Balance & adjustment; thanksgiving; social equilibration. Partnership; marriage; public relations; enemies; persuasion; sublimation; yielding.

♏ *Scorpio the Scorpion*   Fixed   Feminine Water Sign   210° – 240°
24 October to 23 November   Vegetation death; seedlife; survival; endurance. Death & regeneration; passion; separation; others; losses; inheritance; metaphysical.

♐ *Sagittarius the Centaur*   Mutable   Masculine Fire Sign   240° – 270°
23 November to 22 December   Hibernation; advent; inner life; meditation; expansion. Realization; higher mind; religion & philosophy; sport; freedom; action; rebirth.

♑ *Capricorn the Goat*   Cardinal   Feminine Earth Sign   270° – 300°
22 December to 20 January   Preservation; patience; reality; self-concentration. Perfected matter; ego objectives; organisation; power; success; society; government.

♒ *Aquarius the Waterbearer*   Fixed   Masculine Air Sign   300° – 330°
20 January to 19 February   Waiting; fasting; Lent; observation; planning; abstraction. Social consciousness; humanitarian; collective; progressive; cold; altruism; utopian.

♓ *Pisces the Fishes*   Mutable   Feminine Water Sign   330° – 360°(0°)
19 February to 21 March   Swelling seed; purifying rain; serenity; potential. Sensitivity; receptivity; self-sacrifice; psychic; karma; seclusion; hospital; dreaming.

Six of the signs are single signs and six are double signs. The single signs are Aries, Taurus, Leo, Virgo, Scorpio and Capricorn, whose images are centralized, strong, singular and refer to specific traits. Aries the Ram is initiatory and single minded. Taurus the Bull is stable and secure. Leo the Lion is strong, powerful and dominant. Virgo the Virgin is naive and discriminatory. Scorpio the Scorpion is potent but secretive. Capricorn the Goat is tenacious, tough and independent. The double signs are Gemini, Cancer, Libra, Sagittarius, Aquarius and Pisces. They are duplicatory in image and quality. They usually describe multiple personifications or dualistic concepts, and occasionally both. Gemini the Twins is a mirror-image split left-right around a vertical axis which is imitative, reflective and indicative of sibling relationships. Cancer is two emotional values, one above the other but spiralling or rotating continuously, like the Wheel of Fortune. Libra the Scales is a weighing and reciprocation of left to right, with the Scales itself as an intermediary mechanism, indicative of the counterbalancing in ideological relationships. Sagittarius the Centaur (half man-half horse) is a split of upper and lower natures. The lower horse-like influence is athletic, outdoor, sensual and materialistic, while the upper archer is directed to higher philosophical, religious or psychological matters. The two halves vie for prominence. Aquarius the Waterbearer shows two snakes wriggling in opposite directions, one above the other, and is unconsciously thinking in counterpoint to conscious words and acts. Pisces the Fishes are two emotions swimming in opposite directions tethered together at the tail, describing conflicting but interconnected feelings. Three of these double signs are attached to each other and Cancer, Libra and Aquarius have separate halves. Often such elementary clues contain interpretive data of great use.

The Horoscope

We see the solar system from the Earth (geocentrically), even though we know that the Sun is at the centre. Einstein proved that there are no absolute vantage points in the universe, so living on Earth we view the rest of the universe from this relative centre. As we see the solar system from within its plane, all planetary movements appear to follow a line around the circumference of an imaginary sphere surrounding Earth: the *Celestial Sphere*. All planetary movements are projected onto

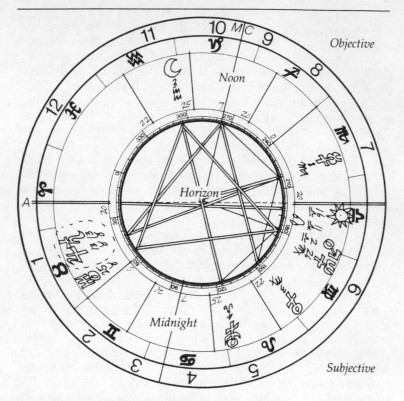

Figure 5: The Astrological Horoscope
The horizon is the dashed horizontal line across the horoscope, and the ASC is to the left. The MC is the position of the Sun above at noon and the centre of the field of consciousness. The upper half is conscious, and the lower half is unconscious. The planets move in a counter-clockwise direction round the circle. The houses are numbered round the outermost ring.

this celestial sphere along the strip of zodiac constellations.

Our *Horoscope* ('hour-pointer') locates us in space and time. It is a circular diagram (Figure 5) showing the relative positions of the Sun, Moon and planets against their background of the zodiac at the exact time and place of our birth. The centre of the horoscope represents our actual location at birth.

The horoscope circle is symbolic of the path of the Sun and planets around our birth place. The Horizon is a horizontal line across the horoscope. The horizon divides the celestial sphere into two equal hemispheres; above and below. The upper hemisphere and planets residing there are objective, conscious and direct influences reaching us directly through the atmosphere. The lower hemisphere and planets below the horizon are subjective, unconscious and indirect influences because they must pass through the entire mass of the Earth to reach us. The Sun passes across the upper hemisphere during the day and the lower during the night. The oppositions of light and dark, objective and subjective, conscious and unconscious, direct and indirect are primary divisions in life.

To the left of the horoscope is the Eastern Horizon where the Sun rises in the morning. To the right is the Western Horizon where the Sun sets in the evening. The Sun rises at the left, culminates directly above at noon, and then sets at the right, passing under the Earth at night.

The horoscope is our personal measuring device for life cycles. The degree of the zodiac on the eastern horizon at the time of birth is our *Ascendant (ASC)* or Rising Sign. The Ascendant shows our orientation relative to the zodiac and the planets at birth. It is our personality (mask), physical appearance and birth itself which is the interface between the upper conscious and lower unconscious halves of our horoscope and being. As movement around the circle is clockwise for the planets, influences which originate in our unconscious instinctual hemisphere must pass through and be transformed by our personality before they become conscious.

The noon position of the Sun is the *Midheaven* or *MC* (medium coeli = middle of the heavens). This highest point of the sky is the culmination of Sun's daily path where it shines directly through the atmosphere and produces the most heat and light. The MC, our ego-consciousness and life objectives, derives its power as the centre of our field of consciousness.

The Lower Midheaven or IC (immum coeli = bottom of the heavens) is opposite to the MC. At the IC, planetary influences must pass through the entire mass of the Earth. This is the centre and focus of the unconscious hemisphere of your horoscope: the realm of instincts, dreams and the Id, as defined by Freud.

The Descendant (DSC) is opposite the Ascendant and is the position where we sublimate the self through partnership in the world.

From midnight at the IC until Noon at the MC, the Sun gradually rises in the sky. This left hemisphere and its resident planets are coming into consciousness as the realm of the self.

Our personality as shown by the Ascendant is the centre of the field of the self. As soon as the Sun or any other planet reaches the MC it begins to descend in the sky. The loss of heat and light from its maximum point at the MC parallels a decrease in consciousness. The right side shows influences of which we are becoming unconscious, and is the realm of the not-self, or the outside world. The MC/ego is the mediator between us and the world, as well as the potential unifier of the two halves of the horoscope.

The Houses

The zodiac signs rotate in relation to the quadrants of our horoscope, so we may have any of the twelve signs occupying the Ascendant. The natural, *archetypal* relationship between the signs and houses is when the first degree of Aries is the degree of the Ascendant, which occurs once each day when the horizon coincides with the beginning point of the zodiac. At all other times, the zodiac is in a unique relation to the horizon. The exact degree and sign on our Ascendant are determined by the time of our birth. The Ascendant moves at an average of one degree every four minutes through the signs. The relationship of our birth time to the position of the zodiac defines the *Houses* of the horoscope.

In Life★Time Astrology, the *signs of the zodiac are divisions of space* and the *houses are divisions of time*. Houses are designated by the numbers one to twelve (Figure 5) and are determined by our birth time and the latitude of our birth place.

The first astrologers thought that the houses were equal like the spokes of a wheel. When it was realized that the Earth's orbit and planetary paths were all elliptical, it was clear that the houses varied in size and in the time it took them to pass the Ascendant. This gave rise to unequal house division systems. The only places on Earth which have twelve equal houses naturally are on the Equator. The farther north or south of the Equator we are born, the greater the distortion of the twelve houses. This reflects the fact that the seasons are equal in length near the Equator, but vary to greater extremes the closer to either polar region our birth place is located.

The most accurate and popular system of house division was developed by the monk Placidus in the seventeenth century. The Placidean System locates the house divisions, called *cusps*, by calculating the time taken to cover a given space on the ecliptic. This was the first house system defined by time.

The horoscope of signs and houses is our orientation in space and time. The position of the sun relative to the zodiac shows the time in the year of your birth; the position of the signs relative to the Ascendant shows our orientation relative to the zodiac; and the houses show the qualifying effect of our position on Earth.

The movement of the Sun through the houses each day indicates the time of day for which the horoscope is erected. The Sun is on the Ascendant (1st House cusp) at sunrise; on the MC (10th House cusp) at noon; on the Descendant (7th House cusp) at sunset; and on the IC (4th House cusp) at midnight. The intermediate house cusps divide these four quadrants into three segments each, making a total of twelve in all.

The position of the MC in the zodiac indicates the Sidereal Time (Star Time, abbreviated ST) at birth, the relation of Earth to the stars independent of the latitude. The MC moves approximately one degree every four minutes throughout day and night, and the Ascendant, due to latitude, moves at a variable rate. Therefore, our MC/ego moves at a constant rate, while our ASC/personality moves variably depending upon the day and place of our birth.

In traditional astrology the sequence of signs beginning with Aries is analogous to the sequence of houses beginning with the 1st House. The qualities of the signs are directly translated into the modes of the houses, which are considered the field of action of the signs. The houses are the signs manifest in the mundane 'real' world. The house interpretations are unclear because, although they are numbered, their sequence is not utilized. Many modern schools of astrology either undervalue or eliminate the houses due to the difficulty in defining them accurately and the greater difficulty using them intelligently.

Life★Time Astrology is based upon a revaluation of the Houses because their sequence is essential. Everyone has the same ten planets, but the exact sequence and phasing differentiates one person from another. Every day the Ascendant and the MC of Earth pass all planetary positions in our horoscope in sequence. Every year the Sun passes this sequence and every month the Moon. The sequence of houses provides a time structure which orders interpretation and the reading of our horoscope. Life★Time Astrology is unique in ascribing to the sequence of twelve houses our life process from conception to death. The sequence is biologically correct and psychologically consistent.

The sign qualities derived from seasonal identifications form a unity with the houses of our individual lives. Their interaction is the key to a *human ecology* and their synthesis requires the introduction of the primary dimension of astrology — Time.

★Chapter Two★
Life★Time Astrology

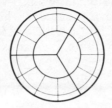

Astrology is knowledge of Time. Whatever differences exist between us, we all live in time: we are all conceived, born, live and die. To understand life it is necessary to understand time.

Space is composed of three dimensions and time is movement through them. We believe that time is absolute; that wherever time is measured, it is always the same, as one discrete moment succeeds another at a constant rate. The only measure of time is by clocks which, placed anywhere in the universe, should agree with each other. The accuracy of mechanical clocks reinforces the notion that a minute, second, hour, day, month or year is the same for everyone. In reality, these statements are not true!

Time is not absolute, but relative. Einstein discovered that clocks in motion slow down and that the faster a clock moves, the slower it registers time. A clock travelling at near the speed of light would virtually stop. Time does not exist apart from and therefore is relative to an observer. Time is a democracy of regular motion, where a majority of clocks are chosen to be accurate! (See Fraser, *Voices of Time*, p. 415) Because everything in the universe, including each one of us, is constantly in motion, we all have our own relative time sense (Many references are given in my book, *The Round Art*, p. 107-113). The 'relativity of time' is important because under varied physical and emotional conditions, and certainly as we age, our time sense changes. Sometimes we seem to exist outside of time altogether, as have mystics and visionaries throughout history. When we are active and interested, time passes quickly, but when we are passive and bored, it passes slowly. For example, days at school when

we were young lasted forever, but the decades pass by instantly
to the aged. The awareness of duration and location within the
temporal continuum is called *biological time*.

Biological time is the relationship between metabolism and
perception. Metabolism is the rate at which our body processes
food and oxygen – the rate at which we live – and is judged by
body weight, respiration rate, food consumption and age, and
as it changes, our time sense changes. When metabolism increases, the rate at which images are processed by our eyes and
brain increases, and this produces an overestimation of duration and the feeling that time is passing slowly. If we process
six images per second normally, when we receive nine images
per second in an excited state, it seems that each second of clock
time lasts 1 1/2 seconds. When our metabolism decreases, our
eyes and brain receive less images in a given time, which produces a tendency to underestimate duration and a feeling that
time is passing rapidly. If we process six images per second
normally, when we receive only three images per second in a
sedated state it seems that each second of clock time lasts only
half a second. As metabolism decreases, time sense accelerates!

Youth and old age are characterized by high and low
metabolic rates. Time passes slowly for the young and faster for
the old as our time sense changes as we age! At conception the
metabolism of our fertilized ovum is a rapid molecular rate and
dramatic changes in state occur second by second. After conception our metabolism gradually slows down until the
moment we die. Death of old age is when our body slows down
so much that it stops.

Our overall metabolic rate changes during life and is constantly altered by short-term changes of metabolism and
perception. Stimulation and tranquilization produce local
changes in metabolism and in our time sense. Excitation,
pacification, changes of mood, the consumption and digestion
of food, drugs, exercise, sex, external and internal stimuli all
momentarily alter metabolism. Smoking a cigarette, drinking a
cup of coffee or walking up a flight of stairs temporarily increases our metabolism; we feel younger. An alcoholic drink,
tranquilizer or rest reduces our metabolism, inducing the
slowness of old age. Temporary alterations continuously
modulate our average metabolism. As we age our body loses its
ability to consume and process oxygen and it takes us longer to
recover after minor accidents. A wound to a child disappears
many days before a similar wound to an adult.

Another factor which foreshortens time perception is Memory. Every day we compare our perceptions with memories of all previous days; our entire past exists in each continuous present moment. Today's experiences are added to a pool of life memories and as we grow older this memory pool increases. The significance of each present day is proportional to the total number of days we have lived. For example, the first day of our life is one out of one, or 100 percent of our life; experiences on this day are very vivid and extremely important. The second day is compared to a memory of the first, making it 1/2. The third day is 1/3, then 1/4, 1/5 and so on. At one year old each day is 1/365 of our life. After ten years each day is only 1/3650th of the whole. By the time we are thirty years old, each day is only 1/10,000th of our life! *As we age, each successive day is a smaller proportion of our whole life.* The mathematical series describing this compaction of life in time is a logarithmic progression.

As we age, time appears to contract, to compact and to pass more quickly. An hour in old age is not the same as an hour in childhood. It is easy to remember how, when a child, one day lasted for ever; though now weeks, months and years seem to fly by.

Our Time Sense

Implications of the contraction of time are manifold. Because the earliest events in life are given more importance in perceptual time, they have a deeper and more profound significance. Psychologists verify that events during childhood and gestation largely determine our psychological 'set' for life. Freud believed that the most critical experiences in life happened between the ages of two and five years old. Psychoanalysts try to discover our earliest critical events, when they occurred and what they mean, but the paradox is that, while the earliest events are most important in determining life psychology, it is exceptional if we remember any events that happened before the age of five years old! It never occurs to us to wonder about what happened during gestation. Have you ever thought about how you were conceived?

Most early memories are of mundane situations, like lying in a pram in the sunlight. Difficult events in childhood which are charged with emotional or physical pain are suppressed, blocked and forgotten. The purpose of many therapies is to unblock suppressed reality by reliving past traumatic events by utilizing dream interpretation, hypnosis, suggestion, free association, statistics, games, tests and other methods in an attempt to rediscover important facts of life. The problem all methods have in common is that information must be retrieved from us, but without a clear memory of our entire life, our understanding of ourself is incomplete. Often we just cannot remember what happened, and no one else can do it for us. The problem of access to memory is the great abyss of psychotherapy.

Life ★ Time Astrology is a method for reconstructing life; it applies the relativity of time and memory to astrology by grading the horoscope circle with the process of our life. The two limiting events of life are conception and death. As our time sense is related to metabolism and age, the intervening time is graded by logarithmic progression with the unit of time being the lunar month of 28 days. The lifetime of the ovum from which we are created is one lunar month and our entire lifetime is one thousand such lunar months, or seventy-seven years. The time scale of the ovum is one thousand times faster than the time scale of an adult at the end of life. To put this another way, at seventy-seven years old our life seems to pass one thousand times faster than it did at conception! This is the acceleration of life through time.

In Life ★ Time Astrology our life is graded with a logarithmic progression which uses the sequence 1, 10, 100 and 1000 as an arithmetic progression uses 1, 2, 3 and 4. When life is graded from 1 lunar month to 1000 lunar months in Table 2: The Logarithmic Progression, two intermediate times are significant.

Table 2: The Logarithmic Progression

28 days	280 days	2800 days	28000 days
1LM	10LM	100LM	1000LM
Conception	Birth	7 years	77 years
GESTATION	CHILDHOOD	MATURITY	

Ten lunar months after conception is nine calendar months, the full term of gestation and the moment of birth. One hundred lunar months after conception is seven years old, which many consider the end of childhood and the beginning of the age of reason. These two intermediate divisions in life create three developmental stages: *Gestation*, from conception to birth; *Childhood*, from birth to seven years old; and *Maturity*, from seven years old until death. Although unequal in clock time, they are equal relative to our memory, metabolism and biological clock. Everyone lives through these three developmental stages in life.

During *Gestation* the *Body* is created within the mother. The fertilized ovum travels up the fallopian tube and attaches itself to the wall of the mother's uterus, where its further development ensues. During gestation we pass through many developmental stages directed by our genetic code, which guides the creation of our physical body. While we gestate we perceive everything our mother thinks, feels, senses and intuits, and there is a reciprocal communication from us to her. These earliest influences are integrated into our body.

At birth we are transferred to a new environment in the air. *Childhood* begins with the circumstances of birth, when gender, physical appearance, manner of delivery, the effects of those present and their actions combine to create our *Personality*. During the seven years of childhood our personality is created within the home and family system. As the circumstances of gestation determine physical reality, the circumstances of childhood determine emotional reality.

During *Maturity* we integrate our personality with our body and project their combination into the outside world to work out our various possibilities. Creation of the *Soul* is determined by an ability to act out our life objectives and to understand our being in time as a whole. As the Body is created within the mother and Personality within the family, the soul is the whole of life created within the world as a reflection of the universal process of all life. To identify with the soul is to transcend life.

The three octaves describe the transformation of personal reality and consciousness. Gestation is pre-personal and sub-conscious (collective unconscious), Childhood is personal and self-conscious, and Maturity is transpersonal and super-conscious. Throughout life we relive the evolution of consciousness of all humankind, from pure instinct to transcendence.

The triple octaves of Gestation, Childhood and Maturity occupy the circumference of the horoscope circle. The circular representation of logarithmic time grades the houses of your horoscope from conception to death and combines the mechanism of biological time with the astrological horoscope (Figure 3).

In our horoscope the Ascendant, which is equivalent to the birth moment, orients the octaves to the houses. When the three octaves are further divided into four parts each, the periods in our life when certain developments occur correspond to the succession of twelve houses in the horoscope. These astrologically defined phases exactly match the rigorously derived phases identified by the psychologist Piaget in his clinical studies (See Ruth Beard, *An Outline of Piaget's Developmental Psychology*). The meanings of the houses are derived from the developmental ages of the average person.

The houses are numbered in a counter-clockwise direction from our Ascendant. We must go backwards four houses in a clockwise direction to the cusp of the 9th House for conception. Ahead of the Ascendant four houses, at the cusp of the 5th House is seven years old, the end of childhood and the beginning of maturity. Maturity extends from the cusp of the 5th House to the cusp of the 9th House. Conception and death coincide at the 9th House cusp.

Conception and death, the beginning and end of life, seem unrelated to each other except as limits to life, but there is a profound connection between them. At conception the fertilized ovum links into a code which determines the development of our entire life − our pattern in time as the formative cause of our existence. (See Sheldrake, *A New Science of Life*) At that moment life is all potential. At the instant of death the entire life passes before our eyes in an instant; a dramatic replay of our whole life which constitutes a '*last judgement*'. At death our life is all actual as all its potential has been utilized. The principle that any moment between conception and death is a stage in the transference of potential to actual reality is essential to the analysis and interpretation of the horoscope. In the ancient world the beginning and the end were symbolized by Alpha and Omega, the first and last moments, and as the ouroburos snake forming a circle with its tail in its mouth. Both are symbols of the wholeness and eternity of life.

A traditional problem of astrology is that the sign Scorpio and the 8th House are attributed to death, but they are only two-thirds of the way through the sequence of signs and houses. Sagittarius and the 9th House are attributed to self-realization and rebirth. In the Life ★ Time scale the borderline between the 8th and 9th Houses is *both* the moment of conception and of death. The 8th House is the termination of life and the 9th House is the origin of life. Life is a circular process where beginning and end are linked.

To quote T. S. Eliot:

> What we call the beginning is often the end
> And to make an end is to make a beginning.

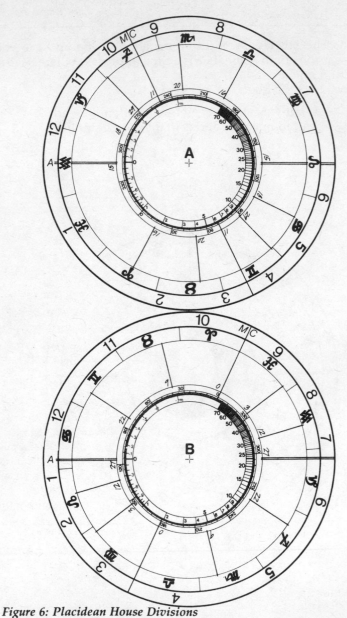

Figure 6: Placidean House Divisions
The two horoscopes are calculated for the same day but seven and one-half hours apart. In Horoscope A the 5th cusp registers at nine years old, while in Horoscope B the same cusp registers at less than five years old, showing two different rates of development in individuals born the same day.

★ Chapter Three ★
The Process of Life

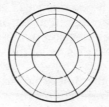

Life is a process which has a definite duration: it begins with conception and ends with death. In order to understand what life means, we must realise that it is a *Process in Time*.

Every intermediate moment in life from conception to death is a stage in the transformation of our potential into actual reality. The sequence of twelve houses in our horoscope describes this process.

Within each of the three developmental stages in life there are four intermediate houses. The twelve houses describe the transformation of life energy and reality. During each house in turn we work to fulfil the demands of an appropriate development, then move on to the next developmental stage. Our energies are continually transferred into more complex and more challenging channels as we age. When opportunity is rejected or misunderstood, the focus shifts backwards upon earlier stages about which we know and within which we are comfortable. Regression is a return to the habits and attitudes of an earlier time in life: if we cannot extend our involvement in the world, we retreat and channel it into something to which we do have access. When marriage (7th House) is too challenging there is a regression to the competition of secondary school (6th House), or when a child finds the demands of elementary school (5th House) overwhelming there is a regression to the baby talk and thumb-sucking of early home life (3rd House). Regressions are not always permanent, but the principle operates in us all.

The duration of each house in sequence mirrors its importance in life, as they successively occupy more time. The houses in gestation last weeks, while in maturity they last decades. Life is cumulative and as we age, memories of all past experiences accumulate within our psyche, whether we are able to recall them or not. The experience of each house is built upon a foundation of experiences from all previous houses, so we must remember earlier developments and incorporate them into new attitudes. The old is never discarded, but becomes the foundation of the new.

The mathematics of the time scale is such that each house in turn is almost equal in duration to the entire preceding time, from the beginning of the house all the way back to conception. There is a proportion approaching unity between the house we are in right now and our entire life up to the beginning of that house.

We all pass through the same sequence of developmental stages in life. Mechanisms learned and formed in each stage can happen out of sequence, and the ages at which the houses begin vary from person to person.

Since we all develop at varying rates, Table 3 shows The Archetypal Ages of the Houses presented as an average scale. The positions of the house cusp positions in our horoscope determine the duration of the developmental times to which they correspond. For simplicity we should understand the average times and process first; then the real variations in timing may be applied to our horoscope.

Table 3: The Archetypal Ages of the Houses

House	Archetypal Ages	Degrees from ASC	Key Words
	GESTATION		
9th	Conception to +7wks	240–270	Mother's self realization
10th	+7wks to +12wks	270–300	Recognition of conception
11th	+12wks to +22wks	300–330	Idealism and planning
12th	+22wks to Birth	330–360	Isolation and sacrifice
	CHILDHOOD		
1st	Birth to 7mos	0–30	Personality and self-assertion
2nd	7mos to 1yr 8mos	30–60	Physical sensory reality
3rd	1yr 8mos to 3yrs 6mos	60–90	Mobility and communication
4th	3yrs 6mos to 7yrs	90–120	Home and family emotional system
	MATURITY		
5th	7yrs to 13yrs	120–150	Self-consciousness and education
6th	13yrs to 23yrs 5mos	150–180	Discrimination and health
7th	23yrs 5mos to 42yrs	180–210	Partnership and world affairs
8th	42yrs to Death	210–240	Separation, metaphysics, death

When the horoscope is divided into twelve houses using the time-based Placidean House system, each house registers at a specific age. Figure 6 shows two horoscopes constructed seven and one-half hours apart on the same day. Houses smaller than an equal 30 degrees show developmental phases which are compacted, while larger houses show longer than average times of development.

The Ascendant sign at birth determines the sequence of signs and their relationships to the stages of our life. In the beginning just knowing the ascending sign in a horoscope is enough to describe the stages of a life accurately. Eventually it is critical to know which part of a sign is on the Ascendant as a fine-tuning mechanism.

The *Ascendant* defines the relationship between the horizon and the zodiac. The rotation of house ages and twelve sign qualities shows the permutations of viewpoint available to us. It is possible to have any of the twelve signs in any of the houses, but the sequence of signs and houses remains the same. Each house is occupied by one, two or three signs, depending upon its length. For example, the 5th House is the time from seven years old to thirteen years old and is occupied by the signs Pisces and Aries. The Pisces part of this house, up to the age of ten years old shows feelings of isolation and sacrifice at school, but when Aries begins at ten years old, there is an increase in personality strength and self-assertion. The qualities of the signs are adapted to the times of the houses and their archetypal developmental objectives. Aries qualities produce self-assertion at the time in life when its sign registers. In the 7th House it would affect partnerships, in the 11th House planning and idealistic attitudes.

If we have Aries on the Ascendant at birth, we experience the sequence of houses in synchronization with the traditional signs, as Aries is on the Ascendant at sunrise on the Spring Equinox. Throughout life developmental phases would be archetypal. We would have earthy Taurean characteristics in its natural time of seven months old to one year eight months old, and Libran balancing qualities in the 7th House time of partnership. With the opposite sign Libra ascending, each house would be occupied by its opposite sign quality. This would describe a character associated with Libra, ie. balancing qualities, equilibrium and partnership.

In the following description of the archetypal sequence of the twelve houses we must understand that everyone experiences variations of the same sequence. We all make use of the same set of cyclical qualities, but at different times in our lives and for different durations.

The signs which occupy each house are the primary influence on our character. They carry the quality which provides the background framework of the developmental stages. The second factor is the planets in residence which further qualify the meaning of the houses. The more planets in one house, the more complex and important is the corresponding time in life. The planets are influences we receive from other people, mechanisms within ourself, and the relationship between the two. The planets catalyze an event which binds a developmental age, signified by the house, to the quality described by the sign. The precise role of the planets will be discussed in Chapter Four.

The Process of Life begins at conception, the only true beginning of life. The importance of this earliest time of life cannot be overstated. All other astrological systems, even those which attempt to grade the horoscope circle, do not even mention conception and gestation, much less recognize their importance in interpretation and in life (Cf. the systems of Rudyhar and Huber). Most current psychological theories also ignore development prior to birth. As a result, the description of the events of gestation initially seems foreign, although women who have had children understand easily. The feminine perspective is essential to wholeness.

We are conceived as a result of a sexual act between our parents, carried within our mother for about ten lunar months and then born. All autonomic and regulatory body systems are created during gestation; the influences we receive are incorporated into our physical body and affect us always.

The function of the Process of Life is to describe life through time, but very few individuals ever contemplate the reality of their lives in this way. The only time we are likely to do so is just before we die.

Most of us are trapped within a present moment which knows neither past nor present as we have forgotten the past and dread the future. While 'live in the present' sounds a profound statement, our life is a process. To attain a larger perspective and to transcend time, we must understand the peaks and troughs, the incidents which counterpoint the ebb and flow, and the people who interweave their lives in ours. To be whole we must reconstruct our life from conception to the grave.

(For ease of understanding, the zodiac sign which corresponds to each house is shown in brackets at the righthand margin.)

The Process of Life

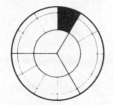

The 9th House   *(Sagittarius)*

Conception until seven weeks after conception
During the fertilized ovum's lifetime of one lunar month, the time scale is molecular and the entire pattern of our life in time has registered. The three spiral germ layers of the ovum form a pattern similar in time to the three major developmental stages or *Octaves* of our cellular life. In fact the lifetime of the ovum is a microcosm of our lifetime, compressed one thousand times.

By the end of the first lunar month, the fertilized ovum has travelled up the fallopian tube into the mother's uterus and attached itself to the uterine wall. By the end of this house our major bodily systems are fully operative, the liver can process waste and the embryo technically becomes a foetus.

The medical profession assumes that a mother cannot know of her child's existence until at least thirty-eight days after conception. Obviously, many women know that they are pregnant soon after, if not at, conception. The more sensitive a mother is to the subtle energies of her psyche and body, the greater the likelihood that she will have discovered her baby's existence early on in the 9th House, and the more sensitive her child is to these influences.

A mother has already begun a dramatic hormonal transformation that changes not only her body but her life. All her attitudes register upon us during this time: the way in which she realized that something was happening, what symbolism her thoughts took, who she turned to for verification and the overall quality of these circumstances provide a key to our own orientation mechanism within the world. A mother's attitudes towards religion, parental wisdom and individual philosophy during this first phase of gestation are very intense and important, as the women's movement recognizes.

The 9th House is the ability to orient oneself within the world as a reflection of our mother's realization of our existence.

The Midheaven (MC)

Seven weeks after conception or thirty-three weeks before birth

The Midheaven (MC) registers at approximately forty-nine days after conception. By this time the development of our bodily components is essentially complete: sex is determined, the face is fully human, features are recognizable, and we live and move within the amniotic fluid. Around the forty-eighth day the first true bone cells replace our cartilege skeleton. When this physical development is reached, a mother becomes aware that she is pregnant.

Hindus and Buddhists believe that the soul enters the physical body forty-nine days after conception. The now human body accepts its *karma* (traces of past lives), a metaphor for its genetic inheritance and astrological pattern in time which has become tangible. During this first stage of gestation the early brain components, the R-complex, the limbic system and the neocortex are developed, recapitulating their historical sequence.

The MC is our ego and is symbolized by the position of the Sun at noon, when it is hottest and brightest. The ego is the centre of consciousness, our objectives in life and our ability to exercise will in life. It is the focus of all conscious activity. The quality, strength and complexity of our ego is determined by the sign of the MC and the planets in aspect to the MC. When the MC is in Gemini, for example, our objectives are often doubled; when in Capricorn they are practical and material; when in Leo they are speculative; when in Pisces they isolate us or expose us to external influences. Planets near or in aspect to the MC show objectives we manifest.

Before this time even if a mother intuits or dreams that she is pregnant, she does not know for sure. The moment of verification is distinctive as a differentiation of our foetal reality and her own consciousness. A mother becomes conscious of her child in the same way that we become conscious of ourself. Whether she makes this discovery as a result of her own realization, requires outside opinions or doesn't trust herself are all metaphors for our own route to self-discovery in life.

The 10th House   *(Capricorn)*

Thirty-three weeks to twenty-eight weeks before birth
By the time our mother has realized the fact of our existence, we are a miniature version of our grown self in many ways – development during the 10th House is quite mechanical, as are our movements.

The 10th House is traditionally our parents and often begins with our father being told of our existence. Our mother announces the change in her life, the adoption of new physical conditions and begins to prepare the environment for the new arrival. Practical matters to be handled at this time include the choice of doctor or midwife, dietary and physical regimes, whether to deliver in hospital or at home, mechanically or naturally. There are many decisions to be made, adjustments in life-style to be considered and practical issues to be confronted.

All our parents' concerns foreshadow our ability to make arrangements and our way in the world. When our mother is reluctant to telling our father about her pregnancy, it will follow that we resist making our creative objectives known to the world. When our parents broadcast the fact, we will expect great publicity to attend our life objectives. A neutral response would imply little impact upon the outer world and little direction. If our parents did not want us at all, we will feel threatened by the world. The realizations and actions which follow can range from open to totally suppressed, and from natural to superficial. An instrumentally determined pregnancy would predispose us to a life influenced by machines. The way our mother deals with our existence determines our attitude towards life objectives.

The 10th House is our ability to confront reality as determined by our parents' reactions to the discovery of our existence and their subsequent actions.

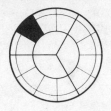

The 11th House   (*Aquarius*)

Twenty-eight weeks to seventeen weeks before birth
At the beginning of the 11th House movements change from being marionette- like mechanical actions to being graceful and fluid. The increasing rhythm of these movements coincides with the 'quickening', when the mother recognizes the movements within. The placenta is of primary importance now as an intermediary between the mother's body and the foetus. None of the mother's bodily systems directly exchange with that of the baby – rather, the placenta exchanges carbon dioxide for oxygen, waste for nutriments and provides minerals, vitamins and hormones for foetus and mother. The umbilical is a closed loop carrying separate blood and the vessels filter out large cells, unwanted whole protein and bacteria (See Flanagan, *The First Nine Months*).

The middle period of gestation is occupied with plans. Our mother projects all possible variants of gender, appearance, character and life onto us, running through infinite possibilities one after the other. The variety and breadth of her viewpoint reflects our increased movements inside her. Practical matters have been largely resolved, the reality of the pregnancy has been accepted, but limitations of activity and increased size do not occur until the end of this time. The mother is in a unique position to free herself from the outer world and focus upon her inner world. Her relationships become less sexual due to the natural satisfaction of her state, and she creates and maintains altruistic friendships with those around her. Talking with other women who have carried and birthed children benefits her and may culminate in an interest in groups and organizations which teach, assist, comfort and understand her state, feelings and thoughts. Her responses to the possibilities of this time can range from ignorance of any relationship at all to a profound recognition of the interconnections permeating every step in the gestation process. She can focus upon herself or upon the universal state of childbearing and birthing.

Towards the end of this house she not only feels different than others, but is physically, emotionally and mentally separate from her former self. This can lead to a unique understanding of others, compassion and sympathy for people in general and progressive thinking, all transmitted to us.

The 11th House is our ability to abstract and detach ourself from the physical world and ascend into the realm of ideas and plans.

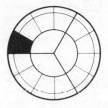

The 12th House   (Pisces)

Seventeen weeks before birth until birth
At this time our mother begins to gain weight, which in turn restricts her mobility. The amniotic fluid is exchanged regularly while it cushions us, supports us, facilitates exercise and evens our temperature. We live within this watery capsule totally protected from the outside world. Our mother becomes more and more dependent and her sensitivity to external influences increases as psychic contact with us increases.

As birth approaches, the self-sacrificial element of the 12th House becomes stronger. Examinations by doctor or midwife become more regular, as does the realization that birth itself is approaching. As our mother's psychic faculties, fantasies and dreams are all in full operation, total absorption in birth is complete. While husband, friends, midwife, doctor and other children support her, she realizes that she will give birth alone. The acceptance and release of her deepest instincts coincides with our final development. The inability of the uterus to expand any further begins pre-delivery time. Our mother is totally alone, yet carries us within her. Her choices of birth technique and circumstances reflects our later reliance upon or independence from the inner life or the outer life. The more she bypasses her own instincts and relies upon mechanical direction, the weaker will be our instinctual contact.

The last eight weeks of gestation are particularly important because the ten degrees immediately above the Ascendant are the hidden elements of our personality; those influences, dreams and fantasies which lie or even remain just near the surface of consciousness. The mechanism is derived from the distortion of the Sun at sunrise. Instinctive maternal responses represent the best possible outlet for these influences, and natural birth tends to allow these instincts their proper role. With the end of this house, the Octave of Gestation is complete and our transition into an independent existence in the air follows.

The 12th House is the relationship between forces acting upon us from outside and our inner psychic attitudes.

The Ascendant

Birth

The Ascendant occurs when the first breath is drawn at birth. The manner of birth and its implications determine the way in which personality functions. The body which formed during gestation is tangible and physical, but personality, the essence of which is formulated at birth and develops throughout childhood, is a process. It is a mask which contains instincts, habits, mannerisms, expressions and fantasies, and is our vehicle of adaptation to the world.

Personality is determined by the nature of our birth, physical appearance, gender, and the actions and projections of those people present or affecting the birth from a distance. The zodiac sign on our Ascendant shows the atmosphere and attitude existing in the birth environment. Cancer shows warmth, maternal influences and emotional reactions as environmental and then personal qualities. Scorpio shows separations in birth and subsequent treatment. Taurus determines a totally physical view of birth and of the personality (A complete listing of signs on the Ascendant and their influences appears on pages 180-181.)

Planets near the Ascendant show people apart from the mother who are present and become direct components of one's personality. Often sub-personalities are derived from the delivering doctor, young anaesthetist, worried grandfather or pushy grandmother. Planets in aspect to our Ascendant show people who have an indirect influence upon our birth. If the aspecting planet is below the horizon the influence upon our personality is unconscious, while if it is above the horizon it is conscious. These influences might emanate from a nervous father at home or younger children wondering what was happening. All the influences coming directly from those present and those making distant projections determine the sub-personalities we possess. Once these influences have been identified, we can discover exactly who these individuals were.

As personality is a process, the process of birth itself is a key to understanding the Ascendant. When birth is rapid and easy, the resultant personality manifests itself fluidly both in short and long-term situations in life. Whether in the local pub or in lifelong working associations, personality flows easily. A difficult labour which requires great effort by the mother produces a hardworking personality. The longer and harder the labour, the more stress and strain on the personality. When a doctor or midwife must help delivery, our personality requires assistance from others to assert itself. When birth is accomplished by forceps or caesarean section, we require the physical intervention of another (doctor) to allow our personality to function. When an entire team of doctors and hospital staff is necessary, the resultant personality needs collective situations for awakening personality, such as mass movements, gurus or religious revivals. The more people present at a birth, the greater the collective influences upon the personality.

In addition to the physical conditions of delivery, our attitudes are determined by the reactions to our birth and to us of those present. Modern birth movements stress the importance of who is present at birth and the general atmosphere of all births. Anaesthetics, local or general, produce numbness, vagueness or great sensitivity to certain influences. Induction exposes our personality to an overstimulation by external forces and generates a compulsive attitude. We would feel that others were compelling us through external circumstances to emerge from within, before our time. These birth 'complications' are interventions in what should be, but rarely is, a natural process. The medical profession has accepted and encouraged such intervention as routine, and as a result is implicated in problematic and violent personalities exhibited by many people today.

The degree and manner of involvement of those present at our birth determines the closeness or detachment of our personality to others. If the doctor was hurrying things along so that he could play golf, our personality would reflect this by continually rushing into self expression.

The Ascendant also governs the personality aspects of physical appearance, gender and initial health. When the mother is surrounded by her family and friends, there are many sympathetic supporters who respond to us at birth. Reactions to our gender and appearance should be various and full, although in institutional births these responses are lacking. The closer we are to others at birth, the more related we feel to our gender and body.

The implications of birth and subsequent treatment have such a profound influence upon one's whole life-view that attitudes towards childbirth affect entire generations of children. Natural methods and the increasing awareness of women and men create natural awareness in children. Rigid suppressive, assembly-line birth techniques produce zombies.

The Ascendant is our personality which is derived from the manner of our birth and the influences of those participating in and surrounding it.

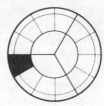

The 1st House   *(Aries)*

Birth until seven months old

The 1st House is the time during which we assert ourself in the world. Primary concerns are nourishment, warmth and attention. The ability to communicate these needs, the difficult and harmonious adaptations we experience, and our treatment within hospital and home, determine our ability to assert ourselves during life. If we are coddled, watched and surrounded by a supporting family and parents we expect such support throughout life. During this time of mother-child bonding, if we are rejected and left in the back room, we feel isolated whenever we try to assert our personality.

During this time we are not free to move your own body and

others must see to our wants, which are basic and self-oriented. As we do not focus light properly until about three months old, we identify others on an energetic level, then on a visual level, accepting those who satisfy our needs. Our instinctive reactions to mother, father and others are related directly to satisfaction, and our personality reflects these external influences.

Since personality is a adaptive mechanism, the primary activity during this time is to adapt to life. Our instincts have total domain and gratification must be immediate.

The 1st House is the ability to assert one's personality within the family.

The 2nd House   (Taurus)

Seven months old until one year eight months old

In the 2nd House we are immersed and imbedded in the physical world. Our body is a primary object and everything is investigated as it enters our space. Objects are tasted, touched, observed and put down. Often this stage begins when we are weaned from mother's milk and begin taking solid food. Our focus is centred upon pure sensation, before the subject-object split in perception which characterizes the next house.

As bodily control increases, the range of sensations is extended. Bad tastes, unpleasant odours and textures are rejected and good tastes and pleasant sensations are appreciated. Objects possessing the strongest sensations are preferred. The broader the range of sensual material to which we have access, the freer and wider our sense of physical security. This includes physical relations with parents, brothers, sisters and our environment. Everything, including the body, has an object-like quality at this time, and flexibility and response to the physical world is now defined. Senses do not yet striate into levels, but remain open to each new object and sensation; being touched and touching in turn are primary transactions. When access to objects is limited, our connection with the world is restrained. As these mechanisms determine our eventual attitude towards property, possession and the physical world, the freedom of sensation is vital.

The 2nd House is the ability to apply energy to the purely physical world and relate to the use of our senses.

The 3rd House   (Gemini)

One year and eight months until three years and six months old

In the 3rd House we apply energy to objects in order to communicate. Many things are perceived simultaneously whereas previously only one object could be accepted at a time. The relative positions also begin to matter. Objects fluctuate between being extensions of our reality and possessors of their own independent life. This subject-object duality is the most prominent characteristic of the time, and leads to differentiation.

We associate the sounds learned in the 2nd House with actions. Even sounds themselves seem like possessions to be played with. Names of people and things are identical to the people and things themselves; a name is our access to the person or object it describes.

We learn to walk and this animates our world as the range of impressions increases dramatically. Dependence on others lessens and the ability to connect thoughts to actions allows us to communicate with them. Nearby people are models upon whom we pattern our attitudes. As the speed of adult perception is logarithmically so much slower than ours at this time, our primary models are other children. When adults read a newspaper, it seems to take them aeons. A balance between child and adult models achieves the widest range of experience in communication. When those around us communicate with words, we follow suit if we can. When parents baby-talk, for example, we learn an irrelevant vocabulary, for whatever means of communication we observe, we mimic and integrate.

Whenever the outer world becomes too difficult to understand, we enter a parallel inner world of magic. If words are misunderstood, we simply label the object with our own words or sounds. Such natural difficulties in communication send us back into the 2nd House stage of sucking or physical contact, and we blame the words themselves. The verbal faculty relies upon transferring rhythmic sucking and chewing movements into language. Singing, dancing and games ease this transference of energy into the communicative sphere. The more time we spend alone, or the more problematic language becomes, the more highly developed our fantasy world.

The 3rd House is the ability to communicate.

The 4th House   (Cancer)

Three years and six months old until seven years old
In the 3rd House language is still basic and unexpressive, but in the 4th House we react to our ability to communicate. We realize that words produce particular responses from parents and siblings – some words produce laughter, others a reprimand. Home should be a place where the full range of communication may be presented, but permitted actions and reactions determine our emotional 'set' for life. The valuing mechanism is emotion: our feelings about home, church, country or nature are conditioned by those prevailing within the family, and made manifest by our parents. We recognize that our family has its own views of the world, or that family views bear little resemblance to those of the world outside. When a questioning of family attitudes is not permitted, our feelings are reserved from expression. This is a reversion back into the 3rd House, where certain words had no value and merely described objects.

Our parents influence our feelings as their attitudes are guidelines whether we accept or reject them. Our emotional patterns are a blend and compensation of our parents', and we realize that the family system is held together by feelings which are not necessarily consistent nor just. We can relate more strongly to one parent than the other, but must gradually take their relationship with each other into consideration. The ability to comprehend these complex relationships determines the kind of home and family system we seek or avoid in later life.

The parent with whom we create the strongest bond is often the carrier for our eventual marital role. In single parent families, one parent must portray both roles.

The Sun and Moon are the influences of our father and mother in the horosccope and their placement conditions these parental-emotional valuations. The position of these luminaries can exaggerate, parallel, negate or have no effect upon this house according to their positions.

Emotions are the glue of family relationships, and our feelings are important for our family as well as for us. When our feelings are blocked or unexpressed, we revert back to the 3rd House of instinctive thinking – we just don't feel at home.

The 4th House concerns feelings about our ability to communicate within home and family.

The 5th House   (Leo)

Seven years old until thirteen years old

We develop our personality in the first four houses of childhood and in the 5th House exteriorize ourselves into the outside world and become self-conscious. This coincides with primary education.

The major expressive device is game-playing, as games are a natural way of expressing our ability to relate to others. The particular games we choose or are forced to play define a range of possibilities: some games provide us with a channel for our energies, while others do not allow expression. Some of us prefer to make up our own rules, some only play by commonly accepted rules, some must receive their rules from others, and some refuse to allow others to play with them at all. The kinds of games we play and our attitude towards rule-making determine our personal relationships. Those friends with whom we play and establish rules are those with whom we form affectionate contact. Personal relationship is the accceptance of game-playing.

Games may exchange energy, demonstrate physical proficiency or intellectual superiority, provide an outlet for emotions, or any of these in combination. The best games contain all of these. The framework within which relationships develop is school where we learn the rules that our social class, religion, geographical area or country hold to be important. We choose to abide by certain conventional games, while others are ignored or resisted. The open-mindedness of games contracts with the rigidity of school discpline. A well-adjusted child balances the two.

Once out of our parents' domain, teachers and those who play games for a living become primary role models for action and thought. This often tends to hero-worship of ideal individuals. The preoccupation with school or games sets a pattern which we follow in later life, especially in sexual relationships. When game-playing and school are difficult, there is a regression to the security of home and mother in the 4th House.

The 5th House is to accept and play games as a way of expressing ourself and forming relationships with others.

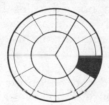

The 6th House   (Virgo)

Thirteen years old until twenty-three years and five months old
The 6th House is the discrimination and physicality of self-conscious adolescence. Puberty accompanies this time during which the transition to secondary education is completed, and the great struggle is between the games we learn and the reality of the world.

Parental identifications which were transferred onto teachers or heroes during the 5th House are now assimilated. The medium is the body, as our role-playing now involves sexuality – the way in which we relate to our body determines the nature of work relationships. If we are governed by sensual responses to objects, including our body, then we expect to work for or to serve others; if we control our sensations, we can expect to manage and be served by others at work. Our degree of physical involvement determines the intermediate ground between the two extremes. We have to make choices, accept responsibility for our own decisions and create a physical reality.

Many of our choices are physical: we must choose clothes, diet, hygiene and information. Our health reflects the overall balance of physical necessities. Difficulty in decision-making leads to disease. The many games and speculations available in the 5th House become limited and we must decide on what is essential.

It is not possible to separate ideals from realities before this time, so complete control over the world seems possible until tangible impediments intervene, such as mental or physical limitations, lack of financial mobility or class barriers. Systems that we learned contrast and permute with the actual mechanism of the world of school or job. Game-playing attitudes and techniques must be channelled into working situations. Flexibility is valued where specialization formerly was encouraged. We either accept or reject control over our own life.

Relationships which obeyed rules become subject to experimentation beyond familial and social codes. Sexuality is mainly fantasy at the beginning of this house, and the fantasies either are eliminated in favour of real physical relations or remain fantasies forever. The contrast of the girl-next-door with the Playboy centrefold can be outgrown here or become a lifelong fantasy. Often our choices are binding, as when we produce children from early sexual experiences. To resist experiment produces naivete, but unreasonable experimentation produces premature commitments. The ability to synthesize the impressions of early life, to organize ourselves into a consistent whole rather than a collection of parts, is the object of this time. Criticism towards others counterpoints our self-criticism; we may be accurate and objective about others, but not about ourselves. If we cannot make choices or organize ourselves, we revert back to the gameplaying attitudes of the 5th House.

The 6th House is the ability to adapt to the world in physique, health, work and sexuality.

The 7th House   *(Libra)*

Twenty-three years and five months old until forty-two years old
Now we are directly opposite the time when our personality
registered at birth in the logarithmic time scale. The way we see
ourself is the opposite of the way we really are, and the polarity
promotes objectivity. Our personality was conditioned by
parents, brothers and sisters, and early environment, and now
must be reconciled with the outside world. The equilibrium we
seek between inside and outside manifests in our choices of
partnerships, both marital and professional. We leave the subjectivity and unconsciousness of the lower half of our
horoscope and emerge into the upper, conscious and objective
hemisphere. The synthesis involves blending both positive and
negative traits developed and enacted during our first twenty-
three years five months.

Partnerships are a summation of our appearance, parental
relationships, education, ability to communicate, attraction,
ambitions and conflicts. Our partner is the balancing agent in
this complicated equation as someone who seems to possess
the characteristics we lack, yet desire to possess. These
characteristics are projected onto our partner, whether or not
they actually carry them. Often it is more important to discover
what we think and feel about a partner than what he or she are
really like.

The 7th House is opposite the 1st House, which governed
self-assertion in the months after birth. We seek a partnership
which counterbalances the strength of our personality. It is the
process of partnership which is important, and the growth it
allows and encourages is all-important. As we act out and
become familiar with the opposing characteristics of our partner, they are gradually integrated into our whole being, just as
a parallel process occurs to them. Excessive strength or
weakness in either partner reflects a similar imbalance *within*
each partner.

Business relationships parallel our personal relationships: efficient business requires that employees sublimate their individual drives for the good of the whole. Yet every individual wishes to advance and maintain his or her own influence. The individuality of each partner dovetails with the collective job. The higher up in business one progresses, the more necessary is an image of the whole operation.

At present marriage is a contractual agreement, subject to moral and legal controls. Subsequently, many marriages are transactions where little beyond sharing lodging or children is held in common by way of growth and evolution. The rules of behaviour within relationships should allow both partners the latitude to grow, yet also must hold them together in common interest. This is true whether heterosexual or homosexual relations are involved. It is necessary to define roles and then play them. The success of relationships hinges around foresight determining the interweaving demands of each individual as well as the whole marriage. The liberation of women and men from stereotyped family roles is important, but it must be remembered that it is we ourselves who make and break these roles and rules.

When our personality is very complex, it becomes necessary to expand beyond a nuclear relationship. This may mean a succession of growth partnerships or a desire to form a relationship with the world itself. Public figures often sacrifice personal relationships in favour of their career.

An inability to relate to others forces a regression back into the unconscious lower half of the horoscope. We may then find that partnerships become work (6th), game-playing (5th), protection (4th), childlike (3rd), purely physical (2nd) or alone in self assertion (1st). At best, all the elements described by the early houses are present in a blended form.

The 7th House is the ability to form permanent relationships.

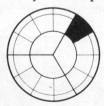

The 8th House   (Scorpio)

Forty-two years old until death
The 8th House is the last house and governs the gradual

withdrawal from life. As it is opposite to the 2nd House entrance into the physical world of the senses, the 8th House is the release of our grasp upon the sensual world; we experience the results of our life's work and all outstanding debts are paid. By the end of this time we should have 'made our peace' with the world.

This is old age, when we must gradually relinquish or delegate control over our own affairs. The end of the 7th House is the time of maximum acquisition, but as we progress through the 8th House the desire to accumulate must be transformed into a willingness to let it all go. Detachment from the world accompanies ageing. A dependency upon the feelings, thoughts, will and even physical support of others increases. After a lifetime of being in control, it is hard to relinquish direction of our affairs.

The gradient of energy declines during this last phase of life, and our activities reflect this. A healthy increase of interest in metaphysics, religion and the intangible is a way of transferring the focus away from youthful gratification towards the symbolic acts of old age. Friends pass away; old places do not seem the same; the activities of middle age are tiresome; the physical world dissolves into an internal, spiritual world which lies behind appearances. In senility, the inner world literally encroaches upon and dominates the outer world.

The primary effect of ageing is that our time sense becomes so highly compacted as our metabolism slows down towards a stopping point that the world appears to fly by. All we can do is sit and watch it happen. By the time we have reacted to a situation, it has passed. The mind moves faster than the body can react. While driving, we see our automobile hitting the post but cannot act in time to avoid it. The deterioration of the senses is the slowing down of perception – our understanding just cannot keep up with the speed of perceptions around us.

The 8th House and the death which terminates it represents the most critical time of life. We should be able to detach ourselves from the world gracefully. The necessity to release control and property, when understood, generates the conditions for a positive death. When matters are left undone and grasping is prominent, death is painful torment. The primary objective is to channel our diminishing energies into their intangible places, to pass on our understanding of life and the world to those who are younger, and to maintain an interest in the last great transformation.

The 8th House is the separation from life as we approach death.

The Higher Octave

The process of life from the 9th cusp-conception point until the end of the 8th House of separation and death defines our mundane life. Life is a circle in time. As T.S. Eliot stated so beautifully,

> We shall not cease from exploration
> And the end of all our exploring
> Will be to arrive where we started
> And know the place for the first time.

In order to understand life, we must see it in its entirety in time. The joys, sorrows, meaningful moments and trivial enjoyments, the complexity and simplicity, the loves and fears, protagonists and allies must all be unified into a *Life*. Until we comprehend the whole, we cannot pass beyond ourselves.

Most people live mechanical lives: they are conceived, born, mature and die. When we see them walking down the street, we do not have to be an astrologer to predict where they came from or where they are going. They never attempt to extend their reality beyond their physical, personal situation. Their actions and feelings are dictated to them by the world, and they are locked into time and cannot, nor do they wish, to get out. They may struggle briefly in early life, but ultimately they bow to the pressures of the world in order to conform.

The life just described is similar to the horoscope circle because they both exist in one plane. Like the sheet of paper on which the horoscope is drawn, the circle becomes a line when you hold it at certain angles. For most, life is a continuously repetitive orbit round the circle. At its most mechanical, life is a straight line of definite length, but with no height or width. Time acts as an absolute constraint and flexibility is minimal if not non-existent as a mechanical life is lived around the periphery of the horoscope circle. At the end of life is the return to the beginning, but without the knowledge that it has happened.

The two-dimensional version of reality is similar to the way in which most men and women understand our solar system. The common belief is that the planets and their moons orbit the Sun, which is fixed at the centre. In fact, the Sun itself is only

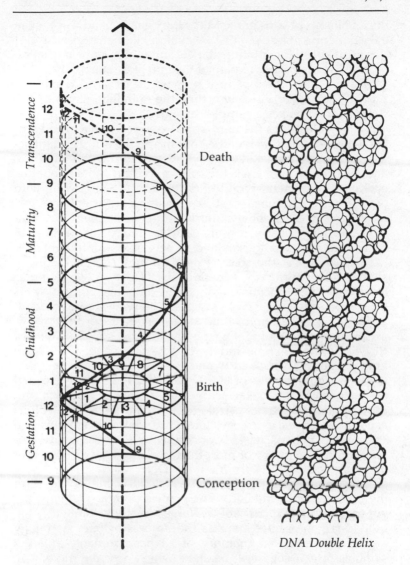

Figure 7: Cylinder of Life ★ Time Astrology
When the horoscope is extended in time along the central axis, conception is at the bottom and transcendence at the top of the cylinder. As we age, the cylinder fills with perceptions and memories. The present is the surface of the contents, which most take to be the whole. Outer life events are at the surface of the cylinder, while inner events are within the cylinder.

one of billions of suns in the Milky Way galaxy, and it orbits the galactic centre at a speed of 1.69 million kilometres per day! At this great speed the orbiting planets and moons appear to spiral around the central bright path of the Sun like filaments enwrapping a live wire (See the illustration on pages x and xi and also on the back cover). Through time the spiralling circus of our Solar System makes a complex cylinder.

Figure 7 illustrates the horoscope extended into a cylinder of life, where conception is at the bottom and the transcendent octave at the top. As we live the cylinder fills up with memories, and the present moment is the surface. Within and without this cylinder the planets spiral, reflecting and synchronizing with our life pattern in time. Most perceive their life as only the surface of the cylinder above a murky fluid, while the realized individual perceives a crystal-clear cylinder forwards and backwards in time and is able to go beyond its confines at will.

The diagram of the solar system through time is distinctly similar in structure to the genetic code DNA-RNA, which is also a pattern which functions in time. The language of astrology is a sister to the language of genetics. The twelve basic units of DNA are divided into four bases, similar to the twelve astrological signs and four elements. Both the spiralling path of the solar system in time and the double helix spiral of DNA are energy patterns which carry and record the form of the entire developmental process of life. A slice through DNA is a coded message called a gene, which guides biological assembly and development, just as an astrological planetary position with its aspects describes a life mechanism and the event through which it expresses itself. Consistent to Rupert Sheldrake's revolutionary concept of morphic resonance, the formation of organisms is not determined by DNA alone. There is a developmental pattern within time which is carried by DNA on the physical level. Similarly, the planets do not create events, but merely act as carriers of the large-scale development of all individuals, presented here as the Process of Life. Astrology describes the pooled memory of all past humans, and the symbols of astrology are the signs which describe the twelve stages of development.

The ability to understand all life presupposes an understanding of our own life process. To describe our life as a cylindrical spiralling of the solar system extends the perspective of the two-dimensional circle we take to be the form of the solar system. An analogous process is necesssary to move our life to a higher level of reality; *A Transcendent Reality.*

To gain access to the Transcendent Octave of development, we must extend our reality beyond the confines of the three-dimensional world of the senses. The process of conception and gestation describes our creation, and this is the pattern of our transcendent reality as well. The way in which our parents conceived us is a metaphor for the way in which the masculine and feminine sides of our nature blend together creatively. The way in which our mother realizes that she is pregnant is a precedent for the way in which we first discover our creative nature; the process of pregnancy describes how creativity manifests itself.

The Transcendent Octave is the higher level of Gestation, so if we can reconstruct our gestation, we can understand the transcendent process. If our gestation was fluid and satisfying for our mother, then the same will be true of our transcendent reality. Problems during gestation reflect blockages which may constrain us from utilizing higher perceptions, or an attempted abortion is a tendency to end the creative process prematurely. The events of gestation provide a pattern which we enact in living out our creative potential in life.

The Gestation Octave both begins and ends life in time: it completes and encloses the circle, yet provides the possibility of being free of the circle. The point of access to the Transcendent Octave of the horoscope is the 9th House conception point/death point. The way we are conceived is a pattern of the way we enter the transcendent octave, and we must pass the barrier of death before we can leave the confines of mechanical life. The passage of this barrier is initiation.

Initiation

Initiation was a ritual to which both women and men were exposed. The initiate was removed from his or her parental home, stripped of childhood identification and subjected to severe tests of patience or strength. Often the initiate was required to find and kill a totem animal, which meant a life or death struggle. Upon successfully passing the test, the initiate was educated as to the history and inner tradition of the whole tribe or religion. He or she received a new name, a new identity and status as an individual.

One object of initiation was to force the initiate to realize that it is essential to accept a higher purpose (i.e., the survival of the entire tribe) which transcends personal value in life. Strength lies in the whole life or whole tribe or whole culture, and not just in one part, an idea which would be helpful today. The shock of the physical test and pain increased the force of the ideas imparted. Initiation provided a direction and purpose to life which was lacking in the unconsciousness of childhood.

The classical initiation process is extinct, but there are ways in which the initiation process is available to us. One of the most obvious initiations is the bearing and birth of children; the women's mysteries of virtually all cultures in the world. The initiation began with a young girl's first menstruation and culminated with the birth of her first child. Women's mysteries were as painful and traumatic as the more overtly violent men's mysteries and possibly even more powerful.

First menstruation is a biological signal that a woman is of age and can conceive. It is an evocation of the ripening of the ovum from which the woman herself was conceived. As the ova ripen within her young body, so she herself is ripe for life. Menstrual blood was sacred, and elaborate taboos, usually in the form of isolation, were observed to protect a woman and her tribe from each other. The first sign of creation within her was met by a ritual separation – a symbolic 'death' in relation to the tribe. She could never be the same again. Similarly, gestation is an initiation process to the mother.

When a woman conceives her first child, she irrevocably changes the pattern and orientation of her life and she 'dies' to her former life. Her thoughts, feelings, intuitions and senses during pregnancy are an inner change which accompanies her outer, physical change. The element of life or death affects both her and the child she will bear, especially at birth. A woman can know what it feels like to risk her life for another.

A woman relives the process of her own gestation when she is pregnant. Through the Life ★ Time Scale her own gestation may be outlined as a base upon which to build an initiated reality for herself and her child. It is less necessary to manipulate the child-carrying process than it is to understand who she is and what are the implications of her behaviour and the choices she makes. Initiation is the ability to accept reponsibility for creativity beyond one's own life.

The initiation of man is a very different process, although of similar roots. Men cannot carry or bear children. The mysteries of creation are idealized, abstracted and ritualized. The act of male orgasm is a dying release and the struggle of the one sperm out of millions to survive the trial in reaching the ovum is highly symbolic. The test of strength in initiation evokes these procreative acts, providing a springboard to a higher purpose in life.

There are many ways in which to experience initiation. Since it is the symbolic death of a previous life attitude, the process can occur through near death; by physical shocks or accidents; by emotional traumas; intellectual crises of conscience; with psychedelic drugs or plants; through meditation; or through the religious impulse. Events of this kind are never planned, but are accidental. Sometimes the effect of peak experiences are immediately suppressed or forgotten, but once we have seen the vulnerability of life, we are never the same again. This is true whether or not we choose to act upon the experience.

The actor or actress who is able to eliminate personality to don other roles fulfils the conditions of a metaphorical death and rebirth. The historian who studies past civilization eventually transfers his 'reality' back into a former time. His success is dependent upon leaving the contemporary world view in order to adopt the viewpoint of a chosen historical era, then to synthesize the two worlds separated by time.

Psychedelic plants and drugs also remove one from 'normal' reality in space and time. As psychedelics increase bodily metabolism through their chemical action, the resultant trip is quite literally a journey back into life. Faster metabolism is a quality of youthful perception, and as it increases our perceptual age decreases. We see the world as we did as a child. Astrologically we travel clockwise back against the natural direction of the signs and houses, towards the Ascendant and further, into gestation. Potent doses send us back into the womb. The loss of personality experienced with psychedelics occurs when we pass back through our own birth! When psychedelics are properly understood and administered, they provide an opportunity to relive life and experience existence without personality – to transcend ordinary life.

Our own sexuality links conception and death. Orgasm is a symbolic death; an opportunity to experience our conception during life. The connection between sexuality and creativity is determined by the nature of the sexual act between our parents, which is evoked whenever we make love. Sex is an initiation, as the practice of eastern 'tantric yoga' verifies. Reconstruction of the sexual act which conceived us is a primary key to our own creativity, sexuality and entrance into the transcendent octave of reality.

Psychoanalysis, psychotherapy and other analytic processes can be initiations, as we track our life backwards towards gestation with the benefit of a trained guide. Glimpses of the whole can happen through association, hypnosis, the recreation of archetypal situations via psychodrama, movement, words or symbols, and can occur through the presence of a sympathetic listener. Correct bodily movement in athletics, running, stretching, dance and sex often provides breaks through into transcendence. Yoga, martial arts, Tai Chi, meditation and other techniques developed in the East are specifically oriented towards the identical aim of unity.

Initiatory processes induce reality beyond the physical and release creative potential. The process of using the logarithmic Life★Time Scale is another means to this end. It is most helpful as a pattern which may be used together with other techniques. Once the breakthrough into the higher octave of transcendence has been accomplished, the four gestation houses take on greater additional meaning.

The Higher Octave Houses

The time of gestation, which begins with conception and ends with birth, is a pattern of our own creative processes and potential transcendent development. As transcendence, creativity and sexuality are three aspects of the higher life, the energies which drive these processes are the same.

The nature of our conception can be reconstructed using Life★Time Astrology. Our father and mother are the masculine/feminine, positive/negative and sperm/ovum combinations which produce us, and each parent contains both polarities. It is possible that our father was active or passive, that our mother was passive or active, or any permutation of the two opposite roles of the life force. Whichever parent was responsible for the impulse to conceive us registers as the creative motivation in our life. Our other parent represents mechanisms within us which are acted upon. The manner of our parents' courtship and seduction mirrors our own creative mechanism. It may have been accidental, planned, one-sided, equivalent, bored, highly sexual, asexual, purely physical, extremely emotional, intellectual, violent, detached, attached, athletic or lazy. Whatever the circumstances, our access to creativity will reflect the nature of conception as a relationship between our parents.

The physical act of conception is a metaphor for our ability to make creativity manifest in the physical world. Either parent may have had the primary inclination to create, but not the necessary strength or will to follow through. Analysis of our conception moment provides a key to our own sexual motivation as well as to our creativity.

The Higher Octave 9th House

The higher octave of the 9th House reflects the first seven weeks of gestation, when our mother gradually realized that she was pregnant. This also occurs after our first initiatory, creative or sexual experiences. The feeling of pure life pulses through us, as though no one had ever made love, painted a picture or realized the implications of their beliefs before. The breakthrough made running long distances is a higher octave of physical activities, and we must push through impulses to stop before the breakthrough is made. The 9th House refers to the religious, philosophical and psychological perspective within which a larger perspective of our life and views may be contained. A mother's ability to understand her new creative state sets a pattern of behaviour for our transcendent, creative and sexual experiences.

The Higher Octave MC

This reflects the moment our mother realizes that she is pregnant. This is the moment our ego registers, our mother becomes conscious of her new objectives and the soul enters our physical body. The quality of our mother's consciousness is equivalent to the nature of our own self-consciousness in life. Our mother's projections and reactions at that time, the people she consulted, their reactions and her ability to broadcast her successful creativity determine the strength and quality of our ego. If she required a doctor to tell her that she was pregnant, then we will need such verification from a protective figure like a family doctor or psychoanalyst to justify our own life objectives. In previous times the mother or other women would have recognized pregnancy, but in the modern world pregnancy is usually determined by chemical test or doctor's examination. The return to natural methods is important in more than the obvious ways! If our mother kept her pregnancy secret initially due to confusion over paternity, then we would keep our life aims secret. Our mother's reaction to pregnancy is a direct metaphor of our place in the world.

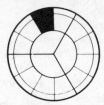

The Higher Octave 10th House

The higher octave of the 10th House reflects our parents' organizational abilities in the world after accepting the fact of our conception. Their responses and actions show how we organize and manifest life objectives in the real world. Higher perceptions from the 9th House must be integrated into our mundane life. If our parents stress practical matters during gestation, our life will be conditioned by practical matters. If they espouse more profound attitudes our life philosophy emphasizes higher values.

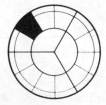

The Higher Octave 11th House

The higher octave of the 11th House sees our mother forming idealistic attitudes reflecting her relationships with others. Her involvement with or abstraction from those around her, and especially group values, determines the pattern of our collective life in the world. Our mother once transcended physical concerns in gestation to purify and project high values onto us, and we must extend our world view beyond mere security. Once we have stepped beyond physical reality to higher aims in the 10th House, we must transmit them to the public. This starts with our immediate family, extends to local groups and then the public at large. The contrast between personal and collective ideals generates higher utopian aims, communal activities and inventive social systems.

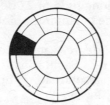

The Higher Octave 12th House

The higher octave of the 12th House reflects a receptive and sacrificial orientation of our mother in the last phase of gestation. Once we transmit our ideas into the world, we must reap the consequences of our actions. In contrast to the physical transformation of the 8th House, these ultimate karmic influences describe the spiritual impact of our life and its ideals upon others, inwardly and outwardly. This indicates to what extent we are willing to sacrifice ourself, even physically, to higher aspirations. If a mother is willing to obey even the most subtle signals emanating from us during the last phase of pregnancy, then we can respond sympathetically to the finest spiritual values.

With the completion of this last house, life is complete on all four octave levels of existence; Gestation, Childhood, Maturity and Transcendence. All potential we accepted at conception has been translated into actuality and the process of life is complete. In reconstructing life with the Life★Time Scale, our understanding of it in time is complete.

Orientation In Time

The exact time of birth determines the position of the signs relative to the sequence of house ages and both sequences can easily be dated. Table 4, Log Time Scale Dates shows the ages of every degree of the horoscope, correlated to the exact Ascendant in our horoscope.

The horoscope blank on the frontispiece of this book shows the degrees of the zodiac from the beginning of Aries at 0 degrees to the end of Pisces at 360 degrees and the beginning of Aries again. Every sign position translates into an equivalent number of degrees from 0 Aries. This number is called Absolute Longitude. Table 5 shows the absolute longitude of all twelve signs:

To find the absolute longitude of 27 degrees Gemini (Figure 8), add 27 degrees to the beginning point of Gemini, which is 060 degrees.

27 + 60 = 87 degrees absolute longitude

An Ascendant of 6 degrees Sagittarius translates into 240 + 6 degrees or 246 degrees absolute longitude. With practice one can translate either way easily.

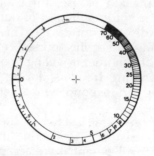

Dating Disk
Photocopy this page and cut out the dating disk, or have a photocopy on acetate. Superimpose this disk over horoscopes with 0 on the ASC to read correct dates in life directly from the wheel.

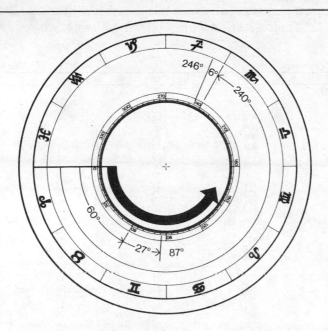

Figure 8: Absolute Longitude
Absolute Longitude is the distance in degrees from 0 Aries to any planet or personal point, measured in the direction of the signs.

Table 5: Absolute Longitude

Degrees	Sign
000 – 030	Aries
030 – 060	Taurus
060 – 090	Gemini
090 – 120	Cancer
120 – 150	Leo
150 – 180	Virgo
180 – 210	Libra
210 – 240	Scorpio
240 – 270	Sagittarius
270 – 300	Capricorn
300 – 330	Aquarius
330 – 360	Pisces

Table 4: Life★Time Astrology Time Scale

Degrees from ASC	Week	Degrees from ASC	Week	Degrees from ASC	Year	Month	Degrees from ASC	Year	Month
240°	4	300°	12	00°	00	00	60°	1	8
241		301		01			61		
242		302		02			62		
243		303		03			63		
244		304		04			64		
245	4	305	13	05	0	1	65	1	11
246		306		06			66		
247		307		07			67		
248		308		08			68		
249		309		09			69		
250	4	310	15	10	0	2	70	2	2
251		311		11			71		
252		312		12			72		
253		313		13			73		
254		314		14			74		
255 9th	5	315 11th	16	15 1st	0	3	75 3rd	2	5
256		316		16			76		
257		317		17			77		
258		318		18			78		
259		319		19			79		
260	5	320	18	20	0	4	80	2	9
261		321		21			81		
262		322		22			82		
263		323		23			83		
264		324		24			84		
265	6	325	20	25	0	6	85	3	2
266		326		26			86		
267		327		27			87		
268		328		28			88		
269		329		29			89		
270	7	330	22	30	0	7	90	3	6
271		331		31			91		
272		332		32			92		
273		333		33			93		
274		334		34			94		
275	7	335	24	35	0	9	95	4	0
276		336		36			96		
277		337		37			97		
278		338		38			98		
279		339		39			99		
280	8	340	26	40	0	11	100	4	5
281		341		41			101		
282		342		42			102		
283		343		43			103		
284		344		44			104		
285 10th	9	345 12th	29	45 2nd	1	0	105 4th	5	0
286		346		46			106		
287		347		47			107		
288		348		48			108		
289		349		49			109		
290	10	350	32	50	1	3	110	5	6
291		351		51			111		
292		352		52			112		
293		353		53			113		
294		354		54			114		
295	11	355	35	55	1	5	115	6	2
296		356		56			116		
297		357		57			117		
298		358		58			118		
299		359		59			119		
300	12	360	40	60	1	8	120	6	10

Degrees from ASC	Year	Month	Degrees from ASC	Year	Month	Degrees from ASC	Year	Month
120°	6	10	180°	23	5	240°	75	11
121	7	1	181	23	11	241	77	5
122	7	2	182	24	4	242	78	11
123	7	4	183	24	10	243	80 ·	6
124	7	6	184	25	4	244	82	0
125	7	8	185	25	10	245	83	6
126	7	10	186	26	4	246	85	4
127	8	0	187	26	11	247	86	11
128	8	2	188	27	5	248	88	8
129	8	4	189	28	0	249	90	5
130	8	6	190	28	6	250	92	2
131	8	8	191	29	1	251	94	0
132	8	10	192	29	8	252	95	10
133	9	0	193	30	3	253	97	8
134	9	3	194	30	11	254	99	7
135 5th	9	5	195 7th	31	6	255	101	7
136	9	7	196	32	2			
137	9	10	197	32	9			
138	10	0	198	33	5			
139	10	3	199	34	1			
140	10	5	200	34	9			
141	10	8	201	35	5			
142	10	10	202	36	2			
143	11	1	203	36	10			
144	11	4	204	37	7			
145	11	7	205	38	4			
146	11	10	206	39	1			
147	12	1	207	39	11			
148	12	4	208	40	8			
149	12	7	209	41	6			
150	12	10	210	42	3			
151	13	1	211	43	2			
152	13	4	212	44	0			
153	13	8	213	44	10			
154	13	11	214	45	9			
155	14	2	215	46	8			
156	14	6	216	47	7			
157	14	9	217	48	6			
158	15	1	218	49	5			
159	15	4	219	50	5			
160	15	8	220	51	5			
161	16	0	221	52	5			
162	16	4	222	53	6			
163	16	8	223	54	6			
164	17	0	224	55	7			
165 6th	17	4	225 8th	56	8			
166	17	8	226	57	10			
167	18	1	227	58	11			
168	18	5	228	60	1			
169	18	10	229	61	3			
170	19	2	230	62	6			
171	19	7	231	63	9			
172	20	0	232	65	0			
173	20	4	233	66	3			
174	20	9	234	67	7			
175	21	2	235	68	11			
176	21	7	236	70	3			
177	22	1	237	71	7			
178	22	6	238	73	0			
179	22	11	239	74	5			
180	23	5	240	75	11			

Every house cusp and sign cusp must be translated into degrees from the Ascendant. Then the ages at which the house and sign cusps begin can be read directly from Table 4. The example of John Lennon's horoscope shows this:

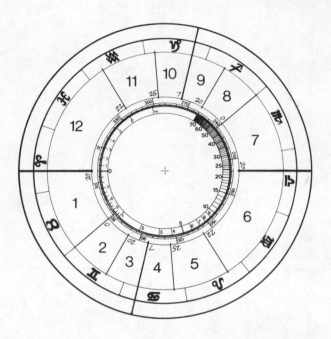

Figure 9: Dating House and Sign Cusps
Align 0 on the dating disk with the ASC and read off the ages of the house and sign cusps to the nearest year. In childhood, simply estimate the ages when a cusp falls between even years. In gestation, the time is measured in months before birth and it is necessary to round off to the nearest month.

(When a cusp is more than 240 degrees from the Ascendant, the age must be in the table for Old Age. Sometimes the 9th cusp is beyond the age of a hundred years old. In this event, the 9th cusp is not dated.) To date the house cusps during gestation, the results are in weeks before birth:

Table 6: Dating House Cusps

Cusp	Zodiacal Position	Abs Long	Minus ASC	=	Degrees from ASC	Age in Yrs and Mos
Ascendant	20 Aries	020	− 020	=	000	Birth
2nd House	00 Gemini	060	− 020	=	040	00yrs 11mos
3rd House	20 Gemini	080	− 020	=	060	01yrs 08mos
4th House	07 Cancer	097	− 020	=	077	02yrs 07mos
5th House	25 Cancer	115	− 020	=	095	04yrs 00mos
6th House	22 Leo	142	− 020	=	122	07yrs 02mos
7th House	20 Libra	200	− 020	=	180	23yrs 05mos
8th House	00 Sagittarius	240	− 020	=	220	51yrs 05mos
9th House	20 Sagittarius	260	− 020	=	240	75yrs 11mos
9th House	20 Sagittarius	260	− 020	=	240	− 40weeks
10th House	07 Capricorn	277	− 020	=	257	− 35weeks
11th House	25 Capricorn	295	− 020	=	275	− 33weeks
12th House	22 Aquarius	322	− 020	=	302	− 27weeks

(Since the 9th cusp/conception point is the end of the first lunar month lifetime of the ovum, four weeks must be added to the figure in the table to arrive at the approximate conception time.)

This completes the dating of the twelve house cusps in the horoscope, showing the ages at which Lennon passed from one developmental stage to the next. The following calculations allow one to date the twelve sign cusps in Lennon's horoscope.

Table 7: Dating Sign Cusps

Taurus	00 Taurus	030	− 020	=	010	00yrs 02mos
Gemini	00 Gemini	060	− 020	=	040	00yrs 11mos
Cancer	00 Cancer	090	− 020	=	070	02yrs 02mos
Leo	00 Leo	120	− 020	=	100	04yrs 05mos
Virgo	00 Virgo	150	− 020	=	130	08yrs 06mos
Libra	00 Libra	100	− 020	=	160	15yrs 00mos
Scorpio	00 Scorpio	210	− 020	=	190	28yrs 06mos
Sagit	00 Sagittarius	240	− 020	=	220	51yrs 05mos
In Gestation:						
Capricorn	00 Capricorn	270	− 020	=	250	− 36weeks
Aquarius	00 Aquarius	300	− 020	=	280	− 32weeks
Pisces	00 Pisces	330	− 020	=	310	− 25weeks
Aries	00 Aries	360	− 020	=	340	−14weeks

This completes the dating of the twelve signs in John Lennon's horoscope and shows the ages at which he passes from sign to sign in his life. We can see the interpretation in Chapter Eight when Lennon's entire horoscope is interpreted.

★ Chapter Four ★
The Cast of Characters

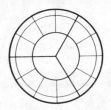

The ten planets represent the *cast of characters* in life. The characters are parents, siblings, relatives, doctors, neighbours, friends, lovers, enemies, associates, partners, children and else of importance. Each character enters life, plays his or her role, and then leaves at a time corresponding to an equivalent planet's position in the horoscope. Some roles are permanent, some sporadic, but most are played by a succession of characters. The Sun is originally our father, then becomes a teacher, then an employer, then we become a father ourself. All characters influence our whole being and play their part in forming our character. A key to the discovery of our essential nature is to use Life★Time Astrology to identify and understand all the characters, their various guises, their times of appearance, and their meaning as they enter and leave life. Each of the ten planets registers at a specific time, manifests through an outer event or an inner realization, and is carried by a character or characters. The event, the character and their interaction are reflections of our being.

When we relate to someone, an image of them is created within which reflects the way we see and feel them (Figure 10). Through time they and we change, mutual attitudes change and our internal reflection of them changes. A central development in life is the balance of the way people really are as opposed to our attitude towards them.

Since life begins at conception, some of the central characters – parents, family and their friends – precede us onto the stage of life. Initially they do not realize our potential existence and play their parts uninfluenced by us. We have no control at all over those who determine the earliest and deepest levels of our identity. A primary paradox of life is that by the time we question those who affect our gestation and childhood, their influence is already past. For better or worse, parents and the events surrounding conception and gestation cannot be changed. Only an understanding of them and attitudes towards them can alter. To discover why we are who we are, we must put our past into perspective by determining who was present in our early life, how and why they behaved as they did, and what it all means.

The most important correlation of planets to characters is that of the Sun to father and the Moon to mother. The Sun is not only our father, but also all the ways in which we relate to him and to the idea 'father'. The Sun is anyone with whom we have a paternal relationship, as well as the father within. The concept 'mother' means much more than the personal qualities enacted by our own mother. It includes all mothers and all maternal feelings. Our mother has her own unique personal qualities, but she also partakes of the mother archetype. She may not even carry any of the receptive, nurturing or protective qualities, but she shapes all attitudes to such qualities.

The planets function as *archetypes*. Archetypes are patterning structures which carry and transform psychic energy, and are the symbolic expression of instinctive processes like love, hate, fear, flight, nurturing and repulsion that are inherited from all humanity. Each planet is an archetype through which instincts are channelled. Likewise, each planetary archetype carries both the positive and negative characteristics available. Venus is loving and lovers, but also the rejection of relationships when badly aspected. Venus may also generate its opposite Martial qualities in frustrated love.

Each planetary archetype is carried by many people in life. For example, in the early part of life all maternal qualities are projected onto a mother by child-parent bonding. Gradually we experience others who possess motherly qualities, like nannies, grandmothers, aunts and teachers. Our own mother is the primary subject of the mother archetype, but we discover that there may be other women more protective, receptive or open than our own mother: our mother may possess none of these qualities! The total feeling towards all our 'mothers' is eventually the basis of our own personal value system; the mother in us. We all possess mothers, fathers, brothers, sisters and the entire range of people we know inside ourself.

Figure 10: Planetary Personifications
These cartoon figures show general planetary correspondences within the family. The Sun is father; Moon is mother; Mercury is baby; Venus is sister; Mars is brother; Jupiter and Saturn are grandparents. The outer planets show generational influences: Uranus is explosive events; Neptune sensitive situations; Pluto is forceful circumstances; and the Node is groups, including the whole family. (Illustration by John Astrop)

As we age, our attitudes towards parents, friends, siblings and others change as they themselves change. With movement through our horoscope houses in succession, planets in residence are affected by the qualities of the developmental stage signified by each house. The nature of each planet and its characters change according to the house of residence and the sign qualities occupying the house. Venus in the 12th House could be a midwife or mother's friend; Venus on the Ascendant could be a nurse or mother's helper; Venus in the 2nd House could be a favourite object or toy; while Venus in the 3rd House could be a sister or playmate; etc.

The house of residence changes the quality of events in addition to changing the character indicated by a planet. Since Venus is relationship, the house and age of Venus' registration qualifies the type of relationship in question. Venus in the 3rd House at two years old is communication with a sister or playmate, while Venus in the 7th House at thirty-two is a love relationship.

A planet's house position qualifies whoever carries its affect. Early in life, events are most often caused by those around us; therefore, the planets *are* other people. Later in life, events are more likely to be a result of our own actions, if not directly caused by us. Mars accidents would happen *to us* when in the 2nd House, but would be caused *by us* in the 6th House. It is important to know whether we or others cause the critical events in life, even though we ultimately must take responsibility for them all.

The sign location of a planet qualifies its action and character. Each planet rules a sign or signs and their equivalent house or houses. When a planet resides in the sign it rules, it functions at its purest and most archetypal. The Moon rules the sign Cancer and the 4th House, both of which govern mother, home, family and emotions. When we have the Moon in either of these positions, our maternal relationship is archetypal. Mercury rules the positive Gemini and the 3rd House of communication, walking and talking; and the negative Virgo and the 6th House of discrimination, criticism and decision-making to define our position in the world.

Table 8: Planetary Rulerships

Planet rules		Positive Sign and House			/Negative Sign and House		
Sun	rules	Leo	&	5th House			
Moon	rules				Cancer	&	4th House
Mercury	rules	Gemini	&	3rd House/Virgo	&	6th House	
Venus	rules	Libra	&	7th House/Taurus	&	2nd House	
Mars	rules	Aries	&	1st House/Scorpio	&	8th House	
Jupiter	rules	Sagittarius	&	9th House/Pisces	&	12th House	
Saturn	rules	Aquarius	&	11th House/Capricorn	&	10th House	
Uranus	rules	Aquarius	&	11th House			
Neptune	rules	Pisces	&	12th House			
Pluto	rules	Scorpio	&	8th House			

When a planet resides in the sign opposite to the sign it rules, like Venus in Scorpio or in the 8th House, it is in detriment and it functions negatively.

Planets located above the horizon in a horoscope are conscious and those below the horizon are unconscious. Venus represents a relationship, so Venus above the horizon is a conscious relationship and Venus below the horizon is an unconscious relationship. The naturally objective, active and vital Sun, when below the horizon, still carries those qualities but we are unaware of possessing them. When the naturally subjective and receptive Moon is above the horizon, our maternal side is prominent but we are conscious of its behaviour.

Planets located in the left, eastern half of a horoscope are self-oriented and planets in the right, western half are oriented to the outer world. Jupiter as the indicator of life philosophy would be exclusive when in the left side and inclusive when in the right side of the horoscope. Planets near the Ascendant in a horoscope affect personality and planets near the MC affect objectives and aims in life.

Aspects are geometrical relationships between planets and will be explained in the next chapter, but they should be mentioned here. Planetary influences can operate alone, but usually affect each other mutually, combining planetary influences. Saturn is inhibition and Venus is relationship, so the Saturn/Venus aspect is 'inhibited relationship'. Planets naturally combine with each other, just as in nature the elements are rarely found in their pure state, but abound in compounds and complex combinations with other elements.

When any planet is in one of the double signs Gemini, Cancer, Libra, Sagittarius, Aquarius or Pisces there is more than one individual carrying the planetary influence, and a duality results in the equivalent event.

The planets are considered either masculine, feminine or neuter. Women and men are composed of both masculine and feminine qualities, and the overall balance of masculine-feminine varies dramatically through life. Women exhibit objectivity, consciousness and vitality, in the same way that men exhibit subjectivity, unconsciousness and passivity. If masculine planets are dominant by sign and house position in our horoscope, masculine qualities predominate whether or not we are biologically male or female. The planets are paired in masculine-feminine dyads which depend upon each other for wholeness. The only exceptions are Mercury, which signifies neutral intelligence, and Uranus, which is originality and independence.

The Sun is the ability to understand and integrate all influences in life into a conscious and objective whole, while the Moon promotes feelings and emotions which generate the internal value system in life. The Sun differentiates as the Moon integrates. The geometrical aspect between the Sun and Moon in our horoscope describes the nature of our parents' relationship, as well as forming a pattern for our own relationships and the masculine-feminine balance within us.

Mercury is the ability to establish communication with both father and mother as a gauge of our intelligence and balance. It is a neutral planet as it combines masculine and feminine, and left and right brain halves.

Venus and Mars are the feminine-masculine polarity manifest in the physical and sexual realm. Venus is passive sexuality which wishes to relate and to be possessed, while Mars is active sexuality which wishes to alter the object of its affection, a desire to change.

Jupiter is a masculine expansion of horizons and Saturn is a feminine contraction of concentration. Their polarity is that of philosophy, religion and psychology versus materialism, pragmatism and science.

The three outer planets take so long to pass through each sign that they indicate transpersonal or generational mechanisms within the psyche. Uranus takes about seven years to pass through each sign; Neptune takes about fourteen years; and Pluto takes about twenty-two years. Everyone experiences a complete cycle of all the inner planets through all twelve signs by the age of twenty-nine years and six months when Saturn has completed its cycle. The planets from the Sun to Saturn are the personal characteristics everyone shares. The three outer planets show influences which affect the masses and the equivalent inner understanding of collective values some people possess.

The Sun   (Rules Leo)

The Sun in a horoscope describes our relationship to the masculine, conscious and vital forces of life as determined by attitudes towards our father. The Sun is this relationship, not the father. As our first physical contact with our father occurs after birth, it is rarely as direct as bonding to our mother. The masculine principle becomes most evident when we begin to focus light clearly at about eighty days after birth and remains objective, rational and detached. This timing reflects the Sun's first complete cycle of 365 days after conception (280 + 85). Although the Sun is often considered the most important planet in a horoscope (or as the only planet in so-called 'Sun Sign Astrology'), this is not the case. Many of us have weak, absent or multiple fathers. The Sun as our father, although central to our life, is also a component of the whole.

With age we realize that our father is not the only man in the world; there are other men stronger, more intelligent, more objective and more masculine. This signals the transformation of the Sun influence beyond those attached to our actual father. The solar image and our vitality depend upon finding ever higher forms upon which to project our life focus and to which to apply energies. Sexual energy, libido, psychic energy or kundalini metamorphoses into purer channels as we age. The energy of sucking in the 1st House transforms into chewing in the 2nd, talking in the 3rd, emotional give-and-take in the 4th, gameplaying in the 5th, competition in the 6th to sexuality in the 7th. When energy is blocked from transforming itself into the next higher level, symbolized by the next house position of the Sun (or any other planet), it regresses. When we cannot find the next gradient of energy, it moves back to a previous house. When there is no outlet for sexual energies, we must return to games to express them. The Sun symbolizes the gradual process of becoming conscious of Self, energy and life.

In early life, the Sun is carried by those who organize or control our environment. This may include, in addition to the father, masculine qualities of the mother, grandparents, housekeepers, uncles, doctors, priests and those who exert influence upon the mother. Early paternal projections transfer to teachers, heroes, actors, athletes, politicians, idealogues, celebrities, royalty, impressarios, the wealthy and anyone in authority. From the beginning of Maturity at about seven years old until the Descendant point at twenty-three years and five months, these projections happen often and are natural. Past the Descendant it is time to begin repossessing these paternal projections: We must become a father ourself. The quality, variety and number of paternal projections made in early life define our own masculine nature. Our father and his surrogates provide models of consciousness, and the degree of awareness depends upon understanding this relationship, whether we are male or female. We can and must be aware of our father and his role, even when he is unsympathetic, absent, unconscious or instinctive.

The Sun in a horoscope is vitality, objectivity, consciousness, organization, decisiveness and spiritual focus.

The Moon   *(Rules Cancer)*

The Moon in a horoscope is the ability to value, to feel and to reflect emotions. The structure and intensity of our instinctive value systems is derived and influenced by the way in which we relate to our mother. She carries us within her during gestation and bonds to us at birth. From that time on we begin to differentiate ourself from her. Feelings about one's mother are continually in flux, like the changeable but repetitive lunar phases each month. The time of the Moon's registration in a horoscope shows the time when we relate to her most strongly. In early life she is an extension of our own reality, but with age she occupies a relative position in our affections.

Early maternal projections surround us within the womb yet are also transmitted by grandmothers, aunts, midwives, female doctors, emotional people, women in general and the feminine component in our father. From birth the Moon signifies everyone who protects, nurtures and feels towards us, including nannies, medical people and males within our environment. From school age lunar projections are displaced by teachers or girlfriends, just as home and family are displaced by school and classmates. Beginning at the Descendant, the Moon becomes a pattern for feelings about partnership, sexuality, mating, raising children and the world. Ultimately we must integrate maternal feelings into our whole being. When the traditional childraising function is rejected, variants emerge to take its place, like finding others to protect or being protected emotionally, instinctive return to sport, nature or the land.

The Moon moves rapidly and functions as a connecting agent and catalyst in a horoscope. She reflects and values the other planets and establishes the tone of emotional life through events which bring out our feminine nature.

Mercury (*Rules Gemini and Virgo*)

Mercury is an ability to communicate with and mediate between mother and father outwardly, and our feminine and masculine natures inwardly. Our intellect, intelligence, mental and nervous processes are determined by the fluidity of this communication. As communication requires the acquisition of visual and audial languages, it is essentially imitative. We communicate as we observe and hear others around communicate. Our mind interweaves masculine-feminine by the connecting bridge between the left brain hemisphere which has domain over logical, analytical, mathematical and verbal functions with linear masculine qualities, and the right brain hemisphere which has domain over holistic, mental, artistic and spatial functions associated with feminine simultaneous qualities. When Mercury registers it shows at which age mental development is most critical. Mercury in the 3rd House is adaptable communicative mind, while Mercury in the 7th House is comparative, balancing and team thinking.

During Gestation Mercury is an indicator of our mother's expression of her changing mental state, and may represent her brothers or sisters, friends, confidants or our siblings. In Childhood Mercury connotes other children and teachers; those after whom our own communication methods are patterned. Mercurial influence is also carried by books and the media, especially by television in the present world. Later manifestations include business sense, criticism, scientific work and individual self-expression.

Mercury is a gauge of our breadth of communication formed in early childhood, which is modulated by parental relationships. Even when parental attitudes openly conflict they must combine within us. Mercury ranges from quick wit and easy superficiality to scathing criticism and serious scientific logic. Mercurial events are adaptations, changes of mind, perceptive insights, learning and teaching phases of life.

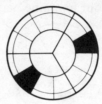

♀ *Venus*   *(Rules Taurus and Libra)*

Venus represents relationships, harmony, love and personal aesthetics as determined by an ability to accept physical situations in life and to make them work, whether furnishing a room, adorning oneself, choosing a partner or making love. Venus is integration and physical attraction.

During Gestation Venus shows a mother's relatedness to herself and others. Venus may be older sisters, friends of our mother's or any women who guide her through gestation and birth, such as midwives, those who teach or espouse natural childbirth and those who write about these subjects. In Childhood Venus indicates other children, aunts, friends of our mother, or even our mother herself. In Maturity Venus describes woman friends, lovers, artists, mates, anyone attractive physically or those involved with beauty, art, clothes and appearances.

Venus indicates relationship to the physical world as amplified by the character of our sexual contact. Relationships with others mirror our understanding of the feminine reality within and the ways of projecting it outside in associations, artistic involvement and indulgence.

Mars   (Rules Aries and Scorpio)

Mars represents the masculine sexual reality and physical situations that we cannot accept and which we desire to change. Mars is never satisfied with what is, only with what can be altered to suit its affections. Mars resists absorption and is assertive, initiatory, passionate, energetic and conflicting. Sexual energy can be channelled into the physical world, but if no outlet is available Mars is violent, overbearing and ruthless.

During Gestation Mars indicates doctors, medical examinations, men in general, aggressive midwives and our parents' sexual contact. At birth Mars is often the doctor in his role as surgeon and intervening agent. In Childhood Mars is active children, men, athletes, medical people, brothers, uncles or craftsmen. In Maturity it is the acceptance of any of the former occupations or roles and those who change the world. On the sexual level Mars is men to whom we are sexually attracted and the masculine aspect of women which attracts us.

Mars is an active desire to change the physical world into our own image, to produce progeny and to assert our own will. The degree of competitiveness in our persona mirrors the strength and nature of inner masculine reality. Mars events are accidents, creative moments, changes, alterations of attitude or situation, transactions we initiate, crises, resoluteness and enterprising moves. When Mars has no viable channel it becomes violent, angry and self-destructive.

Jupiter   (Rules Sagittarius and Pisces) ♃

Jupiter represents expansive influences which are optimistic, positive, generous, enthusiastic, cohesive, philosophical, psychological or religious. Even in negative connections, although being indulgent and lazy, Jupiter is our life view and those who provide patterns for optimism.

During Gestation Jupiter indicates religious influences, grandparents, socialites, prominent people, spiritual or psychological advisors and beneficial midwives or doctors. When registering at birth, Jupiter represents anyone who enlivens or is wise. In Childhood it indicates surrogate parents, nannies, aunts or uncles, grandparents, early teachers, religious trainers or merchants. A registration of Jupiter in Maturity shows those people who determine our world view, psychologists and therapists, advisors, successful or notable people, politicians and those associated with education.

Jupiter indicates expansiveness, openness to new influences and a willingness to adopt educational, religious or psychological standpoints in life. We grow towards the goals we set for ourself; the higher the goals, the greater the possibilities. Jupiter events are expansion in work or philosophy, the advent of wealth and the appearance of people who help us. It is the ability to accept higher tasks which transcend our material appetites.

♄ Saturn   (Rules Capricorn and Aquarius)

Saturn is a self-regulative counterbalance to Jupiter and tests, limits, concentrates, structures, orders, focuses, crystallizes, contracts and conserves. Saturn is acceptance of material and unavoidable restrictions of life. When we resist life's responsibilities, restrictions increase, while the willingness to confront reality enables us to focus and centre ourself.

During Gestation Saturn is restrictive grandparents, serious doctors, pessimists, the authorities and those who inhibit our mother. Registering at birth, Saturn shows over-regulators of the birth process, emotionally restricting people present and the seriousness of the atmosphere. In Maturity Saturn represents teachers, employers, elders, bank managers, authorities and those who seek to form and crystallize our reality. Saturn symbolizes those older, more depressive, more concentrated and more restricted than us.

Saturn is the acceptance and perfection of life through discipline, tests of strength, seriousness, confrontation and resolution of the problems of ageing. Saturnine events are inhibited crossroads, paralysing circumstances, illnesses, troubles and difficulties resulting from changes.

The Outer Planets

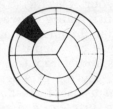

Uranus   *(Rules Aquarius)*

Uranus is the ability to step beyond the purely personal characteristics of the seven inner planets. Uranus represents originality, eccentricity, uniqueness, intensity, inspiration, inventiveness and rhythm which allow you to integrate diverse influences which initially seem divisive, unusual or disconnected. It is the part of you which wants to be unique and free of the fetters of physicality.

During Gestation Uranus indicates anyone who responds in an original way to a mother's pregnancy, including medical practitioners, midwives, childbirth instructors, other women or those who disrupt her natural rhythms or introduce new rhythms such as breathing exercises. When Uranus registers at birth or in aspect to the Ascendant it indicates medical technicians, doctors, anyone who changes existing patterns and acts independently. In Childhood Uranus shows rebels, eccentric playmates, independent friends and ambitious people. During Maturity Uranus represents eccentrics, independent people, reformers, inventors, dancers, technicians, inspired people and fringe medical practitioners. Uranus symbolizes anyone who breaks down our established life patterns in unexpected ways and provides prototypes for our own independence.

Emotional and mental rhythms condition material rigidity and Uranus is the potential to integrate and balance new output. Uranus events are sudden, traumatic, unusual, eccentric and often happen in rhythmic phases.

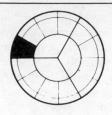

 Neptune   *(Rules Pisces)*

Neptune represents our psychic, sensitive, imaginative, mediumistic and intuitive nature derived from the finer levels of reality and mirrored in dreams, fantasies, idealism, utopian projections and imagination. Neptune shows our sensitivity and receptivity to the spiritual impulse as well as our illusions; the domain of drugs, psychic experiences, ESP and dream states. These are mechanisms which allow existing but hidden principles to rise to the surface of consciousness.

During Gestation Neptune is those near our mother who sense that she is pregnant or act as mediums for her; as often others divine our innermost psychic states before we ourself do. Psychic friends, dreamers, mystics, gurus, dieticians, drug dealers and anyone who exerts psychic influence upon her are also covered by Neptune. At birth Neptune is anaesthetists, hospital nursing staff, the watery medium of birth itself or sensitive participants. An amusing parallel is that the Neptune influence attracted in induced or anaesthetic births is similar when babies are born into pools of water, as one modern practice. Neptune registering in Childhood indicates dreamers, idealists, doctors treating childhood illnesses, fantasy characters, dream images and invented roles, as well as the omnipresent teddy bear or doll. In Maturity Neptune represents those who live in fantasy, illusion, dreams, sickness or sensitives, mediums, tricksters, psychics, astrologers and mystics, in addition to those who are sensitive and who dispense drugs.

Neptune symbolizes those who make us aware that the higher and finer levels of consciousness and reality are available and teach how to gain access to them. Neptune events are particularly difficult to describe as they are vague, internal, dreamy, psychosomatic or spiritual.

Pluto   *(Rules Scorpio)*

Pluto is contact with the masses and transformation, which involves the destruction of existing behaviour patterns and environments as a necessary prerequisite for regeneration. Often Pluto refers to world events which disrupt people and society – world wars, economic collapses, mass movements and superpower politics. Pluto is the effect upon us of the world in which we live and specifically historical transformations. Most of us are affected by mass events without understanding what they are. Pluto shows our relationship to the influences which affect entire generations as well as our own parallel, internal changes. Changes of residence, school, attitude, partnership and other dramatic alterations of importance are governed by Pluto.

Pluto in Gestation shows world events affecting a mother's pregnancy, her contact with public figures such as medical specialists, authorities on childbirth, and even indirect contact with public influences through books or media. Being born during a world war, raised according to Dr Spock or delivered by the LeBoyer technique are examples of such influences. At birth Pluto is people who exert influence, take charge or transform us. Pluto in Childhood is bossy people, parents or teachers. In Maturity Pluto indicates figures who carry generational influences such as politicians, musicians, actors, propagandists and all those who affect us through public opinion or those who change our world.

Pluto is the part of us which responds to the challenges and trials of the masses and participates in public events, either actually or as a surrogate of mass movements for friends or acquaintanceships. Pluto events are gradual but extreme, exceptionally powerful, critical and carry long- lasting influence.

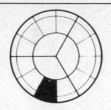

The Moon's Node   *(Rules Gemini)*

A line drawn through the long axis of the Moon's elliptical orbit round Earth intersects the ecliptic at two places, the ascending North Node where the intersection is from south to north, and the descending South Node. For astrological purposes, except in Hindu astrology, only the North Node is used. The Node moves backwards through the Zodiac in a complete cycle of eighteen years. In our horoscope the Node is adaptability, associations, family and groups of all varieties.

The Node at Gestation shows the influence of groups upon a mother, particularly her family. At birth it is the total influence of everyone present. Natural childbirth or women's groups often reflect the Node. In Childhood the Node is other children and our family; in Maturity clubs, social or political organizations, friends, circles of associates and all other groups of people.

The Node is collective influences in life and its events are comings together with others and a desire to link with groups.

Planetary Timing

In Chapter Three the house cusps and sign cusps were dated in the time scale from conception to ninety-nine years old. An identical process is used to find the registration age of every planet in a horoscope.

Every planet must be translated into degrees from the Ascendant, then the ages can be read directly from the table on page 58-59. Table 9 shows the dating of the planets in John Lennon's horoscope (Figure 11).

Figure 11: Dating Planets

The circular dating disk is aligned with the horoscope so that the figure 0 (the birth moment) in the inner ring is on the ASC. Dates during Gestation (the 9th, 10th, 11th and 12th houses) are graded in months before birth. Dates immediately after birth, during the first year of life, are graded in months, and then the scale is graded in years. When a house cusp falls between two years, estimate the date in between. In most horoscopes the conception/death point does not correspond to that shown on the dating disk. Conception point is the actual location of the 9th cusp in the horoscope, not the point on the disk! This reflects the fact that most births are either shorter or longer than the exact full term.

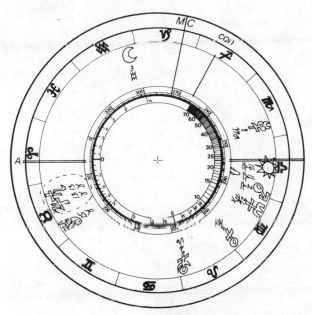

Table 9: Dating the Planets

Planet	Zodiacal Position	Absolute Longitude	Minus ASC		Degrees from ASC	Age
MC	07 Capricorn	277	−19	=	258	−34weeks
Moon	03 Aquarius	303	−19	=	284	−31weeks
ASC	19 Aries	19	−19	=	0	Birth
Saturn	13 Taurus	43	−19	=	24	00yrs 06mo
Jupiter	13 Taurus	43	−19	=	24	00yrs 06mo
Uranus	25 Taurus	55	−19	=	36	00yrs 09mo
Pluto	04 Leo	124	−19	=	105	05yrs 00mo
Venus	03 Virgo	153	−19	=	134	09yrs 03mo
Neptune	26 Virgo	176	−19	=	157	14yrs 09mo
Mars	02 Libra	182	−19	=	163	16yrs 08mo
Node	10 Libra	190	−19	=	171	19yrs 07mo
Sun	16 Libra	196	−19	=	177	22yrs 01mo
Mercury	08 Scorpio	218	−19	=	199	34yrs 01mo

★ Chapter Five ★
Aspects of Life

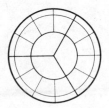

Aspects are angular relationships between planets which connect and blend planetary qualities according to their precise angle as seen from Earth. The pattern of aspects in any horoscope shows how the planets integrate with each other. As aspects link planet to planet, they also connect events to each other, the people to each other and components of our own nature to each other. The simplicity or complexity of life is mirrored in the quantity and quality of aspects. Many aspects indicate the potential for combining many parts of ourself, while few aspects show fewer natural interconnections.

The journey round the outside of one's horoscope is a process in time. The outer events of life follow each other in a counterclockwise direction from cause to effect. The centre of a horoscope is the centre of our being – the hub around which events turn and the totality of all qualities we possess. In the east this is called the wheel or round of samsara (illusion). The periphery is movement through time but the centre is timeless. The strength of aspects is determined by their penetration into the centre and by the nature of the planets combined (Figure 12). Individual aspects are differentiated by their angle and type of reception. Similarly, radio reception is influenced by the angular relationships of planets in relation to the Earth: 60 and 120 degree angles produce disturbance-free fields, while 90 and 180 degree angles produce disturbances and static (For reference see the work of Nelson), like their equivalent angles produce either harmony or static in the horoscope.

The *Conjunction* is an angular relationship of 0 degrees and is the aspect of unity (Figure 12a), when two or more planets oc-

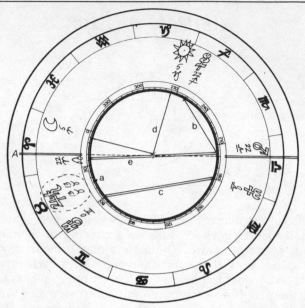

Figure 12: Aspects
Aspects are defined by their penetration into the centre of the horoscope. (a) is a conjunction between Jupiter and Saturn in Taurus, which remains bonded to the periphery of the circle; (b) is a sextile between Mars in Libra and Mercury in Sagittarius, which is peripheral; (c) is a trine between Uranus in Gemini and Neptune in Libra, which penetrates halfway to the centre; (d) is a square between the Sun in Capricorn and the Moon in Aries which tensions the centre and forces a change in direction; (e) is an opposition between the Node in Aries and Mars in Libra which passes through the centre and splits the horoscope in two.

cupy the same position in the zodiac. Their qualities are blended and they register at the same time in our life, which can make it difficult to differentiate them. When one planet is in aspect to a third planet, the other usually is also. The closer planets are to each other, the more firmly they are bonded and the more closely integrated are their qualities. Conjunctions are totally bound to the periphery of the horoscope and are in the causal sequence of life.

The *Sextile* aspect is an angular relationship of 60 degrees, one-sixth of the circle and is a peripheral aspect, only penetrating one-eighth of the way into the centre (Figure 12b). As each sign occupies 30 degrees of the circle, sextiles skip signs. A planet in Gemini makes sextiles to planets forwards to Leo and backwards to Aries. A planet in Scorpio makes sextiles backwards to Virgo and forwards to Capricorn. Sextiles are movement slightly ahead or behind. Masculine and feminine signs alternate through the zodiac, and sextiles connect feminine to feminine and masculine to masculine. The sextile is the aspect of mental or sexual relationship, and tends to involve surface rather than essence.

The *Trine* aspect is 120 degrees, penetrates half-way into the circle, and mediates between the periphery and the centre, resulting in fluid communication, balance and support (Figure 12c). The trine is communication which is neither superficial nor central; close contact, but not too close! The trine connects planets of the same element and their ease of relationshiip is due to this similarity. Earth sign Taurus trines the other earth signs Virgo and Capricorn, and the air sign Gemini trines the other air signs Libra and Aquarius. The structure of the octaves of the time scale is based upon triangles and the trine aspect connects a development in one octave with the equivalent stage of another octave. A planet in the self-assertive 1st House may trine another planet in the self-exteriorizing 5th House or the self-realizing 9th House. The octaves describe the creation of the physical body (Gestation), emotional body (Childhood) and mental body (Maturity), so a trine relates a facet of one body to a similar developmental stage of another body as emotion-to-physical or physical-to-mental or emotional-to-mental. The trine is the most balanced aspect, but also the most static.

The *Square* aspect is 90 degrees, one-fourth of the circle, and is shown as a right angle pointing at or embracing the centre (Figure 12d). The square connects planets on the periphery which tension the centre, but are capable of resolution and produce movement. As the sextile and trine are pacific, the square is a source of motivation and forces changes of direction. Squares connect signs of one gender to signs of the opposite gender; feminine to masculine and vice versa. The masculine Leo is square to the feminine material Taurus and the metaphysical Scorpio. The contrast of gender is disruptive, but its influence provides creativity and energy, just as in life.

The *Opposition* aspect is 180 degrees, one-half of the circle and is the relationship of two planets directly opposite each other (Figure 12e). The opposition creates maximum tension, which leads either to polarization or reconciliation. The energy passes from one end to the other directly through the centre, and as opposites attract each other, there is both an antagonism and complementarity at the same time. The events, people and mechanisms involved are opposed in quality, character and time of life, just as both opposites are represented within our psyche. Usually our focus is upon one of the opposites, forcing the other to be suppressed or projected onto someone or something else outside us. If we cannot integrate the feminine in ourself, we project its contents onto an available woman. The natural polarity of life gives rise to the necessity of the integration of opposites as a way of generating the greatest energy.

There are many minor aspects which may be used in addition to these and which are harmonics of the major aspects. The *Semisquare* is an angle of 45 degrees, one-eighth of the circle and half a square; this aspect carries tension like the square, but performs a mediating function. The *Sesquiquadrate* is an angle of 135 degrees, midway between a square and opposition; it also carries tension but does not penetrate as deeply as a square or opposition. The *Semisextile* of 30 degrees is one-twelfth of the circle or one complete sign; this is the most peripheral aspect and indicates superficial connections. The Quincunx or *Inconjunct* of 150 degrees is midway between the very static trine and very tense opposition and so is variable and irrational.

Complex Configurations

When more than two planets aspect each other, complex configurations result which can be identified by their shapes.

In the *Grand Trine*, three planets are mutually trine to each other, making an equilateral triangle within a horoscope (Figure 13). They are usually in the same element and are identified as Fire, Air, Earth or Water Grand Trines. The Grand Trine is often considered the most positive shape possible, but as a triangle is a rigid shape in geometry, it often shows balance to the point of boredom. The Grand Trine surrounds and encloses the centre of our horoscope, as though we are so balanced that it is impossible to penetrate to your essence. An Earth Grand Trine

Figure 13: Grand Trine
The grand trine is a rigid shape with the Moon in Capricorn trine Saturn in Taurus trine Mercury in Virgo, which encloses the centre and is very static. This grand trine is 'earthy' because all its planets are in earth signs, implying a physically static situation.

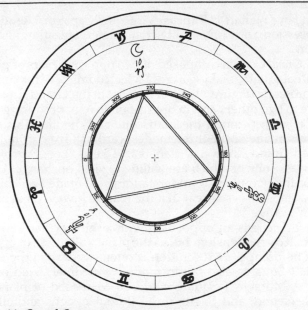

Figure 14: Grand Cross

The grand cross is two oppositions mutuully in square. Each planet is in opposition to one planet and in square to the other two.

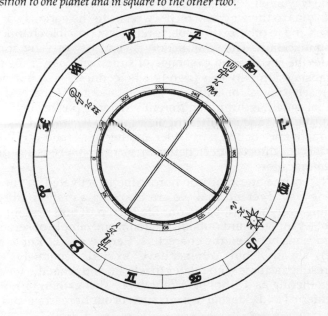

would have planets in Taurus, Virgo and Capricorn, tending to an obsession with physicality, tangible organization and possession.

The *Grand Cross* is composed of two opposing pairs of planets in mutual square, making a cross which dominates the centre of the horoscope (Figure 14). Every planet in the Grand Cross is in square to two others and in opposition to one, producing maximum tension through the horoscope and the life. This shape registers in one of the three modes; cardinal, fixed or mutable. A Fixed Grand Cross has planets in Taurus, Leo, Scorpio and Aquarius, none of which are willing to yield or change. Unless extraordinary outlets or understanding are made available, the internal tension is so great that the planets involved govern the person totally.

The *T-Square* is an opposition with a third planet in mutual square. It carries tension, but as the planets all reside in one-half of the horoscope, its resolution is often easier than the Grand Cross. T-Squares also fall in modes of cardinal, fixed or mutable. A Mutable T-Square could be composed of planets in Pisces, Gemini and Sagittarius, all double signs and all very ambiguous. It is not uncommon to have series of T-Squares in a horoscope.

The way in which all the planets in our horoscope combine is analogous to the way in which we relate to the various parts of ourself and to others: the aspects represent possible channels of communication. The conjunction is similarity of view and attitude; the sextile is an exchange of superficial views; the trine is transmission between friends who connect well, but never approach central or difficult issues; and the square shows mutual agitation through different but not opposite views. The opposition manifests different views that polarize and result in the dominance of one party over another or a stand-off. Where there is no direct aspect between planets, there is no direct communication.

We can imagine that our horoscope is activated in the following way: Pretend that we are throwing a grand party and inviting everyone critical in our life from past and present. We adopt a vantage point outside the room and simply observe the interactions between the characters. Certain people know each other already, but others have existed separately. The interesting factor is who relates to whom, and what the tenor of the gathering as a whole is likely to be. This gathering reflects the internal and external organization of our horoscope and our life! In a horoscope with few aspects and many unaspected planets, we would expect to see a roomful of people milling around, feeling uncomfortable, without attempting to inter- mingle at all. A well-knit horoscope with many aspects would produce a convivial and spirited gathering where everyone gets to know everyone else. Of course, the most interesting specu- lation of all would be if we assumed that everyone was obliged to talk about their relationship to us. . .

Aspect Patterns

The planets naturally form chains of aspects in a horoscope. It is possible for every planet to be aspected to every other planet, or connected through a chain, although this is rare. A chain is formed when two or more planets are in aspect to one base planet without being in aspect to each other. In John Lennon's horoscope (Figure 15) Pluto and Uranus are in aspect to the Moon, but not in aspect to each other. When Uranus is inter- preted in the time scale, the operable aspect is Moon trine Uranus; when Pluto is operable, the aspect is Moon opposition Pluto; but when the Moon is being interpreted, the aspects are Moon trine Uranus and Moon opposition Pluto. The Moon, Lennon's mother, is the link between his ability to change (Uranus) and his ability to be recognized by the masses (Pluto). Thus the Moon is a link in a chain that includes Uranus, Pluto, a square to Mercury and a trine to Neptune.

Chains of planets are webs of relationships in life. At certain times they dramatically connect events, people and parts of us. The aspects are not 'good' or 'bad' as traditional astrology judges them; they simply describe the varieties of communi- cation possible within our whole life. A very easy communi- cation between two isolated trine planets may be less desirable than a web of five planets connected by squares of tension and superficial sextiles. Each event in a horoscope (and life) is con- nected with certain other events, and sometimes the connection is more interesting than either event itself. To segregate any event or person from the whole of one's life is misleading and may be damaging.

Groups of planets function like a psychological *complex*, which is a network of emotionally charged active associations which accumulate and discharge energy. Complexes are natural structures and are pathological only when they lack integration or are suppressed. Just as most people have a number of complexes, so there are usually series of planetary groupings within the horoscope which do not connect with each other. In John Lennon's horoscope there are three clearly defined constellations, which we can call A, B and C. Constellation A (Figure 15) is composed of the Ascendant opposed Sun, two very important positions which are isolated in tension from the rest of the horoscope. Constellation B (Figure 16) includes the MC, Jupiter and Saturn, Venus, Mars, and Mercury. Constellation C includes the Moon, Uranus, Neptune, Pluto and again, Mercury. Mercury, showing Lennon's ability to make connections, is a very important element in the horoscope as it is the only link between these two major constellations.

Complexes vie with each other for momentary control. Since, as we age we move around the horoscope, we move into and out of the influence of all our various complexes continuously. When under the influence of one complex, the others seem to disappear, but in the course of time they reappear and become dominant themselves. Aspect relationships come into and out

Figure 15: Constellation A

The opposition between the Aries ASC and the Libra Sun is separate from the rest of Lennon's horoscope: the energy can only reverberate back and forth between the two.

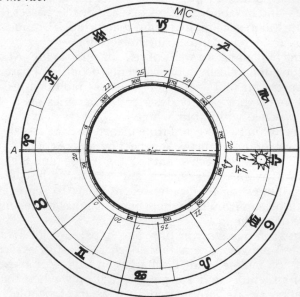

of influence when any of the planets of which they are composed is activated.

Within a constellation, energy flows along the path of least resistance. When two planets are in opposition, but mediated by a third planet in trine with one end and in sextile to the other end, the opposition can be avoided in favour of the easier, but more superficial sextile-trine route. In Lennon's horoscope, the Moon/Pluto opposition can be avoided by moving from the Moon along the trine to Mars and then along the sextile to Pluto, which would be interpreted as avoiding a feminine, emotional, one-sidedness (Moon opposed Pluto) by making communication with other men (Mars) in work relationships (6th House) and showing great vigour and ambition (Mars sextile Pluto). In these cases energy is capable of moving

Figure 16: Constellations B and C
Constellation B is composed of the MC, Jupiter and Saturn, Venus, Mars and Mercury. Constellation C is composed of the grand trine with the Moon, Uranus, Neptune and Mars, and the t-square involving the Moon, Pluto and Mercury. This places great importance on the Moon (the feminine) because it is common to both the grand trine and the t-square. Mercury carries even greater importance because it is the only link between the two major constellations.

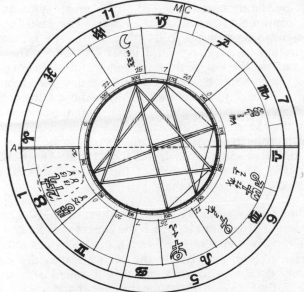

along either of two paths – the healthiest situation of all. There should be a choice between tension and equilibrium as often as possible for true growth, and a recognition that these choices are available. The more aspects to any planet, the more variations of the archetype the planet carries and the broader the view available to us through the planet.

The number of planets in each constellation; the number of individual constellations; the planets which connect sub-constellations; and planets which stand alone: all these criteria are significant in evaluating our life pattern.

Orbs

Aspects are strongest when the angle between two planets is exactly 0, 60, 90, 120 or 180 degrees. A planet's *Orb* is the distance on either side of an exact aspect where the quality of the aspect still functions. Orbs vary according to the size and importance of the planets involved, the aspects involved and the system of interpretation used. Astrologers earlier in this century sometimes used orbs of up to 15 degrees on either side of the planets, making every planet aspect every other planet!

It is important to understand planetary movement, because the horoscope 'freezes' the continual movement of the planets at the specific time and place of birth, but the planets themselves continue to move on their way. The faster a planet moves, the faster it passes into and out of an aspect, the shorter the duration of its effects and less its potency. The slower planets move, the longer their influence and the stronger their effects. The Sun moves about 1 degree per day, the Moon about 13 degrees per day; therefore the Moon moves thirteen times faster than the Sun through the zodiac. You must expect the effects of the Moon to be proportionally less tangible. Pluto takes several months to pass through one degree, so the Moon moves about one thousand times faster than Pluto! The slower the planet, the narrower its orb of influence. Table 10 shows suggested orbs for the planets.

As a planet moves into the orb of another, its effects gradually increase up to the point at which the aspect is exact and maximum strength is generated. When a planet moves into orb it is *Applying*. From exactitude the planet leaves the orb and gradually decreases in strength; this is called *Separating*. In Figure 17, the Sun is in 15 degrees of Cancer and its orb extends

Table 10: Planetary Orbs

Planet or Personal Point	Orb (in degrees)
Sun	±8
Moon	8
Mercury	5
Venus	5
Mars	5
Jupiter	4
Saturn	4
Uranus	4
Neptune	4
Pluto	4
Node	3
Ascendant	5
Midheaven	5
Conception Point	2

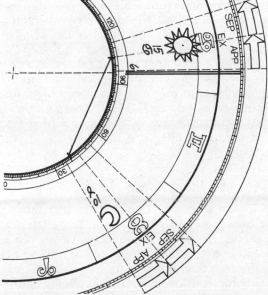

Figure 17: Aspect Orbs
With the Sun in 15 degrees of Cancer, an 8 degree orb means that its domain
is within a zone from 7 Cancer (15-8) to 23 Cancer (15 + 8). Planets aspecting
or passing through this zone enter the Sun's influence at 7 Cancer, become
stronger until they release at 15 Cancer, and lessen in influence until they pass
out of orb at 23 Cancer.

from 7 Cancer (97 degrees absolute longitude) to 23 Cancer (113 degrees). Planets passing through this zone or in aspect to this zone combine with the Sun's influence at 7 Cancer, culminate at 15 Cancer and leave its influence at 23 Cancer.

Within the context of the Life★Time Scale, the orb takes on additional meaning. Movement around the horoscope determines the speed of our perceptions and the duration of an orb in calendar time varies accordingly. An orb of 5 degrees in early childhood represents two weeks, while the same 5 degree orb at sixty years old covers more than six years. Events come and go more rapidly the younger we are; the older we are, the longer events take to manifest. This echoes the fact that wounds heal much faster in youth than in old age (See de Nouy, *Biological Time*), and the results of other experiments in human time perception.

If we allow the standard 8 degree orb on either side of the Sun, and the Sun registers at the age of twenty-eight years old (as in Figure 17), the Sun would influence you from twenty-four years four months until exactitude at twenty-eight years old and end at thirty-three years five months old. The same aspect in gestation would apply, become exact and separate within days! The timing of orbs must be considered in evaluating all aspects when we use the Life★Time Scale. The formation and aftereffects of events in maturity take longer and longer. The table of degree dates on pages 58-59 shows us the time span indicated by an orb at any age. Simply count the number of degrees orb before or after the target age and subtract the difference, as in Figure 17.

Interpreting Aspects

Each aspect is an interaction or process through which two planets are combined and permuted. Interpretation is created by linking planet-via-aspect-to-planet. If Venus represents relationship and is connected by tensioning square to Saturn as inhibition, the resulting interpretation of Venus square Saturn is "a relationship tensioned by or producing inhibition". If Saturn registers earlier, the inhibition precedes the relationship, while if Saturn registers later the relationship produces the inhibition. In our personal life, it is essential to understand this kind of valuation. The people or parts of us involved are the personifications of the planets, as Venus is a beautiful or harmonious person and Saturn is an old, serious or depressed person, so Venus square Saturn is "a beauty inhibited by or inhibiting a more serious person" or "the part of us which wants to be attractive is inhibited by our seriousness". An aspect links sets of ideas, states or people indicated by the connecting planets. In Chapter Six, the Interpretation Tables on pages 134-144 show us the outer material and inner psychological events paralleled by every possible planetary combination. Look at this section, as all aspect interpretation derives from the simple combinations shown.

The action of an aspect is qualified by the age at which it registers. Venus registering at three months old in the 1st House square Saturn is "you as a baby being restricted by grandparents" or "your sister is jealous of the attention you are getting from elders". If Venus occurs at thirteen in the 6th House square Saturn, "your parents inhibit your choice of girlfriends" or "you are discouraged from taking art (Venus) by a scientifically oriented advisor (Saturn) at school". The nature of each developmental house must be attached to the interpretation of planets.

The signs of the planets qualify the interpretation. If Venus is in the security-minded Taurus and Saturn in the social Leo, Venus square Saturn is, relative to Venus at thirteen years old; "a young girl wanting security feels tension with an older man with good social connections".

The connection of planet-aspect-planet qualified by house, sign and age is an association process which describes astrological events accurately and becomes easier with practice.

Sensitive Points

Sensitive points – the positions of exact aspects to a planetary body around the horoscope, whether or not these points are occupied by other planets – are important in Life★Time Astrology because they show all the dates and ages at which natal planets and personal points register. Figure 18 shows the eleven common sensitive points to a natal planet around the horoscope. Whenever any of these points are occupied or passed over by planets, the energy of the base planet, in this case Jupiter, is released. If Jupiter in the birth chart is a generous protector, whenever Jupiter's sensitive points are activated, a similar protective influence is made manifest, either within or without. By using the time scale disk, every sensitive point may be dated exactly in life at the times when each planet and per-

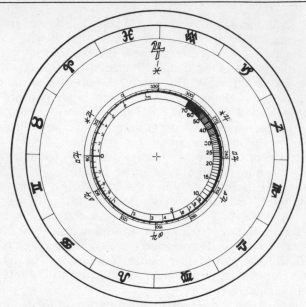

Figure 18: Planet Sensitive Points

sonal point can be expected to produce an effect in life.

Every planet in a horoscope has its birth position and seven major sensitive points. The total number of active points in a horoscope translated into dates in life makes 96 (12 x 8). When the 30, 45, 135 and 150 degree minor aspects are added, as they are on the Life★Time Astrology printouts described in Appendix F, there are 192 points (12 x 16). Sensitive points are distributed either uniformly or in bunches, depending upon the closeness of aspects in the birth chart. Many exact aspects make tight clusters of sensitive points which produce active and potent series of life events separated by less active time gaps. Events which happened many years ago continue to vibrate within us, just as events that are to happen in our future are vibrating in us now.

Sensitive points cover the entire circle of life, but there are so many of them it is unreasonable to use them all. They are useful when we wish to fill in apparently empty spaces and times between the registration of natal planets. To illustrate this process we will calculate the sensitive points that register between Pluto at five years old and Venus at nine years two months in John Lennon's horoscope (Figure 19). The sequence of sensitive points are as follows:

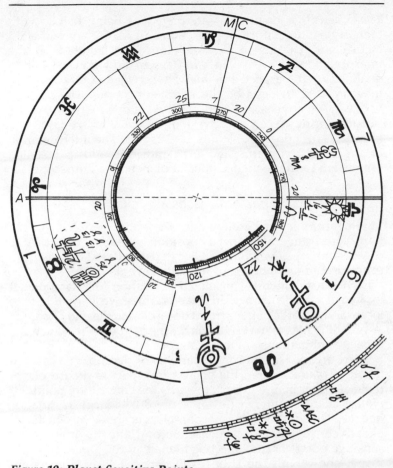

Figure 19: Planet Sensitive Points
The sensitive points can fill out the apparent gap between the registration of Pluto in Leo and Venus in Virgo. Each gap is interpreted as an aspect between the two planets concerned.

*Natal Pluto	4 Leo	4 yrs 11 mos
Square to Mercury	8 Leo	5 yrs 05 mos
Sextile to Node	11 Leo	5 yrs 08 mos
Square to Saturn	13 Leo	6 yrs 00 mos
Square to Jupiter	13 Leo	6 yrs 00 mos
Sextile to Sun	16 Leo	6 yrs 05 mos
Trine to Ascendant	20 Leo	6 yrs 11 mos
Square Uranus	25 Leo	7 yrs 09 mos
*Natal Venus	3 Virgo	9 yrs 02 mos

These sensitive points are interpreted as being in Leo with Mercury, Node, Saturn, Jupiter, Sun and Ascendant in the 5th House and Uranus in the 6th House. In addition to the interpretation of each planet in its sign and house position qualified by the aspect, the intervals between pairs of planets may be used to describe the intervening time. The interval between sensitive sextile Sun at six years five months and the sensitive trine Ascendant five months later at six years ten months is described like a Sun/ASC aspect. The interpretation of the sensitive points and their intervals adds a detailed dimension to the sequence of natal planets in a horoscope.

Time Scale Constellations

The logarithmic time scale grades the entire periphery of the horoscope by age: all planetary positions, personal points (ASC & MC) and sensitive points are located and dated in sequence, producing ninety-one major formative events in life.

Each constellation is considered in relation to a natal planet located at a particular age. In Chapter Three we learned how to locate and date the planets from conception to the end of our life – now it is necessary to determine the sequence in which the aspect combinations are to be interpreted.

There are two sets of considerations for describing a constellation of planets. First, the planets in aspect to a base planet register either before it (back towards the conception point/9th House cusp) or after it (towards the 8th House) in time sequence. The locations of aspecting planets show the "history" of each constellation in sequence. Second, the proximity of the sensitive points of the aspecting planets in relation to the base planet show both the strength of aspect (closer aspects are stronger aspects) and the sequence of the unfolding of the constellation, as the sensitive points register either before or after the base planet.

An analysis of the structure of some of the constellations in a horoscope illustrates this process. As the major horoscope analysis of the book is of John Lennon we can see the final interpretation of these aspect combinations in Chapter Eight. Let us examine a few of the constellations in his horoscope (Figures 15 and 16, p. 88 and 89).

An analysis of the Moon in Aquarius and the 11th House at thirty-one weeks before birth includes aspects to Uranus, Pluto, Neptune, Mars and Mercury. The Moon is first paired with each of the other planets according to whether their sensitive point falls before or after 3 degrees Aquarius. The eventual registration time of each aspecting planet is indicated:

1. Trine from Uranus (25 Taurus) at 10 mos old to   25 Capricorn
2. Trine from Neptune (26 Virgo) at 14 yrs 9 mos to   26 Capricorn
3. Trine from Mars (2 Libra) at 16 yrs 8 mos to   2 Aquarius
4. *Natal Moon at*   *3 Aquarius*
5. Opposition from Pluto (4 Leo) at 5 yrs to   4 Aquarius
6. Square from Mercury (8 Scorpio) at 34 yrs to   8 Aquarius

This is the sequence in which the aspects to the Moon unfold. Each aspecting planet either evokes earlier events or is a preview of later events. Since the Moon is in Gestation, all of its aspects happen later, indicating the first registration of a very powerful lunar-maternal influence. This would amplify the importance of gestation events! The strongest planets in this constellation are the closest aspects in the sequence: Moon-Mars and -Pluto,-Mercury,-Neptune and -Uranus. Their hierarchy of strengths should be taken into consideration when interpreting this constellation.

The next position in Lennon's horoscope is his Aries Ascendant, to which the only aspect is an opposition to the Sun in Libra (Figure 15). When two planets or one planet and a personal point (ASC or MC) are in aspect with each other but unaspected to the rest of the horoscope, they tend to vibrate back and forth. The energy flows from one end to the other and back again. This creates tension through the opposition in Lennon's case and a trapped outlook. As the Ascendant is the birth moment and the Sun registers at the age of twenty-one years ten months old, these two periods are critical in his life.

When the planet chosen as base registers in later life, as Mercury in Lennon's horoscope, an additional timing must be included in interpretation. Planets in aspect to Mercury cover a period of time before and after the actual registration of Mercury. As we age, the orb of aspecting planets becomes indicative of the fact that later events take quite a long time to develop, manifest and then to have their aftereffects assimilated. Mercury receives aspects from the MC, Moon, Jupiter/Saturn conjunction, Pluto and Venus. These planets register as follows, with the addition of the dates of registration of their sensitive points:

1. Sextile from Venus (3 Virgo) to	3 Scorpio at	30yr 07mos
2. Square from Moon (3 Aquarius) to	3 Scorpio at	30yr 10mos
3. Square from Pluto (4 Leo) to	4 Scorpio at	31yr 02mos
4. Sextile from MC (7 Capricorn) to	7 Scorpio at	33yr
5. *Natal Mercury at*	*8 Scorpio at*	*34yr*
6. Opposition from Saturn (13 Taurus) to	13 Scorpio at	37yr 03mos
7. Opposition from Jupiter (13 Taurus) to	13 Scorpio at	37yr 07mos

The Mercury constellation lasts from thirty years seven months (May 1971) until thirty-seven years seven months (May 1978), or seven years! The sequence of planets is absolutely critical in interpreting constellations, as profound differences between horoscopes with constellations containing similar planets occur when the sequence varies. Each constellation describes a very specific series of planetary events which is reactivated whenever any planet subsequently passes over the base planet. The sequence of planets is the most important information conveyed by the horoscope!

This type of aspect analysis must be done for every planet in a horoscope. Each planet is analyzed by sign, house and age; its aspects are determined; the aspect combinations are collated in the sequence of their sensitive points; the original registration times of all the planets are noted; and finally, the interpretation is connected.

This method of analysis is similar to the way in which memory functions. We live life sequentially. Certain periods or events in life carry clusters of associations which preceded or resulted from the primary event. Each of those events in turn has its own past. Whenever similar events, clusters of events or even fragments of events happen, we remember the entire constellation of influences again. Since sensitive points provide the times when primary events and their constellations are likely to emerge again into consciousness, it is useful for understanding the timings and mechanisms of all events in life.

Aspect Interpretation Tables

In the following chapter are brief tables for interpreting planetary aspects. They are as simple and inclusive as possible, because the first necessity is to have material from which to associate freely and with which to build accurate events and people in our horoscope. Every pair of planets has: basic principles and events which are likely to occur; possible negative manifestations when there are squares, oppositions or when they are in unfavourable houses or signs; and personifications of each pair of planets. Remember that all events have both an outer and inner significance and influence upon us. The crotchety old man indicated by Saturn may be inside us already at twenty-one years old!

The use of pairs of planets and personal points is essential to understand the workings of Life★Time Astrology, but the aspect combinations are so exhaustive that they require an entire book to themselves. The best book is *"The Combination of Stellar Influences"* by Reinhold Ebertin (distributed by the American Federation of Astrologers). Its interpretive material is so complete that it has 184 pages and 1117 categories of aspects alone! Figure 20 shows two facing pages of CSI. Ebertin's Cosmobiology Institute in Germany has verified all information with case histories collected by thousands of astrologers.

The left-hand page of CSI shows the base pair of planets to be combined, in this case Saturn/Uranus, together with their Psychological, Biological, Sociological Correspondences and Probable (Event) Manifestations. On the right-hand page are the other planets which can be combined when in the same constellation or when they activate the base pair by transit or direction. The introduction of a third planet makes the interpretation much more specific.

Ebertin bases his system on *Cosmic Structural Pictures* – groupings of planets related by mathematical formulae – where a planet exactly halfway (on the axis) between two others, at the *midpoint*, partakes of the qualities of both. This is a shift away from static traditional astrology and prepares the way for Life★Time Astrology, which treats life as a dynamic web of relations. Using CSI it is possible to compare up to ten planets or personal points with any primary pair of planets. Ebertin's text is essential for more advanced work.

With the survey of aspects, all structural techniques for interpreting the horoscope are complete. All that remains is to combine them to interpret your life story.

0866   ♄ / ♅   S A T U R N / U R A N U S

Principle
Irritability and inhibition, tension.

Psychological Correspondence:
+   The ability to cope with every situation, the power to pull through and to endure, perseverance and endurance, indefatigability, will-power, determination.

-   Unusual emotional tensions or strains, irritability, emotional conflicts, rebellion, the urge for freedom, a provocative conduct, an act of violence.

C   A self-willed nature, tenaciousness and toughness, obstinacy, strong emotional tensions or stresses.

Biological Correspondence:
Inhibitions of rhythm, heart-block, Cheyne-Stokes' breathing. - Unrhythmical processes. - A sudden loss of limbs (a chronic illness in this sense); operations accompanied by the removal of something. (Removal of intestinal parts, spleen, amputation etc.)

Sociological Correspondence:
Violent people.

Probable Manifestations:
+   Growth of strength caused through the overcoming of difficulties, difficult but successful battles in life for the purpose of overcoming a dangerous situation. (Operation).

-   Kicking against tutelage and against the limitation of freedom, the tendency to cause unrest within one's environment, a quarrel, separation, the use of force, interventions in one's destiny, the limitation of freedom.

Figure 20: The Combination of Stellar Influences
The left page describes the Principle of the combination Saturn/Uranus, the Psychological Correspondences, Biological Correspondences, Sociological Correspondences and the Probable Manifestations. The right page describes the interaction of Saturn/Uranus and each of the other planets and personal points (From The Combination of Stellar Influences by Reinhold Ebertin).

SATURN/URANUS ♄/⛢

0867= ☉ Physical exposure to severe tests of strength, the power of resistance, rebellion, inflexibility. - Separation.

0868= ☽ Strong emotional tensions and strains, states of depression, inconstancy. - The sudden desire to liberate oneself from emotional stress, separation from members of the female sex.

0869= ☿ The making of great demands upon one's nervous energy, the ability to hit back hard under provocation, the ability to organise resistance, the act of separating oneself from others. - Necessary changes.

0870= ♀ Tensions or stresses in love-life often leading to separation.

0871= ♂ An act of violence, the occasionally wrong use of extraordinary engergy, undergoing great efforts and toil. - A violent or forced release from tensions or strains, the stage of challenging others for a decisive contest or fight. - Injury, accident, deprivation of freedom.

0872= ♃ The ability to adapt oneself to every situation, a fortunate release from tensions. - A sudden turn (in destiny), the misfortune to get into difficulties. - Losses, damage to buildings, motor damage.

0873= ♆ The inability to face emotional stresses, falsehood or malice caused through weakness. - A resolve to resign oneself to the inevitable, the abandonment of resistance, weakening strength, separation, mourning and bereavement.

0874= ♀ An act of violence or brutality - The desire to overcome a difficult situation through extraordinary effort. - Rebellion against one's lot in life, harm through force majeure.

0875= ☊ The inability to integrate oneself into a community, provocative conduct. - Joint resistance to a common opponent, separation.

0876= A Being placed in difficult circumstances, the fate of standing alone in the world. - The suffering of difficulties caused by others, experiencing emotional suffering together with others, mourning and bereavement.

0877= M Making the highest demands upon one's own strength, rebellion, provocation. - The act of separating oneself from others.

★ Chapter Six ★
Interpretation Tables

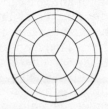

Interpretation tables list the range of possible manifestations of each planet in every sign of the zodiac, in every house of the horoscope and in aspect with every planet. Each planet in a horoscope must be evaluated by combining these three categories:

1. Planet in sign (the quality of the planetary operation)
2. Planet in house (the time and developmental stage of life)
3. Planet in aspect to other planets (connections to other events at other times in life)

Within each category there are a range of possible manifestations, ranging from the most positive to the most negative. Choice is based upon the following criteria.

First, each planet has a quality which can be naturally difficult or easy. The planets Sun, Venus and Jupiter are positive in most circumstances; Mars, Saturn, Uranus and Pluto often show tension, negative energy or difficult situations; and the Moon, Mercury and Neptune are neutral and easily influenced. In addition, the outer planets, Uranus, Neptune and Pluto, carry generational influences which everyone receives.

Second, the types of aspects involved in connecting planets must be considered. Conjunctions are neutral aspects of unity where the quality of the planets joined are simply compared to each other. Sextiles and trines produce supportive or positive connections which equilibrate the planets combined. Squares and oppositions produce tension which tend to static in combined planetary influences.

Third, the location of the planets in a horoscope condition

their interpretation. Planets in gestation represent very deep and archetypal influences which have a primary effect upon the body; planets in childhood represent emotional influences which are familial in origin and are carried in the personality; while planets in maturity are mental and affect the individual soul or entire being. The octaves range from the general to the specific through a life time. Planets near or in aspect to either the MC or the ASC are of particular importance as they condition our world view and personality, respectively, and convey this importance within a constellation.

Fourth, the old system of rulerships of planets indicates the strength or weakness of a planet by sign and house position, as described on page 66. Planets are strongest in those signs (and equivalent houses) which they rule and weakest in those opposite signs and houses. The other signs and houses are neutral. For example, Venus rules the active sign Libra and the 7th House, and the passive sign Taurus and the 2nd House, and is weak in detriment in the active sign Aries and the 1st House and the passive sign Scorpio and the 8th House.

In Figure 21 we wish to interpret Venus as a base planet. Venus is in Pisces and the 6th House, is trined by Jupiter and the MC, squared by Saturn and sextiled by Uranus, and registers at the age of eighteen years old. By sign and house position Venus is neutral. Venus in Pisces would be "longing for love, romance, feeling oriented" and Venus in the 6th House would be "work loving, puritanical, modest". The combination indicates a romantic longing for love is hampered by a puritanical love of work. As Venus registers at eighteen it refers to a young woman or lover. The aspecting planets are evaluated separately, and then accumulated and blended into an entire picture. Venus is a positive planet in its own right. Uranus is a tense generational influence connected by a positive sextile; Saturn is negative and also in a very tense square aspect; the MC is objective and conservative (in Cancer); and Jupiter is positive and connected by a supportive aspect. Therefore, we have two positive planets, including the base planet Venus, two neutral and one negative. The combination is slightly better than neutral. The aspect types are three positive to one negative. According to these valuations, the constellation should be better than neutral in the Aspect Tables.

In the Aspect Tables each planetary pair has a positive list of keywords, a negative list of keywords in brackets and a series of personifications who might be involved in the aspect. As our

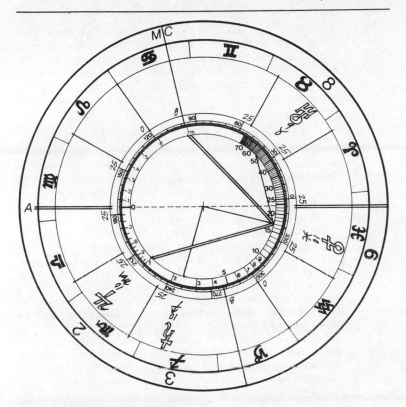

Figure 21: Aspect Interpretation
Venus in Pisces is the base planet in this constellation, and registers at seventeen years old. The MC trine extends back from seven months before birth; the Jupiter trine goes back to one year old; the Saturn square comes from two years and four months old; and the sextile to Uranus extends ahead to fifty-three years old. The Venus configuration synthesizes the earlier events and leads to the Uranus manifestation later in life. Using the date disk from the frontispiece, all aspect combinations may be evaluated and dated in this way.

base Venus registers at eighteen years old and is in the octave of maturity as is Uranus, the MC is early in the octave of gestation, while Jupiter and Saturn are in the emotional octave of childhood affecting the personality, the event is emotional but with a strong bearing upon the overall life direction. The four combinations are:

1. *Venus trine MC:* The neutral keywords are "objective love, attachment; artistic inclinations" with the personification being "an artist, an admirer, or a lover", showing an affair, and evoking the conservatism inherent in the mother when she discovered she was pregnant. This in turn could well show a concern about the possibility of an unwanted pregnancy.

2. *Venus trine Jupiter:* The slightly above neutral keywords are "popularity, good form sense, happiness" with the personification being an "artist, social person, expansive lover", implying a relationship. As Jupiter registered at one year old when there was positive contact then separation (from an uncle), this implication is carried here. A more positive constellation could indicate marriage, while a more negative could imply laziness and arrogance.

3. *Venus square Saturn:* The neutral keywords are "reserve, economy, loyalty to an older person, fear of illegitimacy" with the personification "older lover, lonely people, widower", showing us that the lover is older and that there may well be the threat of an unwanted pregnancy, producing reserve. The original registration of Saturn is back the 3rd House time of talking, so there is an uncommunicative influence and childishness in the relationship.

4. *Venus sextile Uranus:* This aspect is projected ahead to thirty-three years old and shows "arousal, eccentric impulses, musical and artistic talent" carried by one who is an "artist, musician or eccentric lover".

The total picture shows the subject at eighteen years old involved with an older artistic woman in a love affair. He is wary of committing himself for fear of illegitimacy, but this situation sets a precedent for a later eccentricity at thirty-three years old when sexually he is more adventurous. This shows us how the tables are used.

Favourable or Unfavourable Aspect Combinations

This table is used for determining whether positive or negative aspect interpretations govern constellations. Majority rules.

☉		☽		☿		♀	
SU/SU	+	MO/SU	+	ME/SU	+	VE/SU	+
SU/MO	+	MO/MO	+	ME/MO	+	VE/MO	+
SU/ME	+	MO/ME	+	ME/ME	+	VE/ME	+
SU/VE	+	MO/VE	+	ME/VE	+	VE/VE	+
SU/MA	?	MO/MA	–	ME/MA	–	VE/MA	?
SU/JU	+	MO/JU	+	ME/JU	+	VE/JU	+
SU/SA	–	MO/SA	–	ME/SA	–	VE/SA	–
SU/UR	?	MO/UR	–	ME/UR	+	VE/UR	+
SU/NE	–	MO/NE	?	ME/NE	?	VE/NE	+
SU/PL	+	MO/PL	–	ME/PL	+	VE/PL	–
SU/NO	+	MO/NO	+	ME/NO	+	VE/NO	+
SU/AS	+	MO/AS	+	ME/AS	+	VE/AS	+
SU/MC	+	MO/MC	+	ME/MC	+	VE/MC	+

♂		♃		♄		♅	
MA/SU	?	JU/SU	+	SA/SU	–	UR/SU	?
MA/MO	–	JU/MO	+	SA/MO	–	UR/MO	–
MA/ME	–	JU/ME	+	SA/ME	–	UR/ME	?
MA/VE	–	JU/VE	+	SA/VE	–	UR/VE	?
MA/MA	–	JU/MA	+	SA/MA	–	UR/MA	–
MA/JU	+	JU/JU	+	SA/JU	–	UR/JU	+
MA/SA	–	JU/SA	?	SA/SA	?	UR/SA	–
MA/UR	–	JU/UR	+	SA/UR	–	UR/UR	?
MA/NE	–	JU/NE	?	SA/NE	–	UR/NE	–
MA/PL	–	JU/PL	+	SA/PL	–	UR/PL	+
MA/NO	+	JU/NO	+	SA/NO	–	UR/NO	–
MA/AS	–	JU/AS	+	SA/AS	–	UR/AS	?
MA/MC	+	JU/MC	+	SA/MC	–	UR/MC	?

♆		♇		☊		AS	
NE/SU	–	PL/SU	?	NO/SU	+	AS/SU	+
NE/MO	?	PL/MO	–	NO/MO	+	AS/MO	+
NE/ME	–	PL/ME	?	NO/ME	I	AS/ME	I
NE/VE	–	PL/VE	+	NO/VE	+	AS/VE	+
NE/MA	–	PL/MA	–	NO/MA	+	AS/MA	--
NE/JU	?	PL/JU	–	NO/JU	+	AS/JU	+
NE/SA	–	PL/SA	–	NO/SA	–	AS/SA	–
NE/UR	–	PL/UR	+	NO/UR	?	AS/UR	?
NE/NE	?	PL/NE	+	NO/NE	–	AS/NE	–
NE/PL	?	PL/PL	+	NO/PL	+	AS/PL	?
NE/NO	–	PL/NO	+	NO/NO	+	AS/NO	+
NE/AS	–	PL/AS	+	NO/AS	+	AS/AS	+
NE/MC	–	PL/MC	+	NO/MC	+	AS/MC	+

Principles	Spirit; mind; energy; wholeness; holism; ruling; individuality; life; vitality; organisation; consciousness; libido; kundalini; objectivity; conscious life; sympathy.
Sign	*Interpretation*

Aries Exalt	Assertion; energy; boldness; leading; warlike; impatient; sporty; enterprising; egotism; pride.
Taurus	Perseverance; materialistic; practical; secure; physical; obstinate; possessive; jealous.
Gemini	Dextrous; articulate; educable; dual; identity crises; nervous; glib; superficial; moody; changeable; vicacious.
Cancer	Domesticity; shrewd; conservative; parental; comfortable; religious; psychological; feeling; deepness.
Leo Rule	Confident; domineering; assured; rising in life; publishing; protection; speculative; teaching; bossy; arrogant.
Virgo	Efficient; detail oriented; orderly; attentive; critical; fault-finding; service; demanding; healer.
Libra Fall	Balancing; relaxed; consistent; sociable; political; charming; amenable; unitary; unreliable; lazy; dominated; loyal mate.
Scorpio	Passionate; dependent; moody; vindictive; jealous; forceful; self-destructive; dynamic; tempered; magnetic; imperturbable.
Sagittarius	Aspiring; free; sloppy; imaginative; success broad; undisciplined; open; realised; exploratory; hedonist; split.
Capricorn	Goal conscious; egocentric; inhibited; dutiful; hardworking; selfish; industrious; loyal; inflexible; noble; material.
Aquarius Det	Abstract; humanitarian; knowledgeable; human nature; understanding; social; methodical; help from others; selfish.
Pisces	Compassionate; universal; loving; addictive; empathetic; poetic; deceitful; absorptive; negligent; restricted.

Personifications	Administration; ruler; governor; politician; leader; captain; speculation; public figures; father; grandparents; doctor; personalities in media; official; famous people.

House	Interpretation
1st	*Childhood* Attention; parental approval; strong will; vitality; awareness; recuperation; temper; selfishness; physical health; compulsive.
2nd	Endurance; humour; enjoyment; gentle; constant; sensual; secure; withholding; stubborn; solid; possessive; indulgent; parents protect.
3rd	Quick mind; verbal; curiosity; versatile; adaptable; learning; change; siblings; expression; inquisitive; charming.
4th	Secure family; emotional base; pride; parents; beautiful; possessive; domestic; natural; love of comfort; benevolent.
5th	*Maturity* Self-expression; self-conscious; boastful; domineering; leading; artistic; practical; fastidious; virginal; discriminating
6th	Methodical; analytical; naive; simple; critical; fussy; studious; verbal; practical; fastidious; virginal; discriminating.
7th	Subliminative; partnership; adaptive; vain; worldly; constancy; associations important; popular; dependent; diplomatic; friendly.
8th	Separative; insular; intense; metaphysical; mysterious; secretive; obstinate; intense; suspicious; esoteric; fanatical; fearless.
9th	*Gestation (Transcendence)* Mobile; enthusiastic; changeable; dualistic; spiritual-religious; inspired; foreign; moral; positive; open; imaginative; unreliable.
10th	Pragmatic; paternal; practical; calculating; reserved; tight; depressed; self concentrated; reversals; tenacious; clinging; hardness.
11th	Idealistic; grouped; observative; detached; friendship; intuitive; planning; cranky; independent; reformative; erratic.
12th	Sympathetic; impressionable; secretive; retiring; solitary; estranged; institutional; drugged; sacrificial; passive; reserved; odd.

Moon

Principles	The feminine; mother; feeling; emotion; home; family; reflection; rhythm; instinct; change; protective urges; catalytic action; child-raising; integration.
Sign	**Interpretation**

Aries	Volatile; restless; haste; rashness; powerlust; primal; lusty; rebellious; spontaneous feeling; impatient
Taurus Exalt	Constancy; art appreciation; enjoyment; firmness; caution; protection; stubborn; gardener; wealthy; lazy
Gemini	Unpredictable; vacillation; talkative; multiple relations; sentimental; imitative; inconstant; instinctive
Cancer Rule	Related; secure; obsessional; clannish; indigestive; ulcerated; hypersensitive; restrained; inhibited; dissolute
Leo	Gambler; fertile; childlike; amusing; luxurious; social; magnanimous; open; impressive; sporty; entertaining
Virgo	Exacting; methodical; hardworking; neat; clean; retiring; emotionally critical; serving; perfectionist
Libra	Reactive; close partnership; charm; elegance; need approval; public relations; dependent on others; social
Scorpio Fall	Death wish; licentiousness; control; bias; seriousness; extreme jealousy; revenge; domination; subtlety
Sagittarius	Imaginative; foreign feelings; kind; hedonistic; jovial; lofty; traditional; travel; mobility; holier-than-thou
Capricorn Det	Austerity; unforthcoming; reserved; materialistic; ambitious; egotistic; personal bias; selfish; calculating
Aquarius	Unsolitary; civilised; humane; cold; inane; abstracted; detachment; political; frigid; unreliable
Pisces	Yielding; restless; seductive; poetic; secretive; occult; sympathetic; vulnerable; lonely; mysterious; too open

Personifications	Mother; women in general; midwife; grandmother; aunt; wife; emotional people; gynaecologists; obstetricians; cook; collector; domestics; gardener.

House	Interpretation
	Childhood
1st	Self-awareness; influenced; impressionable; impulsive; strong personality; susceptible; maternal strength; corpulence; irritable
2nd	Stable home; comfort; physical focus; food; deep emotional ties; beauty; firmness; stable; possessive; jealous; habitual; growth
3rd	Manifold emotional expression; mobile; change in mother; fantasy; dreaming; curious; fond of siblings; restless; contradictory; superficial
4th	Familial; affectionate; impressionable; depth of feeling; domestic; unconscious; mediumistic; attached; sensitive; smothered; withdrawn
	Maturity
5th	Speculative feeling; intuitive; confident; passionate; vain; impressive; romantic; imaginative; hedonistic; warm; popular
6th	Head rules heart; psychosomatic; practical; careful; correct; naive; pedantic; coldness; reserved; modest; restrained; undemonstrative
7th	Emotional dependence; compromising; evasive; irresponsible; fateful partners; vivid expression; sensitive; mother figure; fickle
8th	Separation; destructive relations; intense; death of mother; possessive; reserved; deep; psychic sensitivity; resentful; dependent
	Gestation (Transcendence)
9th	Vivid inner life; moody; striving; idealistic; changes; fullness; frank; free; restless; alert; emotional attachment; careless; offhand
10th	Recognition; paternalism; repressed; patient; dutiful; sobriety; ungratified; depressed; cautious; reserved; loyal; possessive
11th	Friendly; little meaning; group activities; woman friends; idealism; influenced; opinionated; many plans; sympathetic; hoping; wishes
12th	Moody; insular feelings; isolation; sacrifice; psychic; mediumistic; druggy; induced; easily hurt; hypnotic; reluctant; susceptible; dreamy

Mercury

☿

Principles	Mentality; intelligence; communication; understanding; mediation; neutrality; nervousness; balancing; business sense; criticism; scientific work; logic; self-expression; adaptable.
Sign	**Interpretation**

Sign	Interpretation
Aries	Quick thinking; repartee; creative; rash; mental overwork; decisive; argumentative; impulsive; temper; irritated
Taurus	Logical; material; decisive; common sense; organised; businesslike; blind; secure; structured; obstinate; closed.
Gemini *Rule*	Businesslike; contractual; writer; variety; changeable; inconstant; talented; alert; articulate; perfunctory.
Cancer	Psychological; intuitive; capricious; sentimental; parental ideas; slow mind; conservative; profound.
Leo	Willed; fixed ideas; prudence; planned; foresight; dignified; expansive; broadminded; intellectual; self-centred.
Virgo *Rule* *Exalt*	Unholistic; nervous; collaborative; shrewd; patient; organised; sedentary; precise; scientific; psychosomatic.
Libra	Social; learns through others; vapid; eclectic; unoriginal; reasoned; boring; comparative.
Scorpio	Critical; fanatical; practical; sceptical; cunning; crafty; profound; crafty; sharp; investigative; piercing; acid.
Sagittarius *Det*	Frank; versatile; foresight; unstable; thinking; deeply; manifold interests; philosophical; just; conflicting views.
Capricorn	Organised; practical mind; capable; material ideas; goals conscious; realistic; humourless; crafty; shrewd.
Aquarius	Informed; collective; abstract; cold; inconstant; scattered; quick grasp; scientific; archetypal ideas; occult.
Pisces *Det* *Fall*	Receptive to others; imaginative; plans without energy; irrational; unconscious; karmic; feeling; psychic.

Personifications Siblings; friend; intellects; thinkers; mediators; teacher; writer; artisan; architect.

House	Interpretation
	Childhood
1st	Mental activity; observation; quickness; nervous; precocious; noisy; assertive; enthusiasm; awake; overactive; self-expressive;
2nd	Patience; logic; possessive; deliberate; one-sided; talkative; ponderous; thick; sensible; slow; acquisitive; formal; endurance;
3rd	Versatile; conversant; active; adaptable; imitative; siblings; naughty; facile; clever; friendly; gossipy; fluent; superficial.
4th	Perceptive; familial; thinking feelings; memory; immersible; individual; homely; talk; disputative; irrational; retentive; narrow.
	Maturity
5th	Enthusiastic; creative; extrovert; talkative; bossy; critical; mental competition; games; teachers; conceit; organised; dogmatic; rude.
6th	Specialised; skills; methodical; patient; alert; superior intellect; analytical; critical; sarcastic; naive; tidy; healthy.
7th	Subliminative; teamwork; just; balanced mind; thoughts of others; co-operative; public; intellectual; mediators; opinionated; charmed.
8th	Deep; occult; hidden; spiritualistic; deadly; intriguing; grudge holders; interest in the dead; penetrating; senile; suspicious.
	Gestation (Transcendence)
9th	Deep mind; higher mind; rebirth; ethics; moral; curiosity; knowledgeable; religious; gurus; prophetic; scattered, evasive; free; learning.
10th	Ambition; egotistic thoughts; prestige; power; planning; career thoughts; concentration; patience; reserve; rational; serious; exact.
11th	Interested; detached; progressive; groups; reform; invention; involved; Utopian; planning; inquisitive; eccentric; contrary; work alone.
12th	Influenced; sacrificial; reproductive; dreamy; imagination; retentive; mediumistic; poetic; impressionable; refined; influenced by others.

Venus

♀ | **Principles** | Relationship; harmony; love; aesthetics; physical affection; beauty; art; unity; integration; aberration; bad taste; sentimentality; indulgence; affection; affectation; illusion.

Sign	Interpretation
Aries Det	Aggressive love; outgoing; passion; ardent; creative powers; attractive personality; erotic; self-centred.
Taurus Rule	Love of luxury; taste; constancy; conservative; artistic; musical; loving; indolent; loyal; touching; innate value.
Gemini	Many loves; social; flirtatious; attractive; charming; accommodating; discuss ideas; superficial relations; romantic.
Cancer	Domestic; delicate; feminine; sentimental; indigestible; lush; tender; indulgent; exploited; affectionate; unselfish.
Leo	Premature relations; ardent; fixed affection; fiery relationships; garish taste; squandering; indulgent; pride.
Virgo Fall	Repressed feeling; fastidious; polite; perfectionist; indecisive; shared work; hypercritical; cold exterior; beauty.
Libra Rule	Lively; crafty; companiable; engagements; artistic skill; important affections; bonding; beauty; money; conformist; social.
Scorpio Det	Intemperance; legacies; withholding love; deep feeling; immoral; secretive; serious relations; hatred; indifference; occult art.
Sagittarius	Spiritual love; frank; moodiness; many loves; demonstrative; objective relations; ethical; foreign aesthetics.
Capricorn	Materialistic; distrusting; jealous; maturity; attached; experienced; over-controlled; separate; proud; reserved.
Aquarius	Easy contact; free love; refined; amenable; indiscriminate; unconventional; gay; sponsorship; effervescent.
Pisces Exalt	Longing for love; exploited; tender; gentility; sentimental; musical; romantic; religious; cosmic feeling; suffering.

Personifications	Lovers; maidens; women; the beautiful; artists; musicians; entertainers; clothier.

♀

House	Interpretation
	Childhood
1st	Beauty; personal grace; proportionate; happy; love; demonstrative; popular; love at first sight; social life; clothes; enhancement.
2nd	Physical beauty; objects; needing love; good taste; grasping; deep feelings; personal attraction; possessive; faithful; plodding.
3rd	Love of words; drawing; social; siblings; close relationships; variety; curiosity; friendly with everyone; flighty; fickle.
4th	Deep love; familial; appreciating home; love; dreamy; imaginative; possessive; loyal; tender; flattered; shy; deeply sensitive; stable.
	Maturity
5th	Love-relations; games; pleasure; amusing; hedonistic; vivacious; creative; proud; jealous; romantic; popular; warmth; social.
6th	Work love; critical affections; naivete; friendly co-operation; moral; practical considerations; puritanical; refined; modest.
7th	Great love; affairs; infidelity; attractive; amorous; friendly; artistic; happy marriage; public; charming; gentle; lovable; frivolous.
8th	Strong attraction; love of separation; lust; fanatic love; passion; jealousy; wavering; licentious; sexual; magnetic; charming.
	Gestation (Transcendence)
9th	Love of art, religion, philosophy; wishing; romantic; responsive; scattered emotions; idealistic; imaginings; unstable; cultural.
10th	Social ambition; good relations; legal; cold emotion; faithful; constant; control; formal sense; loyal; undemonstrative.
11th	Abstract love; frigidity; homosexuality; idealistic; progressive; social; kind friend; group activities; women's groups; protected.
12th	Secretive; solitary; masturbative; artistic; seductive; impressionable; sensitive; soft; psychic love; sexual restraint; charitable.

Mars

♂

Principles	Energy; aggression; will; activity; desire for change; conflict; intervention; adventure; impulse; competition; sexual drive; initiatory force; passion; violence; ruthlessness.
Sign	**Interpretation**

Aries Rule	Fighting; spirit; ambition; temper; zeal; independent; irascible; brutal; headstrong; competitive; egotism.
Taurus Det	Work capacity; practical; foresight; executive; acquisitive; industrious; material; skilled; aggressive; strong.
Gemini	Mobility; communicative; sarcastic; versatile gifts; agile; lively; ready; mental; debater; journalistic; rude.
Cancer Fall	Instinctive actions; temper; lacks persistence; irritable; sensuous; tenacious; frustration; ulcers.
Leo ·	Confident; possessive; ardour; frank; domineering; creative; willed; leading; competitive; strong belief; strength.
Virgo	Scientific; orderly; irritable; astute; criticism; skilled; medicine; practical action; perfectionist; fussy; nervous.
Libra Det	Social activities; public affairs; leading; teamwork; dependence on feeling; frank; ardent; idealistic; loving.
Scorpio Rule	Magnetic sex; strong emotions; forceful; selfish; critical; revengeful; occult; sex magic; courage; jealousy.
Sagittarius	Explorational; enthusiastic; strong beliefs; religious; hedonistic; rude; unconventional; adventurous; spiritual.
Capricorn Exalt	Authoritative; directed; independent; energetic; extremely materialistic; possessive; power mad; efficient; controlled.
Aquarius	Organised; inconstant; superficial; masculine groups; perverse; impatient; revolutionary; upsetting; methodical.
Pisces	Addictive; silent work; uncontrolled; over-emotional; romantic; illusory men; seductive; vivid dreams; waiting.

| Personifications | Fighters; soldiers; surgeons; athletes; mechanics; craftsmen; men in general; strong women; engineers; metalworkers; technicians; builders; police. | ♂ |

House	Interpretation

Childhood

1st	Energetic; lively; self-willed; violence; muscular; robust; impulsive; strength of personality; action; impatience; injuries.
2nd	Endurance; practical ability; obstinate; intractable; possessive; purposeful; desiring; tenacious; sensuous; persistence; intense.
3rd	Witty; criticism; scattered; active mind; direct; writing; impulsive movement; anger; argumentative; nervous; talkative; hasty.
4th	Intense feelings; moody; impulsive; instinct; not persevering; domestic dominance; ecology; acquisitive; energetic; uncontrolled; working.

Maturity

5th	Formative power; self assurance; enterprise; gambler; player; athlete; audacious; sexual; artist; speculation; egotism; dictatorial.
6th	Detailed work; organising; tidy; endurance; methodical; critical; skill; energy in work; surgeons; precision; ingenious; frustrated.
7th	Associative; subliminative; cordial manner; work partnership; impulsive; aggressive affairs; joint finance; entangled; passion.
8th	Survival instinct; courageous; sensuous; dissipated; sadistic; craving power; active corporate desire; violent death; illegality.

Gestation (Transcendence)

9th	Sport; convincing others; adventurous; brave; travel lust; social causes; reform; inspired; experienced; extravagant; rude; sloppy.
10th	Famous; ambitious; self-reliant; hard work; realistic; sober; defiant; obstinate; heroic; irritable; cold; unfeeling; reversals; power.
11th	Male friends; reforming; detached; asexual; deliberate; freedom; contradictory; revolutionary; superficial; progressive; perverse.
12th	Energyless; drug desire; alcoholic; secretive; hidden emotions; sensuous; hoping; unconscious; desire; institutions; isolation; unreliable.

Jupiter

♃

Principles	Expansion; optimism; positivity; generous; enthusiastic; philosophical; religious; psychological; travel; wise; justice; harmony; aspirations; amoral; indulgent; sloppy.
Sign	**Interpretation**
Aries	Leading; travel urge; noble; positive; generous; free; spiritual; extravagant; frank; innovative; faithful; foolish.
Taurus	Hedonist; good hearted; indulgent; exploitative; financial interests; stewardship; productive; beneficent.
Gemini Det	Obliging others; many relations; joy; crafty; sociable; free; mannered; empty; legal; curiosity; advanced; friendly.
Cancer Exalt	Pleasure; prolific; deep feelings; charitable; intuitive; receptive; deep love; family important; secure.
Leo	Speculative; grandeur; openness; arts; great energy; positive in games; fond; generous; big hearted; noble; vain.
Virgo Det	Morality; prudent; ambitious; honest; intellectual; conscientious; critical; perfectionist; over-rated; serving; work.
Libra	The law; mildness; open partnerships; advantage through marriage; benign; unfulfilled commitments; psychology.
Scorpio	Metaphysical; passionate; shrewd; striving for possessions; craving pleasure; corporate affairs; mystical.
Sagittarius Rule	Philosophy; religious; humanitarian; esoteric; nobility; foreign; jovial; liberal; psychological; superstition.
Capricorn Fall	Acquisitive; wealthy; recognised; trusty; responsible; integrity; conservatism; austere; tight; materialist.
Aquarius	Impartial; sympathetic; fellowship; human nature; occult wisdom; social reform; intolerant; astrology; broad.
Pisces	Deep emotions; hidden life; drugs; modest circumstances; kind; unreliable; visionary; indolent; illusory; alcohol.

| Personifications | Priests; philosophers; psychologists; psychiatrist; the wealth; lawyer; banker; physician; official; publisher; guru; wiseman; fortune hunter. |

♃

House	Interpretation
	Childhood
1st	Self-sufficient; optimistic; extrovert; fat; aspiring; imbalanced; sociable; well-liked; protection; indulgence; promises; vigour.
2nd	Expansiveness; growth; reliable; wasteful; generous; enjoyment; insecure; trusteeship; liberal; open; exploitable; wealthy.
3rd	Positive mind; optimism; religious influence; intelligent; flexible; versatile; changing; popular; travel; conceited; carefree; sweet.
4th	Receptive; attachment; contented; religious; psychology; family sense; impressionable; congenial; strong home; morality; fortunate.
	Maturity
5th	Creativity; artistic; self-confidence; lead; popularity; vanity; honour; achievements; dignified; intolerant; prestige; dominant.
6th	Ambition; learning; teaching; teamwork; carefree; service; healing; work ethic; morality; conscientious; organisation; professional.
7th	Fortunate marriage-job; justice; popularity; temperance; charitable; social contacts; selfless relationships; judgement; spiritual.
8th	Religious; separated; legacies; funerals; sex values; over-rated; proud; self-indulgent; peaceful death; materialistic; occult.
	Gestation (Transcendence)
9th	Religious; moral aspiration; foresight; plans; expansive feelings; speculative; foreign matters; inner development; justice; balance.
10th	Responsible; productive; material; practical; prominence; recognition; reliable; dignity; standing; domestic affairs; egotist; capable.
11th	Humanitarian; prominent friends; groups; help from others; liberal; obliging; collective goals; invention; ulterior motives; sociable.
12th	Altruism; contentment; solitude; generous; imaginative; inner life; compassionate; spiritual search; meditation; fantasy; crisis.

Saturn

ħ

Principles	Contraction; pessimism; negativity; stingy; concentration; focus; seriousness; economy; inhibition; reserve; unadaptable; formative energy; discipline; limitation; suffering.
Sign	Interpretation

Aries Fall	Selfishness; diligence; reserved; humourless; lonely; mechanical; autocratic; wilful; strong character.
Taurus	Perseverance; method; constructive; money worries; ambition; hard work; father; elders; serious finances.
Gemini	Intellectual; scientific; businesslike; serious; difficult; abstract; inhibited; calculating; detached; systematic.
Cancer Det	Sensitive; self-centred; elderly; paranoid; lonely; jealous; suspicious; estranged; respectful; unstable.
Leo Det	Limited; authoritarian; leader; simple; loyalty; hard work; loss through children; ungratified; resentful; need recognition.
Virgo	Perfectionist; hard worker; serious; materialistic; acting alone; pedantic; detail oriented; attentive; discreet.
Libra Exalt	Industrious; conscientious; impartial; austere; reliable; managerial; corporate; mediative; businesslike; legal; enemies.
Scorpio	Resourceful; restrained; melancholy; metaphysical seriousness; cautious; corporate; legal conflict; perfectionist.
Sagittarius	Moralising; high minded; religious; serious traveller; prudence; law; separation from home; doubts.
Capricorn Rule	Paternal; advanced; suspicious; slow; patience; method; pessimism; diplomacy; materialistic; partial; strong; egotist.
Aquarius	Serious groups; collective; ambitious; organised; responsible; mental work; detached; selfish; domineering; games.
Pisces	Struggle; melancholy; restrained; older friends; retirement; deep meditation; spiritual; withdrawal; distrusting.

Personifications	Doctors; bankers; workers; farmers; workers with metals; scientist; grandparents; uncles and aunts; business people; archaeologists; geologist; miner; computer programmer.
House	**Interpretation**
1st	*Childhood* Ambitious; restrained; obstinacy; responsible; cold; unfriendly; limitation; hardship; lonely; older people; defiance; selfish; serious.
2nd	Material; ordered; possessive; stability; endurance; inhibited; restricted movement; grasping; conservative; inertia; difficulty.
3rd	Difficult siblings; zealous; thorough; unadaptive; shy; disciplined; practical; scientific; critical; mechanistic; clumsy; logic; serious.
4th	Reserved; ambitious; difficult family; love; independent; defensive; repressed; economy; responsible; isolated; secure; reclusive.
5th	*Maturity* Responsible; reliable; loyal; informal; shy; conservative; repressed; unsportsmanlike; strict; serious school; inhibited sexuality.
6th	Critical; correct; responsible; methodical; pedantic; scientific; serious study; detailed; sedentary; inhibited; asexual; misunderstood.
7th	Dutiful; older partner; serious relations; estrangement; impractical; loyal; inhibited; discontented; enduring; hard work; responsible.
8th	Partners' finances, emotions; lack capital; obstinate; transformations; strong; reserved; selfish; occult; concentrative; rebirth.
9th	*Gestation (Transcendence)* Aspirations; serious philosophers; separation; devotion; sincere; hurt; religious; stable; unsocial; achievement; status; morality.
10th	Patience; will power; restraint; ambitious; strong will; concentration; economy; partial; egocentric; cautious; karmic affairs; debts.
11th	Responsible; planning; reliable partner; extravagant expectations; aspirations; false friends; faithful; detached; inhibited mate.
12th	Reserved; lonely; restrained; secluded; nerves; timid; isolated; fear of failure; inferior; depressed; retiring; sacrificial; worrying.

♅

Principles	Originality; eccentricity; independence; rhythm; inspiration; individuality; invention; rebelliousness; dancing; perception; excitable; obstinacy; operations; accidents; changes.
Sign	*Interpretation*

Sign	Interpretation
Aries 1928-1934	Utopian; enthusiasm; unusual; peculiar; odd personality; free; unconventional; intuition; courage; daring; tempered.
Taurus *Fall* 1934-1942	Erratic; sudden changes; unstable finances; independent; ingenious; risk; speculative; premature; reform; original.
Gemini 1942-1949	Mental energy; spontaneous; inquisitive; scientific; methodical; original methods; free thinker; bizarre; comprehension.
Cancer 1949-1956	Erratic feelings; strange mother; impulsive; residence changes; rebel; freedom; excitement; psychic; sensitive.
Leo *Det* 1956-1962	Egomanic; peculiar love; children; individual; licentious; determined; organising; unrestrained; sexually free.
Virgo 1962-1969	Health professions; mechanical; free; subtle; original job; intellectual; revolutionary; ingenious; computers.
Libra 1969-1975	New relationships; divorce; irritable; affairs; free love; magnetic; quick associations; imaginative; restless.
Scorpio *Exalt* 1975-1981	Regeneration; rapid change; destined struggles; violence; danger; ruthless; occult explosion; rebellious; astrology.
Sagittarius 1981-1988	Adventure; astrology; progressive education; reformed; unorthodox; Utopian; excitable; spiritual; neurotic.
Capricorn 1988-1996	Power; great aims; fanatacism; penetration; acquisitive; resolution; headstrong; strange career; radical.
Aquarius 1996-2003	Detachment; trouble; magnification; penetration; spiritual energy; religious change; inventive talent; wayward.
Pisces 2003-2011	Intuitive; peculiar methods; isolated; investigative; occult; mystical; self-willed; strange aspirations; idealism.

Personifications	Eccentrics; inventors; unusual people; technicians; revolutionaries; dancers & musicians; astrologers; radio-TV; electrician; healers; feminists; rebels; surgeons.

House	Interpretation
	Childhood
1st	Energetic; unusual; original; restless; odd; scientific influence; obstinacy; irrational electric; wilful; abrupt; erratic; stubborn.
2nd	Unusual objects; gains & losses; headstrong; determined; jealous; speculative; premature; unsettled; precocious; impractical; lively.
3rd	Inventive; original; precocious; creative; desultory; quick understanding; restless; intuitive; scattered; sharp; witty.
4th	Strange family; peculiar emotions; intuition; wandering; odd associations; homelessness; estrangement; impatient; rebellious; changes.
	Maturity
5th	Enterprise; boldness; creative; originality; peculiar games; dramatic; sudden affections; gambling; adventurous; quick learning; arty.
6th	Peculiar work; individual learning; quick; scientific effort; genius; occult; original; reforming; detailed; foolish; critical.
7th	Eccentric relationships; drug experiences; rebellious; inspired; peculiar marriage view; many marriages; aesthetic; talented; rigid.
8th	Penetrating; investigating occultism; energy realised; danger; fearless; strength; tenacious; great change; rebirth; violence; superphysics.
	Gestation (Transcendence)
9th	Spiritual; enlightenment; prophecy; rebelling; religious reform; advanced ideas; progressive fanaticism; restless; unconventional; danger.
10th	Ambitious; shrewd; concentrated energy; resolute; technical ability; professional; radical ideas; sudden fall; affliction.
11th	Scientific; profound; aspirational; organising; magnification; progressive; intuitive friend; perversity; rebellious; peculiar ideas.
12th	Mystical; revelling; intuition; estrangement; strange disease; visionary; secretive; being misunderstood; yoga; seek liberation; unreal.

Neptune

☊ **Principles**

Sensitivity; psychic; impressionable; fantasy; imagination; dreams; illusion; drugs; mediumship; intuition; idealism; Utopian projections; ESP; transcendental experiences.

Sign	Interpretation
Aries 1861-1874	Inspiration; idealism; unselfish; highly sensitive; far distant; social welfare; confused; mad; insane; addicted.
Taurus 1874-1888	Good taste; formal; unusual objects; idealistic finances; visionary; healing; natural beauty; alcoholism; addiction.
Gemini 1888-1901	Nature love; mystical; magical; inspired; confusion; vagueness; scattered; poetic; quick perception; variety; worrying.
Cancer 1901-1914	Intuition; psychic force; sensitive to home-mother; cherishing; inhibited; susceptible; unstable; suffering.
Leo Exalt 1914-1928	Passionate; easily stimulated; acting; leading; flattery; certain; love of pleasure; misdirected affection; waste.
Virgo Det 1928-1942	Fault finding; hypercritical; work difficulty; psychic communication; chaos; chemical; drugged; preoccupied.
Libra 1942-1956	Uncertain relations; divorce; sensitive partner; drug abuse; psychedelics; strange feelings; disappointed; receptive sex.
Scorpio 1956-1970	Hidden emotions; mystery; sex urge; confusion; clairvoyance; occultism; sensationalism; depression; sickness.
Sagittarius 1970-1984	Higher mind; religious regeneration; travel; foreign ideas; meditation; enlightenment; aimless; inspiration.
Capricorn 1984-1998	Supernatural; meditation; strange objectives; deception; depression; parental sacrifice; mystic reality.
Aquarius Fall 1998-2012	Soul unions; noble aspirations; easy temptation; social theory; group stimuli; independence; intuitive.
Pisces 2012-2026	Mysticism; inner life; mediumistic; neurotic; metaphysical; escapist; druggist; addictable; seductive.

Personifications Psychics; sensitive people; dreamers; Utopians; tricksters; mystics; gurus; dieticians; drug dealers; anaesthetists; chemists; inventors.

House	Interpretation
	Childhood
1st	Sensitive personality; intuition; dreamy; impressionable; delicate digestion; drugs; strange appearance; peculiar relationships.
2nd	Sensitive to form; artistic; sensuous; beauty; soft; imaginative; addictive; moody; strange form; muddled; impractical; lazy; dependent.
3rd	Duality; sensitivity; fantasy; confusion; unrealistic; inspiration; wrong ideas; weak memory; misunderstanding; nicknames; siblings.
4th	Great sensitivity; spiritual perception; deep feeling; inner union; discontent; anxiety; residence changes; addicted; sacrificial.
	Maturity
5th	Beauty; peculiar pleasures; sexuality; acting; exaggerating; romantic; psychological problems; broken family; intuitions; waste.
6th	Psychosomatic; serving; healing power; gentle; deceitful; hypersensitive; addictive; easy; despondent; magnetic energy; inspiration.
7th	Receptive; idealistic relationships; platonic; seductive; artistic; impulsive; harmonious relationships; psychic connections; oddness.
8th	Psychic; spiritual; unconscious processes; mediumistic; depressive; secretive; drugged; wasting diseases; hospitals; disappointment.
	Gestation (Transcendence)
9th	Presentiment; clairvoyance; idealism; over active mind; dreams; unrealistic; wishes & plans; self-deception.
10th	Aspiration without application; deep ideas; uncertainty; lacking reality; family trouble; psychic experiences; scandal; mysterious.
11th	Artistic; idealistic; strange attraction; hopes; wishes; mental change; insincerity; psychic experience; notoriety; theorising.
12th	Reserve; psychic communication; reverie; art; external influences; drugs; hospitals; ill; inducement; craving; alcohol; pessimism.

Pluto

Principles	The masses; transformation; revolution; destruction; force majeure; power; magic; willpower; propaganda; coercion; media; major changes; regeneration; passages.
Sign	*Interpretation*

Aries 1823-1852	Self assertion in the world; power-lust; new ideas; revolutionary person; potential; courageous; dauntless; free.
Taurus Det 1852-1884	Possessiveness; materialist; endurance; utilitarian; genius with materia; art; depending on finances; productive.
Gemini 1884-1914	Inventive; mobility; comprehension; intellectual assertion; science; adventures; ruthless behaviour.
Cancer 1914-1939	Intense personal feelings; familial restraint; compulsive; paternalism; transformed family; liberated woman.
Leo 1939-1957	Revolution in self-expression; change of attitude; exteriorisation; outburst of consciousness; creativity; talent.
Virgo 1957-1972	Health revolution; mental disease; psychosomatic; holistic medicine; workers; reactionaries; punks; birth control.
Libra 1972-1984	Liberation; homosexuality; changes in partnership; social justice; regenerated civilisation; arbitration; delicate balance.
Scorpio Rule 1984-2000	Death and rebirth; regeneration; force; fanatacism; atomic warfare; world war; daemonic forces; transformation; rage.
Sagittarius 2000-	Prophecy; sagacity; exploration; travel; strive for wisdom; philosophical change; psychoanalysis; Utopian aims; religious.
Capricorn 1762-1777	New ideas; practical revolutions; great ambition; corporate; executive; inventive; obsessed; materialistic.
Aquarius 1777-1799	Democracy; mental change; scientific; advancement through friends; psychological; synthetic ideas; intellectual.
Pisces 1799-1823	Profundity; apocalyptic; universal; compassionate; christian fanaticism; born again; mystical; astrological.

Personifications	Revolutionaries; mass media people; politicians; dictators; propagandists; actors and actresses; public speakers; atomic scientists; outlaws; prostitutes.
House	**Interpretation**

Childhood

1st	Power drive; extraordinary energy; assertions; rage; powerful will; hardships; robust; strong parental changes; advanced; rapid growth.
2nd	Great ambition; acquisitive; great gains or losses; dependence on money; insatiable; change material situations; stewardship.
3rd	Ingenious; specialised learning; rapid speech; penetrating mind; resourceful; secretive; strong opinions; strange siblings; gossip.
4th	Strong heredity; unusual task; solitary; deep feelings; magnetic; magic; domination at home; nature love; ecology; occult; secrets.

Maturity

5th	Dynamic emotions; authority; self-awareness; powerful will; force; dramatic expression; great achievements; creative power; talent.
6th	Healing; psychosomatic diseases; working with others; inquisitive; collecting; scientific; energetic; great criticism; fanatacism; zeal.
7th	Fateful partnerships; fame; strong unions; divorces; multiple partners; personal magnetism; dramatic changes; domineering; intuitive.
8th	Fanaticism; tragic events; record achievements; search for meaning; transforming; public death; influential; tenacious; occult; secrets.

Gestation (Transcendence)

9th	Higher knowledge; spiritual regeneration; pioneering; the unattainable; travel; reform; social change; religious fanaticism; atheism.
10th	Dictatorship; struggle for recognition; practical problems; independence; danger; isolation; plans; dramatic change; willpower.
11th	Communal; Utopian communities; reforming; friendship important; sudden death; changes of attitude; exaggerated hopes; popularity.
12th	Isolation; universal; revelatory; destructive; metaphysical; secretive; tempted; suppressed emotions; strange illness; retirement; occult.

Node

| Principles | Associations; alliances; sociability; communal sense; sublimation; fostering; collective influences. |

Sign	Interpretation
Aries	Cultivating friendships; honours; wealth; associative urge; extrovert; social; ardent; enthusiastic.
Taurus	Gain through property; sharing resources; debt; gain by learning and property.
Gemini Exalt	Good mind; language facility; gains from siblings; publishing; writing; words create anxiety.
Cancer	Close parents; soul associations; gain by property; obliging at home.
Leo	Speculative with others; large circle of friends; sporting; clubs; society affairs; wasteful; pompous; love affairs.
Virgo	Scientific associations; teaching; institutional; research; nagging; critical of others; sensitive health.
Libra	Unable to be alone; gregarious; dependent on others; contention; communal sense; social meetings; business success.
Scorpio	Deceptive; secretive associations; esoteric organisations; sexual relations; subversive affairs.
Sagittarius Fall	Legal teamwork; administrative; orderly; communal; mental quality; prophetic dreams; psychoanalysis.
Capricorn	Responsible to others; exploitation; practical groups; unions; professional groups; authorities; social climbing.
Aquarius	Stimulating friends; many friends; social life; inseparable; grasping; helping others communally.
Pisces	Beliefs; religious communities; collectives; institutions; isolation within groups; gaining possessions.

Personifications Associations; groups; clubs; political parties; labour unions; organizations.

House	Interpretation
	Childhood
1st	Self expression; desiring to rule; recognition; social life; personal associations.
2nd	Permanent bonding; alliances; money from others; devoted people; reliable; loyalty; legacy.
3rd	Many associations; ideas from others; important contacts; superficial association; nursery school; short relationships.
4th	Family ties; prominent parental contact; confused ancestry; soul unions; dependent; attached.
	Maturity
5th	Popularity; game-playing; large schools; many loves; affectionate with family; organised; team sports.
6th	Teaching associations; science; health interests; love of animals; serving others; work relationships; honest employees.
7th	Love affairs; teams; public affairs; profit through others; gain through women and partnership; making friends easily; social.
8th	Occult organisations; associations; co-operative effort; socialism; old age home; secret relations; gifts; legacies; violent policies.
	Gestation (Transcendence)
9th	Utopian ideas; idealistic groups; legal affairs; educational interests; dreams; water journeys; political idealism.
10th	Honour; credit; great achievements; business organisations; corporate affairs; deception; material objectives.
11th	Many friendships; supportive family; ideal plans; complex relationships; compulsive joining; social life prominent; helpful.
12th	Secret associations; rest homes; hospitals; nursing staff; teams of doctors; restraint from others; philosophical interests.

Ascendant (AS)

AS	Principles	Environment; personality; birth circumstances; people present at birth; reaction to the world; mask; way of acting; personal attitude; surroundings.
	Sign	**Birth Circumstances and Environment**
	Aries	Restlessness; energy; self-assertive; aggressive; impatient; surgery; forceps delivery; hurrying; ruthlessness.
	Taurus	Stable conditions; security; quiet; beautiful surroundings; women present; midwife; home; domesticity; practical.
	Gemini	Changes; quick birth; talking; many people present; siblings present; nerves; observers; moving around; adaptation.
	Cancer	Moody; home; family contact; humid; caring; feminine; protected; simplicity; sensitivity; anaesthetics; women.
	Leo	Authoritarian; confident; extrovert; active; joyous; open; prominent doctor; purposeful; bold; luxurious environs.
	Virgo	Critical; hospital; doctors; nurses; naivete; first births; virginal; nervous; stable; painstaking; hygienic; observant.
	Libra	Harmonious place; balanced; teamwork; physically easy; obliging; social; talkative; craving approval; women; nurses.
	Scorpio	Disharmonious; humid; hot-headed; brutal; surgical; forceps; violence; force; tragic; Caesarean; circumcision; cautious; angry.
	Sagittarius	Enthusiastic; athletic; joyous; good humour; natural; easy; active; messy; lively; expansive; foreign; recognised.
	Capricorn	Concentration; inhibition; restriction; long labour; serious; restraint; older doctor; reserved; anxious; methodical.
	Aquarius	Communal; detached; serious; idealistic; restrained; cold; progressive; friendly; abstract; mechanical; unorthodox; rhythmic.
	Pisces	Self-sacrificial; drugged; governed by externals; unconfident; anaesthetics; induced; isolated; psychic; dreamy; vague.

AS

Personality

Restless; rash; energetic; self-assertive; aggressive; impatient; quick temper; iniatory; violent; forceful; family ties; the surgeon.

Love of beauty; harmonious personality; security; property; practical; artistic; possessive; obstinate; loving; attentive; attractive; homely.

Quick responses; talkative; vivacious; adaptable; mobile; inconstant; communicative; artistic; highly strung; lively; superficial; boastful.

Sensitivity; rich home life; shyness; dependent; impressionable; sympathetic; mediumistic; gentle; addictive; unable to stand alone; dedicated.

Self-glorifying; courageous; hedonistic; ruling; generous; fun-loving; impressive; joyful; dignity; game-playing; haughty; arrogant; egocentric.

Discreet; cautious; reserved; critical; shy; precise; clean; pedantic; anxious; nervous; psychosomatic illnesses; indigestible; stable.

Balanced; harmonious personality; teamwork; attractive body; charming; flatterable; vain; saccharine; relaxed, gushy; meddlesome;

Aggressive; passionate; separate; metaphysical; reserved; paranoid; cautious; dependent; decisive; secretive; hot-blooded; sexual; magnetic.

Positive; jovial; happy; philosophical; sporty; enthusiastic; expansive; independent; social; lively; sloppy; nature-loving; hedonistic; easy.

Tenacious; repressed; serious; inhibited; materialistic; goal-conscious; hard working, anxious; pragmatic; professional; ambitious.

Reforming; communal; detached; group-oriented; friendly; progressive; own ideas; adaptable; inhibited; cold; moody; changing objectives.

Sacrificial; dreamy; psychic; sensitive; vague; depressed; comfortable; lazy; quiet; isolated; sympathetic; lonely; simple; receptive; induced.

MC

Principles	Ego-consciousness; objectives; focus; spiritual awareness; individuality; aims; profession; honour; confidence; moment of recognition; purpose.
Sign	**MC Registration Circumstances**
Aries	Intuitive; successful establishment of individuality; aware objectives; active assertion; ambitious; domineering.
Taurus	Sensitive; productive; stable; physical manifestation; substantial; tangible; secure; willed; artistic; stubborn.
Gemini	Thinking; dualistic; confused; manifold aims; changing goals; multiple professions; unstable; indecisive.
Cancer	Feeling; sensitive; protective; maternal; devoted; receptive; overemotional; greedy; inferior; tact; simplicity; thrift.
Leo	Intuitive; extrovert; self-conscious; controlled; leading; egocentric; creative; high aspirations; organisation.
Virgo	Sensitive; concerned with health; morning sickness; orderly; diligent; critical; practical; pedantic; hypochondriac.
Libra	Thinking; harmonious; balanced; relaxed; just; co-operation; sharing; craving recognition; reliant; diplomatic; exploitative.
Scorpio	Feeling; separate; considering abortion; wilful; passionate; intense; fanatical; repressive; destructive; suspicious.
Sagittarius	Intuitive; optimistic; material; strive for security; realised; free; mobile; athletic; religious; moral; extreme.
Capricorn	Sensitive; rational; pragmatic; real; selfish; egocentric; disciplined; tough; serious; inflexible; reserved; cautious.
Aquarius	Thinking; idealistic; humanitarian; detached; sociable; rebellious; frigid; scattered; friendly; vague; planning.
Pisces	Feeling; solitary; isolated; lonely; sensitive to others; waiting; hoping; clarity; goal conscious; impressionable.

Personifications   The individual; the Ego.

Ego

Ambitious; successful; individual; assertive;
confident; definite objectives; creative power;
initiatory.

Persistent aims; striving for material security; hard
to please; tenacious; egotism; materialistic;
mentality; aesthetics important; mistrustful.

Love of change; multifaceted; occasionally
creative; facile; unstable; communicative; friendly;
superficial; conflicting goals; charming.

Responsible; tactful; sensitive; dedicated;
concerned; conservative; emotional; slow; stable;
woman dominated; feminine.

Self-exteriorised; confident; open; expansive;
social climbing; optimistic; organisational;
pretence; generosity; leading; selfish; rigid.

Perfected; striving for security; lively; petty;
conservative; hypersensitive; working hard;
service; stewardship; simple means; critical.

Advancing through others; fortunate connections;
equilibration; co-operation; sublimation;
adaptation; exploitation; manners without.

Perseverance; mystical; independent, ambitious;
energetic; ruthless; compulsive; domineering;
purposeful; destructive; acquisitive.

Aspiring; idealistic; high standards; extended
thought; higher mind; philosophical-religious;
ambitious; changeable; Utopian; undependable.

Self confident; lonely; tenacious; overworked;
strong father; sober; unimaginative; prosaic, self-
centred; conscientious; ambitious.

Innovative; Utopian; humanitarian; abstract;
future oriented; modern; aspirational;
undisciplined; new ideas; progressive action;
novelty.

Passivity; hoping for results; luck; susceptible to
externals; feeling alone; insular; simple; modest
aspirations; occasional pleasures.

Sun Aspects

SU/SU — The will to live; power; the physical body; health and energy; bodily and spiritual harmony. Lack of incentive; illness; weakness; changes in direction; being without focus. The body; father and son; grandfather to son; colleagues; man to man

SU/MO — Conscious and unconscious; relationship; inner balance; public life; success. Inner discontent; conflict; unrelated; inner tension; struggle. Man and wife; father and mother; marriage partners; friends

SU/ME — Common sense; understanding; thoughts; practical mind; businesslike; organizational. Unclear; confusion; aimlessness; nervousness. Youngsters; intellectuals; business people

SU/VE — Physical love; beauty; popularity; social life; aesthetics; romantic. Frigidity; ugliness; unpopular; antisocial; tasteless; cold; indulgence. Artist; beloved man or woman

SU/MA — Vitality; vigour; advancement; vocational success; endurance; impulsiveness. Dissidence; violence; headstrong; contentious; daring. Fighter; soldier; doctor; husband; quarreller

SU/JU — Health; recognition; religious; expansive; happy; successful; creative. Materialistic; indulgent; arrogant; illegal, lazy. Wealthy; healthy; prominent; socialites

SU/SA — Separate; concentrated; absorbed; serious; hard worker; ambitious; dedicated. Selfish; inhibited; suppressive; pessimistic; inferior; anxious; weak; negative. Serious people; elderly; sick; inhibited; cruel father; weak father; missing father

SU/UR — Progressive; eccentric; technological; original; free; changeable; dynamic; individual. Obstinate; self-destructive; rebellious; tense; irritable. Innovator; reformer; rebel; technician; trouble-maker

SU/NE — Sensitive; delicate; imaginative; uncertain; refined; inspired; visionary; psychic. Insecure; weak; sick; deceptive; seducible; tasteless. Medium; romantic; dreamer; psychic; sensitive; drug addict; seducer; weak father

SU/PL — Power; attainment; conscious objectives; leading; growing; autocratic; ruthless. Ruthless; arrogant; forced; brutal; fanatical; destructive. Leader; fighter; revolutionary; transformer; martyr; strong father

SU/NO Physical associations; public; adaptive; sociable; popular; educational. Anti-social; disharmonious; unadaptable; unrelated; isolated. Associate; fellow; colleague; witness; relative; dignitary; police

SU/AS Personal relations; physical relations; confidence; advancement; esteem; recognizable. Pushy; disharmonious; disliked; self-seeking; shy; quarrelsome; dependent. Men in the environment; contact; husband

SU/MC Individual; objective; self-knowledge; success; missionary; authority; famous. Egocentric; unclear; arrogant; conceited; uninteresting; misguided. Body and Soul; 'I'; One's own Ego

Moon Aspects

MO/MO Emotional life; feminine relations; changeable things; pleasant moods; motherliness. Emotional suppression; moodiness; separation from mother; unemotional; tension. The feelings; the Soul; mother and daughter

MO/ME Emotional thoughts; perception; judgement; valuation; feminine ideas; discretion. Changeable; lying; gossip; criticism; calumny; ingenuous; highly strung. Intellectual women; girls; authoress; psychologist; traveller

MO/VE Love; devotion; art; conception; romantic; cultured; marriage; graceful. Moody; shy; tasteless; sterile; irritable; loveless. Lover; expectant mother; mother; artist; woman; actor

MO/MA Excitement; intense emotion; frankness; candid; sincere; feeling will; industrious. Impulsiveness; rash; fighting; intolerant; rebellious; irritable. Wife; woman colleague; hard worker; housewife; businesswoman

MO/JU Happy; religious; social conscience; travel; faithful; recognition; positive feeling. Indifferent; negligent; rebellious; unpopular; illegal; marital problems; sloppy. Successful; generous; happy woman; females; bride; expectant mother; official women

MO/SA Self-control; duty; care; attentive; circumspect; lonely; ascetic; critical; ambitious. Depressive; separated; widowed; inferior; melancholy; anxious; estranged. Inhibited people; sad; widow; single parent; female grandparent

MO/UR Subconscious forces; instinct; sudden events; occult; intellectual specialization. Schizophrenia; emotional tension; overstrain; abrupt; exaggeration; anxiety. Restless woman; ambitious; reformists; schizophrenic

MO/NE   Refined; inner vision; imagination; inspiration; relaxation; romantic; idealistic. Frail; self-deception; unreality; weakness; addicted; seductive; supernatural. Sensitive; medium; impressionable people; card-readers; psychic; indolent; the weak

MO/PL   Extreme emotion; one-sided; fanatacism; overzealous; devouring; dynamic; insatiable. Fanatic; sadistic; obsessed; shocking; jealous; demanding; insane demands; upheavals. Emotional people; public relations people; publicists; schizophrenic; revolutionary

MO/NO   Spiritual union; inner relationships; alliances (between women); family ties; devoted. Estrangement; multiple relationships; unadaptable; frustrated; unfamilial; insular. Woman alliances; blood union; associates

MO/AS   Emotional relations; obliging; feminine; adaptable; personal ties; subjective ties. Hypersensitivity; disagreements; moody; changeable; over-reactive; annoyed. Feminine environment; mother; alcoholics; drug addicts; lovers; personalities

MO/MC   Emotional objectives; sentiment; home; family; soul-ties; intuitive understanding. Difficult women; unprofessional; vacillation; unreliable; sentimental; wavering. Women; feeling and emotional people; governesses; mother; soul people

☿

Mercury Aspects

ME/ME   Movement; thinking; mind; news; opinions; perception; good comprehension; understanding; easy. Static states; subjectivity; dullness; lacking objectivity; lying; no communication. Active people; friends; confidants; mediators; intellects; teachers; siblings; the young

ME/VE   Love thoughts; beauty sense; design; feeling intellect; hilarity; art success; writing. Vanity; conceit; hypersensitive; irresolute; squandering; luxury. Lovers; author; writer; beauty sales person; art dealer; aesthete; artist; female friends

ME/MA   Thought power; realized plans; resolution; repartee; enterprise; debate; settling affair. Criticism; nagging; malice; hasty action; speech difficulty; obstinate; cynical. Critic; quarreller; debater; writer

ME/JU   Constructive mind; erudition; literature; business sense; common sense; science; fluent. Negligence; fraud; unreliable; exaggerating; conflict; indiscreet. Speaker; authority; negotiator; businessperson; publisher; traveller; philanthropist.

ME/SA   Mental work; concentration; deep thought; logic;
         organization; experience; industry. Dullness; reserve;
         shyness; estrangement; difficulty; hard infancy; distrust.
         Philosopher; intellectual; scientist; crook; logician

ME/UR   Intuition; astuteness; flexibility; independence; influence;
         mathematics; original mind. Scattered; madness; nerves;
         erratic; eccentric; contradictory. Mathematician; scientist;
         technician; musician; astrologer; lively people

ME/NE   Imagination; fantasy; deep perception; vision;
         presentiments; poetic; idealistic; clear. Faulty judgement;
         paralysis; deception; fraud; dissipated; foolish. Actor;
         fantasizer; dreamer; saint; liar; faith healer; psychic

ME/PL   Persuasion; understanding; cunning; diplomacy;
         influence; wit; slyness. Breakdown; hasty expression;
         excessive opposition; overeager; impatience; crudeness.
         Speaker; politician; fascist; critic; tyrant; propagandist

ME/NO   Joint plans; exchanging ideas; social-business meeting;
         correspondence; relationship. Unsociable; unpopularity;
         closed; blocked; disloyalty. Joiners; groupy; writer;
         organizer; negotiator; networker

ME/AS   Personal ideas; definition; verbal communication;
         meetings; intelligence; talkative. Gossip; misjudgement;
         anxiety; superficial; flighty. Thinker; gossip; organizer;
         friend; administrator; diplomat

ME/MC   Intellectual objectives; observation; self knowledge;
         meditation; own aims; clarity. Aimlessness;
         unselfconscious; changeable; vacillation; dishonest.
         Expressive people; talkers; media people; MCs; Job
         counsellors

Venus Aspects   ♀

VE/VE   Peace; goodwill; love; desire; feeling love; humour;
         beauty sense; art. Unrelated; listless; tasteless;
         aberration; carelessness. Lover; aesthete; beauty;
         model; girl; actor; artist; musician; clothier; nurse

VE/MA   Sexual love; artistry; passion; creativity; lively
         expression; intimacy; prolific. Asexuality; seduction;
         unsatisfied; infidelity; irritable; sexual disease. Lover;
         sexist; seducer; polygamist; active lover

VE/JU   Joyous love; happiness; popularity; form sense;
         marriage; bliss; comfort; gay; hedonism. Laziness;
         lacking feeling; indolence; arrogance; legal conflict;
         indulgence. Artist; filmstar; model; socialite; expansive
         lover.

VE/SA	Dutiful emotion; soberness; loyalty; inhibition; sacrifice; fidelity; economy; reserve. Jealousy; torment; deprivation; lonely; depressed; mother separation. Lonely people; widow(er); illegitimate children; older lover
VE/UR	Arousal; eccentricity; impulse; talent; music; sentimentality; refinement. Repressed sexuality; inconstancy; estrangement; unconventional; loose. Musician; artist; eccentric lover
VE/NE	Rapture; eroticism; mysticism; idealism; platonic affairs; travel; refinement. Seducible; tasteless; infatuation; dreaming; illusion; escapist. Artist; musician; dreamer; visionary; romantic; drug dealer; addict; weak lover
VE/PL	Fanatic love; sensuality; gifted; attractive; compulsive; devoted; talented; magnetic. Lusty; stressed love; sado-masochism; vulgarity; excessive desire. Lover; pornographer; menstruating woman; artist
VE/NO	Love union; adaptation; universal love; ties; obliging; artistic communities. Isolation; separation; unhappy affair; flighty. Lover; marrieds; singles; art groupies; gallery owner
VE/AS	Harmonious love; beauty; attractive personality; adornment; art; taste; gentility. Bad taste; desertion; unsociable; wasteful; indulgent. Woman; mother; wife; lover; artist
VE/MC	Objective love; affection; benevolence; artistic; attached; attractive individual. Vanity; conceit; jealousy; dissipated. Lover; artist; admirer

♂
Mars Aspects

MA/MA	Energy; activity; work; aggression; impulse; resolve; will; decision; accomplishment. Wasting energy; violence; injury; destruction. Fighter; soldier; athlete; craftsman; surgeon; police
MA/JU	Successful creativity; joy; activity; organisation; prowess; rebellion; practicality. Conflict; estrangement; precipitancy; haste; restlessness; dispute. Manager; organizer; jurist; judge; official; athlete
MA/SA	Inhibition; endurance; danger; fanaticism; spartan life; ascetic; tough; Destruction; danger; death; impotence; obstinacy; separation; tests; dispute; illness. Labourer; miner; fighter; killer
MA/UR	Applied effort; intervention; courage; independence; operation; revolutionary; birth. Argument; obstinacy;

emotional tension; stress; nerves; operation; injury; accident. Surgeon; violent people; revolutionary; reactionary; driver; fireman

MA/NE Inspiration; desire sensitivity; escapism; romanticism; fantasy; denial. Destruction; infection; misdirection; drugs; inferiority; smoking; paralysis; narrowness. Sick people; addict; sailor; pathologist; dealer

MA/PL Superhuman force; violence; vigour; great ambition; success; obsession; research. Cruelty; assault; aggression; injury; sadism; homicide; ruthlessness. Dictator; disabled; nuclear scientist; politician; general

MA/NO Physical collaboration; team spirit; union; shared success, progeny; betrothal. Quarrels, lack fellowship; disrupted meetings; eunuchism; dissolution; dissociation. Collectives; communists; socialists; eunuchs

MA/AS Fighting spirit; forced will; teamwork; attainment; resolution; creative work; surgery. Caesarean; forceps birth; operation; fighting; aggression; conflict; dispute; quarrel. Surgeon; soldier; colleagues; boxer

MA/MC Ego-conscious action; order; decision; success; resolution; occupation change; prudence. Excitable; stress; prematurity; purposeless; fever; fraud; agitation; murder. Organiser; leader; politician; leading personality.

Jupiter Aspects ♃

JU/JU Contentment; optimism; luck; financial gain; religion; philosophy; social life. Unlucky; losses; pessimism; illegal; extravagant; materialistic; greedy; corpulence. Lawyer; judge; banker; insurer; physician; uncle; grandparent; publisher

JU/SA Patience; perseverance; industry; diplomacy; seclusion; duty; philosophy; calm; real estate. Vacillation; discontent; upset; failure; illness. Professor; teacher; lawyer; official; politician; relatives; tenant

JU/UR Optimism: fortunate ideas; perception; sudden recognition; bliss; invention; change. Independence; opposition; magnifying matters; arguments; tension; stress. Organisers; inventors; adventurer; optimist; religious zealots

JU/NE Speculation; imagination; metaphysics; idealism; luck; ethics; generosity; profit. Susceptible; dreaming; unreality; enmity; insult; losses; swindlers. Speculator; dreamer; mystic; visionary

JU/PL   Plutocracy; spiritual-mental power; leadership; regeneration; organisation; transfusion. Fanaticism; losses; guilt; failure; legal liability; bankruptcy; exploitation. Organiser; professor; teacher; speculator; dictator; propagandist

JU/NO   Good contact; adaptability; tact; common interest; fortunate union; life force. Lack fellowship; anti-social; selfish; conflict; lifeless. Philosophical communities; fellows; partners; associates

JU/AS   Agreeable; favourable influence; generosity; wealth; cure; success; easy birth; teamwork. Waste; friction; rebellion; hypocrisy; conceit; bragging. Generous people; wealthy people; uncles; grandparents; aunts

JU/MC   Philosophical objectives; conscious aims; contentment; bliss; success; purpose. Risks; unclear aims; changes in life-style; desire for importance. Successes; philosopher; psychologist; priest

Saturn Aspects

SA/SA   Restriction; patience; concentration; industry; crystallisation; earnestness. Hindrance; illness; developmental crisis; depression; inefficiency; sorrow; paralysis. Inhibited people; scientist; father; elderly; farmer; miner; businessperson; doctor

SA/UR   Tension; determination; collected thinking; calmness; technical affairs; travel; endure. Emotional tension; provocation; force; backlash from past; limitation of freedom. Violent people; the dying; amputees; chronically ill

SA/NE   Renunciation; suffering; sacrifice; caution; method; duality; asceticism; patience. Insecurity; illness; pestilence; habit; neuroses; emotional inhibitions; insecure. Ascetics; chronically ill; elderly; druggists

SA/PL   Cruelty; hard labour; tenacity; self-discipline; adepts; martyrdom; struggling; silence. Egotism; violence; divorce; slow separation; murder; self-destruction; loss of money. Scientists; murderers; reactionaries; martyrs

SA/NO   Isolation; inhibited union; maturity; sponsorship; mystery. Unadaptable; difficulty cooperating; death of relatives; depression; inhibition. Elderly persons; mourners

SA/AS   Inhibited personality; difficult birth; early maturity; lonely; isolated; inmates. Depression; wrong outlook; poor family; disadvantages through others; segregation.

Inmates; patients; lonely people; doctors; hospital staff; grandparents

SA/MC   Serious objectives; slow development; separation; self-preoccupation; experience. Emotional inhibition; dejection; illness; insanity; loss of consciousness; despondent. Inhibited people; patients; burden

Uranus Aspects

UR/UR   Suddenness; ambitions; enterprise; creativity; crisis change; reform; many plans. Hard conditions; change; catastrophe; nervous crises; suicidal thoughts; danger. Reformers; inventors; technicians; revolutionaries; astrologer; healer; physicist

UR/NE   Unconsciousness; inner vision; inspiration; mysticism; art; research; journeys; spirit. Instability; confusion; death; revolution; crisis; incapacity; confusion psychically. Mystics; mediums; psychics; revolutionaries

UR/PL   Transformation; revolution; innovation; mobility; reform; mutation; explosion; changes. Impatience; mania; destruction; upsets; subversive activities; enforcement; explosion. Pioneers; reformers; geniuses; explorers; gunmen

UR/NO   Shared experience; sudden attraction; unstable relations; variety; innovation; activity. Disturbance; quarrels; separation; restlessness; flighty; irritable; incidents; dreamy. Politicians; labour unions; excited family; nervous people

UR/AS   Environmental response; invention; new contacts; original; nervousness; rearrangement. Excitable; inconstancy; disquiet; accidents; quick changes; compulsion; rudeness. Excitable people; originals; eccentrics; technicians; neurotics

UR/MC   Original objectives; assertion; fortunate changes; organising; successful; stress. Tension; prematurity; unreliability; temper; upsets, sudden turns of destiny. Yogis; gurus; inventors; physicists; musicians

Neptune Aspects

NE/NE   Spiritual development; intellectual perception; travel; empathy; mysticism; drugs. Hypersensitivity; nervousness; confusion; health crisis; deception; addiction; deceit. Mediums; frauds; sensitives; perceptive people; spiritual people; addicts; dreamers

NE/PL	Supernatural; intensification; active imagination; psychics; parapsychology; evolution. Confusion; torment; obsession; craving drugs or alcohol; loss; possession; falsehood. Mystics; astrologers; psychics; occultists; mediums; addicts; gamblers
NE/NO	Idealistic associations; sensitive groups; mysticism; Utopian associations; spiritual. Antisocial; deceptive; cheating others; deception; sleeplessness; disturbed dreams. Groupies; psychic groups; mystical organisations; magic circles; covens
NE/AS	Impressionability; sensitivity; sympathy; strangeness; refinement; idealism; water birth. Betrayal; weakness; confusion; disappointment; escapism; fraud; illusion; drugs. Anaesthetists; sensitives; mediums; addicts; psychics; mystics; weak people
NE/MC	Uncertain objectives; vagueness; peculiar ideas; Utopian; supernatural; artistic. Feigning; falsehood; acting; numbness; strange ideas; depression; deception. Utopians; parapsychologists; weaklings; actors; the mentally disturbed; psychotics

Pluto Aspects

PL/PL	Inner change; metamorphosis; transformation; propaganda; mass influence; powerlust. Ruthlessness; fanaticism; agitating efforts; weakness; coercion; indoctrination. Dictators; hypnotists; politicians; magicians; public speakers; actors.
PL/NO	Collective destiny; public figures; influencing others; group associations; movements. Tragic destiny; karma; being cramped by others; antisocial; suffering; suffocation. Crowds; mass meetings; armies; political parties; unions; multinationals
PL/AS	Fascinating personality; ambition; magic; unusual influence; control; transformation. Changing environment; dictatorship; ruling others; repulsion; readjustment; injury. Great specialists; fascinating personalities; stars; politicians; public figures
PL/MC	Transformed objectives; individuality; strength; growth; authority; expert knowledge. Misused power; resistance; vindictiveness; anti-social conduct; recuperation; destiny. Transformers; authorities; specialists; magicians; surgeons

Node Aspects

NO/NO   Unions; connections; junctures; communication; approach; groups; clubs; fellowship. Limitations; antisocial; incompatibility; unsocial; unadaptive. Contacts; mediators; relatives; family; associations; colleagues

NO/AS   Fellowship; personal relationships; family contacts; social conscience; charm; loves. Short relations; estrangements; disturbed domestic relations; antisocial; difficult. Family; associates; workmates; fellows; friends

NO/MC   Group objectives; individual relationships; astral relationships; mutual understanding. Inconstancy; differing; individual over collective; difficult collectives; Marxists. Associations; political parties; unions; friends

Ascendant (AS) Aspects

AS/AS   Acquaintance; location; surroundings; the place; body; social relations; personal relations. Maladjustment; feeling lost; misplaced; difficult birth. People in the environment; doctors; midwives

AS/MC   Individual synthesis; higher self and lower self; personality and ego; integration. Impossible synthesis; irreconcilable goals; lack of direction. Synthesisers; strong personalities with direction

Midheaven (MC) Aspects

MC/MC   The Ego; spiritual, intellectual and social impressions; goals; objectives. Egoless; materialistic; goalless; insane. Egotists; people who live in the moment; goal-oriented people

★Chapter Seven★
Your Story

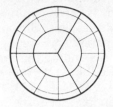

There is unity between the events which begin and end life. At the instant the sperm fertilizes the ovum, a complex life pattern registers and begins its exorable unfolding. The nature of life – physical, emotional, energetic and intellectual – is largely determined at conception and our experiences and environment qualify this inherent reality. It has been reported by many who have almost died that the sequence of events of their life flashed before their mind's eye at death. This is a description of the same pattern in time at the moment of its completion.

In other words, at conception, life is all potential; at death, all potential has been made actual and life is finished. The life process is the translation of potential into actual reality and at every moment past actualities are balanced against future possibilities. The fulcrum point from which you experience this phenomenon is the Present. Life may be compared to a transformer which takes raw energy from the earthly environment and transforms it into finer and finer energies through time, until the process is complete and the body is released at death.

The horoscope is the graphic representation of your life pattern from conception to death. Movement through the horoscope follows life and is *Your Story* – a tale involving everything essential in your life. The rules which govern your story are those which govern all stories and are not generated by particular psychological schools, religions or nations. Your Story is the playing out of your version of timeless archetypal patterns which the code transmitted to you at conception. Since birth you have continually told, retold, altered, permuted, remembered and forgotten your life story. What you tell your partner, children, friends, bank manager, psychoanalyst and yourself are variations of your story. Every time your stories are told, you alter them minutely to suit the audience and the occasion. The only information you have about anyone else you know, or have known, is carried in memory in the form of a story. Obviously the stories you tell about yourself, your past, your family and your parents are totally true! Everyone else is subject to elaboration, to bending the truth to improve content, interest and intelligence, but you yourself do not. But you do! Without an objective view of your life derived from the astrological information in your horoscope, you are left with a view of life as you have told it and distorted it.

The only memories you are likely to have before the age of five are vague scenes of spring days seen from rocking prams, reminiscences of parents and relatives, photographs posed for family scrapbooks, or nothing. If events are remembered at all, they tend to be superficial in respect to your real being. Yet, you possess clearly demarcated characteristics which were formed during the earliest times of life. Of the time during gestation even less is known, as you must rely upon the verity of aged parents for all information. How do you know that what you remember or are told by your parents is true? They also alter their stories through many years of re-telling them to verify their roles as responsible parents and to play down their own shortcomings. The more culpable they might have been, the more likely they are to have forgotten the associated stories. When there was chaos, it was your fault. In remembering and retelling stories about your early life, they redefine their role in your life and extensively redefine your reality by their stories.

To see and understand yourself clearly, you must recognize habitual ways of remembering, and go back to the beginning and reconstruct your life. Reconstruction is integral to psychoanalysis because therapy starts at the present and works backwards into the past. The past is gradually recovered through recall, dream analysis, free association, memory stimulation, psychodrama or hypnosis, and as the analysis goes deeper, the importance of the emerging contents increases. Gaps in early life are often the subject of years of probing and much of the confusion derives from what you 'know' about early events. Is what you know true?

For analysis to be helpful, it is essential to eliminate spurious stories and discover the real motivations of your past. Life★Time Astrology is unique because the order in psychoanalysis is reversed — instead of regressing backwards into life, you recreate your life from the beginning in the order in which it was lived.

The object of an astrological analysis using the Life★Time scale is to recreate the pattern and subpatterns of life. The resulting objective view of the principles and people can be compared to memories, and more importantly, the connections determined by the aspects show how the events in your life interweave. To understand life as a process in time which continues into the future rather than as an isolated present moment cut adrift of true meaning is a great step towards wholeness.

A central issue in astrology is that of contradiction. It is not possible to describe character with absolute statements as though it never changes because no behaviour is static — it is always being modified by age and circumstances. Everyone possesses contradictory feelings, thoughts, intuitions and sensations. To be realistic, astrology must present all sides of your being, at the times when they come into play. Life★Time Astrology does just this. As you reconstruct your life with your horoscope, squares and oppositions or combinations of incompatible planets describe contradictory views, events and parts of you which you always carry within. At one time of life, you feel one way about your mother, while at other times you feel the opposite. This is true of relationships, life's work, children, and virtually all areas of reality, including attitudes towards yourself. Instead of constituting a threat, the tensioning and opposing parts of your nature and life are essential to the whole. You must accept all contradictory parts, understand them and work with them, rather than trying to make them disappear.

In the psychology of Jung, all components of the self of which you are unconscious or unaware constitute the *shadow*. As well as including the dark parts of your nature, the shadow carries all the characteristics you do not want to see in yourself. The usual solution is to project those unwanted characteristics onto people around you, who then become, in your mind, responsible for them. Similarly, events in life which demonstrate your failings are also repressed or attributed to others. When any person or event in life becomes more important than the whole, the strong emotional charge carried is a sign that the shadow is in operation. The inner experience of coming to terms with the shadow (i.e., the negative sides of nature and life) is enacted by everyone in life. In Life★Time

Astrology both sides of your nature are presented in their proper sequence. If the position of Mercury indicates great intelligence, while its opposition to Saturn shows inhibited mental development, rather than trying to decide which you 'really are', you should realize that you are both of these at different times. At times when Mercury is operative you are very intelligent, but at the times when Saturn is dominant you are inhibited. You can benefit from knowing when each of these situations are in operation. If you can accept vices as well as virtues, you are on the path to the unification of the whole self.

Ground Rules

You must accept that life is a story told from your own point of view. Others may set the scene before your arrival, but you are the central character. As you grow into the central role, others may temporarily pre-empt centre stage, or even occupy it for long periods of time, forcing you to accept 'bit parts', but even then you retain your own unique vantage point.

Your story must be consistent. The characters and characteristics as defined by planets, signs, houses and aspects must be created realistically. Each character must have an identity and must develop with the story.

The signs of the zodiac represent a sequence of behaviour patterns. In life you live through all twelve signs and have an opportunity to act out many permutations of viewpoint and behaviour. The difference between you and others lies in the fact that *everyone passes through the various signs at different ages*, and that the planets amplify certain signs and not others. Aries describes 'self assertion'; it is crucial whether you pass through this sign at the age of two or forty-two.

The houses of the horoscope describe the exact phasing of the developmental periods in life. As you age from conception, you pass through the twelve houses in sequence. The change in time sense as you age means that each house occupies a time period almost equal to the time from the beginning of that house all the way back to conception. During each house, you recapitulate your entire previous existence.

The signs overlaid upon the houses describe the qualities which govern each developmental period. The three octaves are three *Acts* of life (Gestation, Childhood and Maturity) and each act contains four scenes (houses).

The first act is gestation, when your mother is the central

character and your father, grandparents, doctors and midwives play supporting roles. Each scene of gestation follows the transformation of your mother, and the signs through which she passes are the sets against which she plays her part. If she passes through the isolating 12th House occupied by the physically secure Taurus, you would feel physically secure when isolated and dependent upon others.

The second act is childhood, which begins when you first appear at the 'curtain-raising' moment of birth. During childhood you gradually adapt your personality amidst the characters who set the scene in the first act, possibly joined by other young characters as the family expands. You vie increasingly for better dialogue and more spotlights. If, to continue the example, you have demonstrative and extravert Leo qualities during the communicative 3rd House, you would become very powerful as soon as you learned to talk and express yourself.

The third act is maturity when, after establishing a physical and emotional milieu, you work out all your various possibilities in the world. Gradually the earliest members of the cast relinquish their roles and their lives, and by the end of the drama they have exited from the stage and you have taken over all their parts, retaining them as the memories of a lifetime. The culmination of the play is the departure of the central character, you. . .

The fourth transcendent octave does not occupy its own stage time, but lies within the higher meaning you are able to impart to the drama as a whole.

The planets are the cast of characters. In the beginning the primary characters are all the 'others' who produce, nurture and allow you to develop many parts. They are the prototypes of your range of roles; early directors and script-writers who determine the pattern and breadth of your first parts. Gradually you integrate their influence into the whole of your role. The Saturn grandfather who attended your birth and worried in the adjoining room becomes the hidden seriousness which only those who know you well can see. The times when planets register in the sequence of houses and signs show exactly when each character makes his or her most important contribution to the whole, as well as those other times when they influence you. As the Saturn opposition showed a fretting grandfather, when Saturn actually registers at twenty-four years old, you worry over the birth of your own child. The quality of life depends upon your ability to identify these significant characters and to integrate their roles willingly into your total character.

The aspects are relationships between house development phases, sign qualities and planetary characteristics, all bound together in your life. The aspects show the web of relationships which tension and equilibrate your being, and they define the pattern and rhythm of the events of your life through time. When there are many more squares and oppositions in the horoscope, life is tense, testing and difficult, but also potentially powerful. When trines and sextiles dominate, life is easy and comfortable but may lack drive, ambition and liveliness. An even blend between the two shows enough balance to provide a stable base to your activities, yet the requisite tension to generate movement and diversity.

Interpretation is information derived from the logical combination of signs, houses, planets and aspects, with which you are now familiar. The most effective way to order and convey this mass of information is as Your Story. The fluency of the story depends upon understanding the basic mechanisms of astrology, so when you cannot remember the meaning of a sign, house, planet or aspect, you should return to the tables in Chapter Six or the appropriate chapter, and refresh your memory. With practice and repetition you can interpret horoscopes at a glance.

The description of Your Story proceeds octave by octave from conception to the end of life, or a predetermined age in the future. You begin by interpreting the relationship between your parents leading up to conception, then conception itself. As you advance through the houses, the positions of the planets determine the rate of movement. Houses without planets are passed over, while houses with concentrations of planets show important developmental periods. In the next section it will be shown how all components of the horoscope are approached and blended together. The house by house process of life is broken down into octaves and the planetary characters and characteristics are also described for each octave.

Each house section is accompanied by example horoscopes which show how to interpret life events accurately. In each case only the relevant planets are shown to eliminate confusion, although in practice all planets combine to generate the astrological whole. When you have a computed horoscope of your own, enter it on the blank in the frontispiece of this book and you can interpret your entire horoscope as you read through this chapter.

Setting the Scene

To begin, you must set the scene for your entrance. It would not do to start anywhere else except the time before you are conceived. First you must identify which of your parents had the impulse to conceive you, why they had this impulse and what is the relationship between your parents at this time.

Conception includes the ovum's lunar month of ripening which begins with your mother's last menstruation; it is fertilized midway through its cycle; and ends when the fertilized ovum attaches itself to the uterine wall, when the cellular body begins developing. In a clockwise movement from conception (9th House cusp) in the horoscope, the circle is the pattern of events which happen to your ovum (Figure 22). The lifetime of the ovum is a microcosm of the process of cellular life. Since fer-

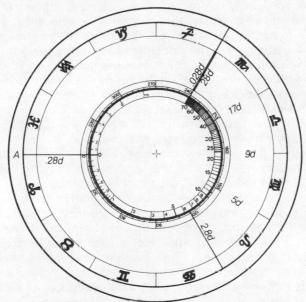

Figure 22: The Lifetime of the Ovum
The twenty-eight day lifetime of the ovum carries the same pattern as the twenty-eight thousand day cellular lifetime. This diagram shows the ovum lifetime which includes the time before fertilization. The divisions are twenty-eight days, two and eight-tenths days, twenty-eight hundredths of a day and twenty-eight thousandths of a day. The ovum is a microcosm of the life of the cellular body.

tilization occurs at an intermediate point in the ovular cycle, you can see in the horoscope how your parents participated in your conception.

The prelude to the story is the relationship between your parents just before conception. The Sun is your father, the Moon is your mother and the point of conception is the cusp of the 9th House. Gestation begins at this point and continues in a counter-clockwise direction. To discover which parent was responsible for the impulse to conceive you, you must move in a clockwise direction backwards from conception point until you find either the Sun or the Moon, as in Horoscope 1. If you find the Sun first, your father was responsible for conception, and if you find the Moon, then your mother was responsible for your conception.

The body is created during gestation, and conception is the creative act which begins gestation. The description of how your parents acted to conceive you also describes the way in which you yourself create; that is, the sexual act of your conception is a metaphor for the principle of creativity in your life. If the Sun-father is primary, the masculine influences within you precede the feminine, but if the Moon-mother is first, feminine influences are primary in your creative and sexual life. Both women and men have an equal possibility of feminine or masculine origin and creative influence at conception.

Now that you know which parent has the initial impulse, it is essential to discover the attitudes of your parents. This information is carried by the Sun and Moon in specific signs, houses and in their mutual aspect, if there is one.

You first determine whether the originating parent is conscious or unconscious of the desire to produce a child. This is indicated by the position of your Sun or Moon: either above the horizon, indicating consciousness, or below the horizon, indicating unconsciousness. Both luminaries above the horizon imply that both parents are conscious of the desire for a child, or even the possibility of a planned conception. If both are below the horizon, the probability is that your conception is instinctive, unplanned and accidental. One above and one below indicates that the conception combines the conscious being of one parent and the unconscious being of the other.

The eastern left hemisphere of the horoscope is the logical and rational physical realm of the self, and the western right hemisphere is the holistic and artistic realm of the not-self. The placement of each luminary/parent reflects whether they acted

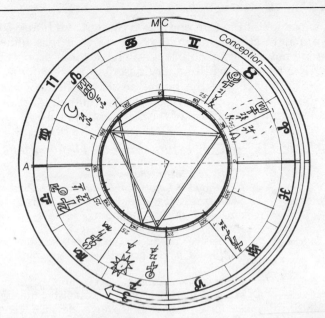

Horoscope 1: Before Conception

Moving back from Conception at the 9th cusp in a clockwise direction the Sun in Sagittarius in the 3rd House is the father responsible for the impulse to conceive. The mother is indicated by the Moon in Leo in the 11th House squared by the Sun, showing tension in their relationship. The Sun is in the unconscious lower half of the horoscope and the Moon is in the conscious upper half of the horoscope, and both are in the left half realm of selfish motivation.

selfishly or selflessly. The left-right divisions in the horoscope could even describe the relative importance of your brain hemispheres!

The sign elements of the Sun and Moon are further definitions. In Earth signs parental reasons for conceiving a child are material; in Air signs as a means of communication; in Fire signs as an energy exchange or common creation; and in Water signs someone to feel for or about. Parental motives influence not only your prenatal state, but reflect the motivating force behind your creative activity throughout life. The elements correspond to the four psychological types of Jung: Fire with Intuition; Earth with Sensation; Air with Thinking; and Water with Feeling. The types of creativity as determined by the prenatal influence are important in discovering your own creative role in life.

The location of the Sun and Moon by sign and house constitute a major determining influence upon your masculine and
feminine natures, as of course we all have some proportion of
both. The sign of each luminary describes the *quality* of their
creative influence and the house describes the *developmental
stage* to which your parents respond. The following key-words
demonstrate the meanings of the signs and houses:

Table 11: Pre-Conception Parental Designations

House Sign	Octave and Interpretation
	Childhood = Emotional Body Through Personality
1st Aries	Self-expressive, impulsive, self-centred, spontaneous (selfish, demanding, restless, tempered, tactless)
2nd Taurus	Possessive, productive, physical, sensual, secure (indulgent, stubborn, jealous, grasping, withholding)
3rd Gemini	Expressive, communicative, mobile, adaptable, active (superficial, nervous, dualistic, moody)
4th Cancer	Familial, protective, sensitive, devoted, receptive (touchy, greedy, timid, overemotional, inferior)
	Maturity = Mental Body Through Soul
5th Leo	Playful, impressive, self-conscious, leading, controlled (egocentric, fixed, conceited, dramatic)
6th Virgo	Orderly, diligent, discriminative, practical, perfected (critical, pedantic, suppressed, naive, hypochondriac)
7th Libra	Harmonious, balanced, consistent, related, just, united (indecisive, vain, unreliable, shallow, lazy)
8th Scorpio	Penetrating, wilful, separate, passionate, intense (fanatical, repressive, jealous, destructive)
	Gestation = Physical Body Through Body
9th Sagittarius	Realized, free, exploratory, mobile, sporty, religious (material, split, careless, extremist, hedonist)
10th Capricorn	Pragmatic, rational, logical, selfish, disciplined, tough (serious, inflexible, reserved, cautious, inhibited)
11th Aquarius	Idealistic, humanitarian, sociable, civilized, intuitive (detached, cranky, frigid, rebellious, unreliable, inane)
12th Pisces	Solitary, reserved, absorptive, patient, secretive, open (druggy, inhibited, negligent, doubting, sacrificial)

(Negative indications are in brackets.)

The house position shows the sequence of parental involvement, as you have seen. The house position by octave shows which 'body' is being influenced by which parent. For example, the Sun in Leo and the 12th House would be leading, impressive and controlled when interpreted by planet in its house, but in the 12th House the Leo characteristics of the father are of the physical body, are solitary and reserved. The father would be dominant, but dominated by external influences; he appears strong in a weak situation. This is how the masculine nature would function. The Moon is in the orderly, naive and discriminative sign Virgo, but also in the expressive, impulsive and spontaneous 1st House. Your mother would appear less dominant, but at this time would be very active and the feminine side would be stronger than it appears. As these parental influences bracket the Ascendant, the resultant character would show a personality carrying the above masculine and feminine sides. If the horoscope is a man's, he seeks a wife (or partner) who is really passive but behaves actively to compensate for his own dominant act which covers up inner security. If the horoscope is a woman's, she seeks men who appear to be active in the world but who are trapped by circumstances. It is important to stress that these descriptions mirror your choice of partners, but only show the character of your parents *from your viewpoint*.

At this stage, the parents are described before either of them is aware that a conception is about to take place. The Sun or Moon, or both, when situated exactly on the conception point, indicate instant realization that a conception has occurred. Luminaries directly opposite or in square to the conception point show resistance to conception and in constructive sextile or trine aspect show active support for the conception.

An interesting fact about families is that the differences between individual children of the same parents are partially determined by the way in which the parents act out their relationship before and during each child's conception and gestation. Parents also age from child to child. First children are inevitably seen in a different perspective from subsequent children. Each child of the same parents has its own unique circumstance and life, even in multiple births, when there can be different parental reactions to each child. If either parent is acting out of character during conception, the resultant child carries divergent characteristics from either parent.

The mutual aspect between Sun and Moon shows the relationship between your parents before conception. If connected by trine or sextile, they possess a stable relationship and communicate well. If in opposition, they may disagree about having children; in square they disagree but are capable of resolving the tension; if conjunct, they have similar views and motives; and if there is no aspect, their relationship is indirect at the time, or that their communication is slight. It is essential to realize that you are describing their relationship at a specific time. They may have intimate contact before conception which is continued after conception, but were out of touch with each other *when* you were conceived. Your being reflects the state of your parents' relationship throughout this time.

At this point you have established your parents' motives separately and now you must discover how conception occurred.

Conception Point

The conception point is the cusp of the 9th House and shows the nature of the sexual act, as well as the prevailing atmosphere within which it occurs. The nature of conception is a metaphor for the way in which your own creativity arises. If your father is passive and your mother active (as shown by sign and house locations of the Sun and Moon) in this moment, creative drive originates in your feminine nature. The sign on the conception point shows the element/type governing creativity. The previously established characteristics of your parents before this time are combined through the medium of conception.

In *Horoscope 1* the conception point is 25 Taurus. The first luminary in a clockwise direction from this point is the Sagittarius Sun in the 3rd House. The father is responsible for the impulse to conceive a child, and since the Sun is below the horizon, he is unconscious of this desire. Location in the eastern half shows that he has selfish motives. Sagittarius Sun is a foreign man who is mobile, active, sporting, philosophical and adventurous; while being in the 3rd House indicates that he is joyful, vivacious, restless, communicative and superficial. The two planets in aspect to the Sun are the adventurous and rapidly communicative Uranus and the separative and serious Saturn. This makes it clear that the father is primarily motivated by a desire to enjoy himself and have sport.

The Moon/mother follows the Sun in a clockwise direction from conception, which indicates that she takes the secondary role in the impulse to conceive. The Moon's location above the horizon shows that she is conscious of the desire for offspring and in the eastern half that she also has selfish motives. The Moon in Leo is a speculative, intuitive and instinctively creative, sociable and ambitious woman. The Moon in the 11th House indicates that she is idealistic, observative, is ready and willing to change and has abundant aspirations. The Venus aspect brings to the connection love and affection; Neptune brings inspiration and seduction; and the Midheaven qualifies these feelings with a strong egoistic sense of objective and deep sentiment.

The Sun and Moon are in square aspect of 98 degrees, which implies tension and struggle between different characters, as well as conflict between duty and pleasure. It also shows a certain incompatibility between inner and outer attitudes, manifesting as great attraction but also combat; and as the Sun and Moon are in fire signs, they both have similar intuitive, impulsive natures which spark each other off. This would describe the creative mechanism.

The conception point in Taurus shows that both partners are motivated by a desire for sensation in the sexual act. As the actual conception is described from the mother's viewpoint, the Taurus qualities of endurance, persistence, being difficult to please, great enjoyment and indulgence are all indicated. The intent of both partners is to have a good time amidst a light-hearted affair. The fact that Pluto is very close to the conception point shows a fated transformation and strong subconscious forces are in operation. The father, just before and probably during conception, is concerned with the political and financial stability of the nation as well as of himself. Pluto always involves generational influences translated into personal involvements, as you would expect as this horoscope belongs to a politician.

You should follow the procedure described in this section when reconstructing your own pre-conception time and conception itself. Locate the luminary responsible for conception, describe it by element, sign and house; then locate the other luminary as the parent acted upon, describe it by element, sign and house; then describe their mutual aspect relationship if there is one; finally analyze the element and sign on the 9th House/conception point with the previous information in mind. This prepares you to interpret the octave of gestation.

Octave of Gestation

Gestation is from conception until birth, during which time you develop from a fertilized ovum to the complex being which is modern man. Influences received from the outside world through your mother interact with internal genetic processes as you pass through the cellular realities similar to simple organisms, invertebrates, reptiles, later mammals and primates. Each stage leaves traces in your final character as woman or man, especially in the convoluted structure of your brain. Biological history is carried within us all, as well as the residue of all our ancestors. Gestation is the '*collective unconscious*' of Jung – a primal inheritance common to all humanity which forms the basic material of every individual psyche. These contents are undifferentiated instincts of survival carried by all humankind.

Throughout gestation your mother is subject to influences from you within her and from individuals and situations around her: her reality during gestation blends these influences. You must identify the origin of the influences which affect her and you during this time.

Planets in gestation and planets which aspect them show influences which affect your mother, and those who carry them when they are external. The four houses of gestation describe stages of intrauterine development described from your mother's viewpoint. Her activities change during the process of the four houses, but the planetary characters tend to remain constant. The number and strength of planets in gestation (or aspecting planets) shows whether you relate to your body directly or indirectly. Once gestation influences and the people who carry them have been identified, you can determine what effect they have upon her and you. As gestation is a collective substratum within the psyche, influences registering here have a very deep and powerful yet general impact upon your reality. In the following description of the planets and their personifications in gestation, remember that they are qualified by their sign, house and aspects and that they refer to both outer and inner influences.

The Sun during gestation is your father; an indication of your mother's consciousness of what is happening to her; her vitality; and paternal support for your mother. Since gestation is described from your mother's viewpoint, the Sun may also be her father or father-in-law, particularly since grandparents often have strong reactions to their children's children. The Sun can also be the doctor who diagnosed your mother's pregnancy; who advised her in gestation; or delivered you, according to where during gestation they register. Generally, aspects to the Sun show relatives on your father's side of the family or his associates. When the Sun is in the double signs Gemini, Cancer, Libra, Sagittarius, Aquarius or Pisces, it is likely that your mother split her masculine projections between your father and her father; her husband and another man; her husband and the doctor; or when there is a question of paternity. Those born during the Second World War in countries where conscription was common and allies or occupying forces abounded are especially subject to this question. Positive aspects to the sun show paternal support for the pregnancy, while tension aspects indicate paternal disagreement or resistance.

The Moon during gestation is your mother herself; her feelings and emotions about gestation; and the quality of her instincts. She must totally alter her life because of your existence and be in tune with the creative energies within her body. Since you interpret this time from your mother's viewpoint, the Moon is also her mother or maternal support. When women conceive and carry children, especially for the first time, they tend to identify with their own mothers in ways previously impossible. The Moon in gestation also implies particular genetic influence transmitted via your mother's family. When both Sun and Moon register during gestation, the luminary closest to or in closest aspect to the conception point shows the deepest genetic influence. The Moon is also other women to whom your mother responds or respects: midwives, woman doctors, friends, mother figures, those who teach birth exercises, counsellers or other women who are mothers themselves.

Mercury during gestation shows your mother's thoughts; her ability to communicate what she thinks; and her perceptions of gestation, culminating in her understanding of the creative process. Mercury is reflected outside by friends of hers who stimulate communication, cleverness and perception, as well as siblings and family. Their function is to stimulate thinking about the gestation process, its implications and creative matters generally. Mercury also shows intellectual attitudes to which your mother is attracted, such as talking and reading which stimulates intellectual roots in the expected child. Mercury also shows anyone who adopts your mother's viewpoint, represents her or performs a mediating function.

Venus during gestation shows beauty; harmony; love; adaptation; relationship; and sociability which manifests in your mother or someone to whom she relates. Venus often indicates a female friend, associate or sister of your mother's who acts as a prototype for your appearance, taste or relatedness. Venus is passive sexuality as mirrored in her relations to others in general, and your mother's reaction to her own appearance as it changes during the nine months.

Mars during gestation indicates a desire to change; activity; conflict; and will as personified by doctors, midwives, aggressive people in general or those with whom your mother has sexual contact. Whether medical advice and personnel are threatening is shown by the position of Mars by sign and aspect. If squared by Mercury, your mother thinks nervously about the coming delivery, and if opposed by Saturn she resists the restriction of gestation or is worried by the possibility of physical injury during birth. A prominent Mars at this time shows a forceful intervention in her own destiny and a wilful response to this challenge of the pregnancy and anticipated birth.

Jupiter during gestation is your mother's ability to accept gestation philosophically; through her own religious beliefs; her particular psychology; or through those who protect her during this time. Jupiter is carried by those who are generous, supportive, optimistic and expansive; typically aunts, uncles, grandparents, counsellers or the religious. Expansion in your mother's viewpoint and her physical size are indicated when Jupiter registers, and its influence is noble, good humoured and broadens her horizons.

Saturn during gestation is worrying; pessimism; restriction; and seriousness which is often imposed upon your mother by doctors, grandparents, financial restrictions, and in some cases the father himself. Saturn are personifications who are older, sicker, negative, depressive or limited in perspective; and who obviously or inadvertently transmit these qualities. Your mother may have to continue working, be isolated, be in the care of her parents, depressed or forced to economize, so the impact of Saturn is to narrow her perspective, not necessarily in a detrimental way. Constraint upon relations with others may derive from illegitimacy, unwished co-habitation, forced tightness or social limitation, or from within your mother herself. Saturn has its strongest effect when it is near the MC or ASC, reflecting an actual or expected limitation of mobility and life as a result of the creative act of gestation.

Uranus during gestation institutes reform ranging from expressive creativity to disruption transmitted by revolutionaries; reformers; creative people who do things their own way; and friends who are independent or inspired and encourage your mother to be so herself. As Uranus is the first of the generational planets, its influence is often carried by more than one person. The sexual-creative appetite shown by Uranus becomes very active during gestation and unless sated manifests as rebelliousness or secretive behaviour. A change in rhythm is Uranus' most frequent indication and eccentricities in thought, action and diet result, if not accidents which threaten your mother's well-being. As a generational influence Uranus also governs prevailing birth and gestation attitudes of the public, birth technology, and those who support new techniques or modern scientific attitudes.

Neptune during gestation increases sensitivity on physical and psychic levels to events in the outer world and to inner attitudes. Neptune often refers to your mother's increased fantasy, dream and psychic life due to your presence within her and the profound communication possible. She is especially sensitive to the effects of diet, drugs, tobacco and the psychic influence of others; particularly in the early stages of pregnancy. Increased openness and vulnerability transform usually dominant women into dependency or unreasonable expectations, if not outright idealism. Often Neptune has no real outer cause and is carried by your mother, or feels as though it is emanating from within her, although there is no way to know for sure. The lack of tangibility characterizes Neptune influences which are transmitted by those around your mother who dispense food or drugs, those sensitive to her needs and others who have similar ideals.

Pluto during gestation is dramatic transformation, and fanatical, magical or extreme influences which derive from the world at large. Great experts and those who propagandize through the media, books and classes, from Dr Spock to Michel Odent, could be such influences. Pluto exaggerates the force of any house within which it resides and shows collective disruptive force as more dominant than that of individuals. The effects of war, changes in residence, near accidents during gestation, traumas in relationship and radical alterations of lifestyle are all Plutonian.

The Node during gestation is the urge to unite with others, socialize or adapt to blood ties, groups of other pregnant women or friends. The Node is your parents' families and other relatives collectively, as well as any groups or alliances.

The 9th House   (Sagittarius)

Conception until seven weeks after conception
The moment of conception is the cusp of the 9th House and its domain is from conception until your mother realizes that she is pregnant about seven weeks later. These influences function after she has conceived but before she know this fact. She experiences the early stages of hormonal biological changes which eventually affect her. Although it is possible for your mother to 'feel' or even to 'know' that she is pregnant during conception itself, the earliest time doctors believe pregnancy can be detected (by them) is thirty-eight days after conception. Planets in the 9th House show influences intimating pregnancy which are received by your mother in the process of discovering that you exist and which set a pattern for your self-discovery in life. The 9th House feels foreign, strange, alien, sentimental, spiritual and active.

When the Moon, Venus or the psychic planet Neptune

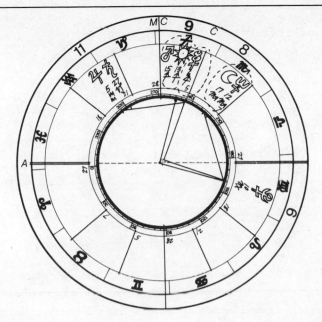

Horoscope 2: The 9th House

register in the 9th House, there is 'woman's intuition' that
something is happening; this may emanate from your mother,
her mother or friends. When any of these planets occur just
after conception, your mother experiences sudden and dramatic emotional and physical changes. When planets occur just
before the MC, your mother senses that she has conceived,
rather than exhibiting true psychic powers.

In *Horoscope 2*, the mother is already sensitized psychically, as
indicated by the Neptune/Moon conjunction in Scorpio just
before conception. Mercury registers just after the conception
point, in Sagittarius, and it indicates that the mother thinks that
something is happening almost immediately after conception.
The sextile to Saturn shows that she has been thinking deeply
about her situation anyway, and the sextile to Jupiter shows
that although she is quite solitary, erudite and interested in
literature, she uses common sense to discover her situation.
The square to Pluto indicates criticism coming from others
(Pluto is the masses, or public opinion) and the necessity to be
diplomatic. The fact that the Sun and Mars register one week
later (indicating the ability to make decisions) and are also
squared by Pluto (showing the effects of public opinion), you

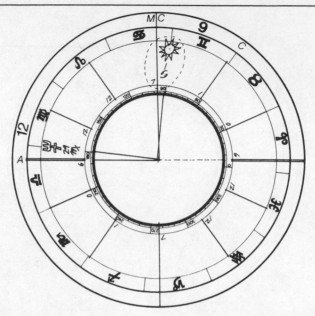

Horoscope 3: The 9th House

can assume that the Sun/father makes a decision to commit himself to the relationship. Both parents sense that conception has occurred before any verification from outside parties. The father acts quickly and arranges to marry the mother. This indicates great sensitivity (Moon/Neptune) followed by inspiration (Mercury) and then resolute action based upon a life philosophy (Sun/Mars in Sagittarius). The parents were unmarried at conception and subsequently married to please families and friends after the conception was realized.

In *Horoscope 3*, the Sun registers in Cancer just before the MC, squared by Neptune in the 12th House. Sun/Neptune is weakness or hereditary sickness and Neptune in the 12th House is sickness requiring hospital treatment; so the total picture five days before the mother realized she was pregnant is that the father was taken to hospital. This translates into a weakness of spirit just before the goal (MC) is reached. The father died of diabetes days before the pregnancy was realized.

The Midheaven (MC)

Seven weeks after conception or thirty-three weeks before birth
When the MC registers, the ego enters the physical body and your mother accepts the reality of pregnancy. By this time you possess all human systems, sex is determined and the face is fully human.

When you are born near the Equator or at certain times during the day, the MC is exactly 90 degrees, a square aspect, from the ASC; the archetypal relationship between the personality/ASC and the ego/MC is a tension between your view of yourself and your life objectives (Figure 23). At all other times, the MC leans

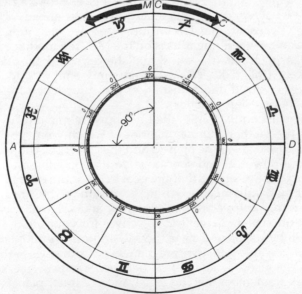

Figure 23: The Ascendant/Midheaven Relationship
The ASC and the MC are archetypally in a 90 degree square to each other: the natural tension between personality and objectives. When the MC leans to the left of vertical, objectives are self-oriented, and when the MC leans to the right, objectives are selfless.

towards the ASC/eastern side at the left or the DSC/western side at the right. The MC leaning towards the ASC shows self-oriented ego-consciousness, while the MC leaning towards the DSC shows ego-consciousness oriented towards the not-self or the outside world.

The element of the sign on the MC shows the way in which your mother discovered she was pregnant. If in a fire sign it was intuited; in an earth sign sensed; in an air sign thought; or in a water sign felt. On a higher level, this is the way in which you discover your own Ego direction in life. For example, if your mother realized her pregnancy because *she felt* she was pregnant, you can expect to evaluate your position in the world by the way you *feel*.

The sign of the zodiac on the MC further qualifies your mother's realization of her new purpose. The cardinal signs Aries, Cancer, Libra and Capricorn show that she initiates action in response; the fixed signs Taurus, Leo, Scorpio and Aquarius show firm and resolute acceptance; and the mutable signs Gemini, Virgo, Sagittarius and Pisces show a desire to change whatever conditions or attitudes exist already. Use the table on pages 132 and 133 for more detailed sign judgement. For example, when Aquarius is on the MC, the mother thought she was pregnant (the air sign); she accepted the idea immediately (the fixity of Aquarius); and she was idealistic, sociable, civilized and transmitted the knowledge to friends (the Aquarius sign qualities).

Planets in conjunction to the MC show people directly influencing the mother and the qualities of which your ego is composed. The stronger the planets and the closer the conjunction, the more powerful and specific is your ego. The Sun directly conjunct the MC means that the goal in life is the establishment of your own individuality, while Uranus on the MC means that your mother responds in an eccentric and original way, producing original and eccentric objectives for your life.

A number of planets near the MC indicates multiple objectives and egos. When there are planets on both sides of the MC, ego-consciousness alternates between selfish to selfless motives. Remember that the registration of inner planets (Sun, Moon, Mercury, Venus and Mars) show influences and events coming from people around your mother or from her, while outer planets (Jupiter, Saturn, Uranus, Neptune and Pluto) show activities attributable to more than one person or large scale events. Those born during the Second World War in

Europe with Uranus or Pluto on the MC reflect the influence of deeply violent transformative events on their mothers at the time. See the analysis of John Lennon's horoscope in Chapter Eight for an example.

Aspects to the MC show people your mother told and those who have an indirect effect upon her as personifications of secondary manifestations of your ego. Aspects from planets below the horizon show unconscious or inner influences, while from planets above the horizon they show conscious or outer influences. If the MC happens to be in one of the double signs, indicating multiple influence already, these objectives become quite numerous. With no planets conjunct the MC, but many planets in aspect to the MC, you would have many secondary objectives in life but a difficulty finding your major focus.

In *Horoscope 4* the Aquarius MC shows a gregarious and popular mother whose husband resisted her pregnancy, as indicated by the opposition by the Sun in Leo. The resultant ego would be attracted to group situations at the expense of, and resisted by, selfish motives in the unconscious 4th House of the home and family. As this horoscope belongs to one of the first astronauts, this judgement is quite appropriate.

In some cases there are no planets conjunct the MC nor any

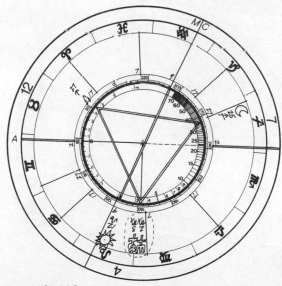

Horoscope 4: The MC

aspects to the MC. The sign governing the MC then becomes the objective, but there is little other support from the remaining planets. This would imply single-mindedness, which reflects the mother being left to her own by others upon realizing her pregnancy. When she wishes to keep her pregnancy a secret, there are tell-tale signs. The isolated signs Scorpio and Pisces show a desire to reserve judgement, and planets conjunct the MC but no planets in aspect indicate recognition of the pregnancy, but a lack of interest in spreading the knowledge.

In *Horoscope 5* the MC is in Scorpio, indicating secretive behaviour on the part of the mother, with Jupiter preceding the MC as a positive but hidden relationship, and Venus following the MC as a passionate attachment. The combination is unaspected. Venus/Jupiter is joyous love and marriage, but the Scorpio negates the idea, so there is a conception occurring outside marriage. Scorpio shows separation from whatever planetary qualities are in operation. The ego indicates a person who is creative, penetrating and intense, who finds others who support this world view, but who finds recognition difficult.

When Mars, Saturn, Uranus, Neptune or Pluto conjunct or aspect the MC traumatic events during gestation may be expected, especially when these planets or aspect points register

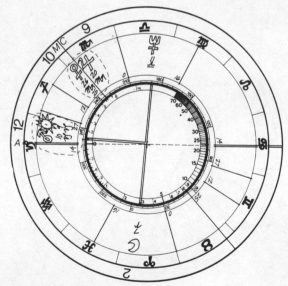

Horoscope 5: The MC

after the MC. This is because planets after the MC show repercussions of the mother's realization of pregnancy. Mars usually indicates a doctor; easy aspects imply that the doctor reassures the mother, while difficult aspects suggest that the doctor is threatening, unhelpful or even damages her. Chemical tests or talk of induction register as Neptune influences, as do dangerous drugs such as thalidomide and others which are supposed to relieve symptoms of morning sickness. Saturn shows restriction or intense concentration resulting from the realization, often through, or as a result of, someone older or more serious. Pluto indicates an extreme transformation accompanied by drama, disruption or even violence. Uranus shows alterations in the mother's rhythm, eccentric circumstances or her desire to continue to be independent in spite of obvious dependency.

When more than one of these planets combine in a difficult square or opposition aspect to the MC and also connect to the surgical Mars, there is a possibility that abortion is contemplated or attempted. It is obvious that when such attempts are made they are unsuccessful, because the horoscope involved presupposes a survivor, but it is necessary to judge the severity of the attempt by the specific planets that make direct aspect connections and the closeness of the aspects. Neptune aspects imply fantasy and uncertainty; Mercury aspects imply a questioning of the situation; the Node is a sampling of friends as a primary response. All these metaphors are carried directly in the ego.

To interpret inner and outer MC events, be sure to examine the planets, aspects (using their sensitive points) and the MC itself in order, moving in a clockwise direction from conception point towards the birth moment Ascendant. The accompanying Horoscope 6 shows exactly how to determine the correct order. When the correct order is followed, the mother and everyone significant in the discovery of your existence and, by extension, your ego-consciousness, can be reconstructed. The events and individuals involved foreshadow the pattern of development of life's objectives.

In *Horoscope 6*, the sequence of planets and aspects around the MC is:

1. Sensitive square from Jupiter (13 Capricorn) to: 13 Lib
2. *MC at:*   *15 Lib*
3. Sensitive trine from Saturn (16 Gemini) to: 16 Lib
4. Sensitive square from Node (18 Capricorn) to: 18 Lib
5. *Uranus at:*   *22 Lib*

All planets and the MC are in the air sign Libra, which means that partnership is the central issue at this time. The Jupiter square is recognition by mother of religious implications in her relationship with the father which created tension between them (Libra is either/or situations). The mother's recognition of pregnancy is a happy and successful fulfilment of her partnership, but soon she is affected by the seriousness of Saturn trine. Saturn/MC shows inhibitions, an older person (doctor or parent) to be considered, but also that the restrictions can be discussed (Saturn in Gemini). The Saturn/Node aspect implies

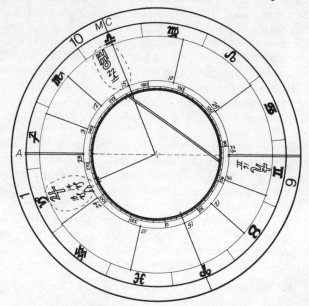

Horoscope 6: A Sequence of Planets Around the MC
Planets which aspect the MC fit into a sequence of events round the discovery of a pregnancy — square Jupiter; MC; trine Saturn; square Node; and Uranus. The order of planets and sensitive aspect points define the processes in life.

difficulty with the parents' families. The final Uranus connection shows an unusual and tense partnership being formed as a reflection of the MC constellation. The Sun and Ascendant in sextile to Uranus but just out of orb promise that there will be creative outlets from the partnership in the end.

After finding the influences acting upon your mother at the MC, you must take her specific response and carry it into the three houses comprising the remainder of gestation: the 10th, 11th and 12th Houses.

The 10th House   (Capricorn)

Thirty-three weeks until twenty-eight weeks before birth
The 10th House reflects the repercussions after your mother realizes that she is pregnant, as the first function is to communicate her situation and attitudes to the world. Her ability to make your existence known determines your life ambitions. The more effectively she and your father organize this communication, the greater chance you have of finding your own position in the world.

This house governs perfected matter and practical concerns: during this time the parents must orchestrate all necessary practical tasks for confronting gestation. Selecting a doctor or midwife, a location for the coming birth, an attitude and technique for childbirth itself, finding a space at home for the baby, planning for the welfare of the mother and making the necessary financial considerations must all be done by the parents.

Planets in the 10th House show who influences your mother during this crucial period. You must remember that from this time on your mother is likely to see doctors, nurses, midwives or childbirth experts and her other associations in a different light than usual. She must assert herself and require that decisions made during this time are consistent to her thoughts and feelings.

Symbolically, this time sees the mother applying the objectives determined at the MC into the 'real world'. As the 10th

House is traditionally considered paternal or masculine, she may struggle for her own way or for control over the circumstances of the birth from her husband or her doctor. A mother's ability to manifest her own objectives physically is an indication of an eventual authority and ability to achieve one's aims in life.

Many planets in the 10th House show multiple influences upon your mother and subsequently various goals in life. In *Horoscope 7* is the registration of the father (Sun) and a woman friend (Venus), both friends (Aquarius) of the mother. Sun conjunct Venus is devotion and love, but Aquarius is dualistic, so the relation between husband and friend is competitive with mother, making her sensitive and insecure from the Neptune opposition. The supporting trines from Jupiter in Libra, as society at large, and the Gemini Ascendant, as a confidant in her environment, imply that there is support coming from outside, but the overall constellation shows detachment and abstraction from the reality of a difficult affair. When Mercury follows at thirty-five weeks before birth in square to Mars, the mother criticizes the father about his misconduct and withdraws sexually from their relationship (square Mars in Scorpio). This configuration shows a person with potential power in the world of ideas or religion, alienated from his feminine, recep-

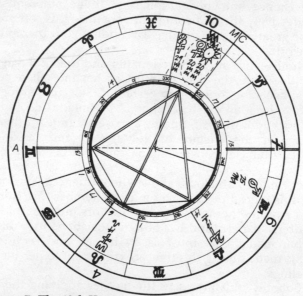

Horoscope 7: The 10th House

tive side due to ill-considered or superficial associations.

An absence of planets in the 10th House shows a natural and uneventful expression of the recognition by the mother of her pregnancy and would indicate general goals without specific personal patterns or definite ideas.

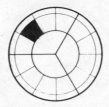

The 11th House   *(Aquarius)*

Twenty-eight weeks until seventeen weeks before birth
In the period represented by the 11th House, the pregnancy is accepted and material matters are resolved, yet it occurs before the mother has any outward appearances of pregnancy. The mother decreases her usual labours and her primary function is to prepare for birth, including communicating with her mother and friends who have already had children. She occupies herself with plans and ideals common to expectant mothers and becomes more careful of her diet, clothing, activities, social life, sleeping and sexual habits – in short, she reconsiders and re-values everything about herself.

While it is perfectly natural and acceptable to have sexual intercourse well into gestation, the 11th House is often characterized by a decrease in sexual appetite: your mother's procreative drive is temporarily satisfied. It is a unique situation; her activities and thoughts centre around her unborn baby, and much of her time is spent musing, planning and speculating about what the child will look like, act like and live like. The mother continues to function in the world but her concentration is both inside herself and outside in the future. Planets in the 11th House show your mother's friends, family and acquaintanceships who affect her ideals. Since you remain quite mysterious to her, she must idealize her experience of you. You begin moving inside her but remain more an idea than a reality.

In *Horoscope 8*, the registration of Mercury in Cancer shows maternal thoughts coupled with unsocial behaviour from the Node opposition. The following unaspected Mars in Leo is a deliberate sexual relationship with a man other than the father. This disruption is followed by the constellation Sun, Pluto and

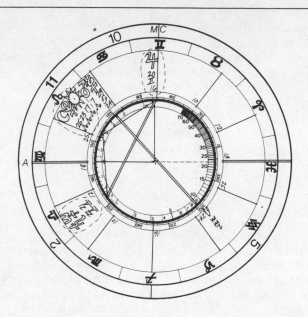

Horoscope 8: The 11th House

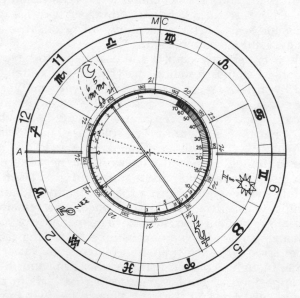

Horoscope 9: The 11th House

Moon in Leo in the 11th House, showing a forceful separation and the consummation with another 'father' who the mother manipulates via the sextile Saturn. She obtains a successful conclusion as indicated by the sextile to Jupiter and the MC. Looking back, one can see the duality of the mother as an integral part of the MC in Gemini. The mother is an actress willing to do anything to manifest her ideals. A similar pattern is lived by the resulting child in adulthood.

Horoscope 9 shows the Moon conjunct Node in Scorpio as the mother's mother recognizing that although there is a strong soul union (Moon/Node), that there is also estrangement due to undermining associative forces (Node in Scorpio). Since Moon square Mars is a desire to unite and also endure surgery, and the opposition to Saturn indicates depression and isolation, the mother attempts an abortion (Mars/Saturn is the death axis according to Ebertin), probably only saved by the contact to Venus as a desire to have children. This constellation conveys a threatening undercurrent from friends and women in general in the child throughout later life, even though the mother eventually married the true father at the registration of the Sun in Sagittarius at 12 weeks before birth. By the time the child was born, the parents considered her a 'love child' and symbol of their lifelong happiness, yet the child when adult carries the mixed feelings of her threatening gestation buried within.

An 11th House devoid of planets indicates that the mother formulated her ideals and attitudes herself, without any prominent exterior influences. This would imply little interest in group and other collective contacts in life.

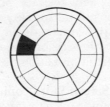

The 12th House   *(Pisces)*

Seventeen weeks before birth until birth
At the beginning of the 12th House the mother starts gaining weight, which increases her sensitivity to psychic reality as well as to her own emotional state. Her inner focus gradually becomes dominant over exterior circumstances while her dependency upon others increases towards the birth time. The

image of Pisces, the sign equivalent to this time, is that of two fishes swimming in opposite directions but tethered together at the tail, symbolizing that the inner world of the mother and her outer world are linked emotionally. The mother's primary function during this stage is to reconcile these two worlds. Increased movement within her balances her decreased outward activity and reflects the psychic rapport between mother and unborn child. As birth nears, the mother's commitment to the inner, relinquishing her own way in favour of her child, her submission to doctors, hospital examinations and her limited mobility all contribute to the self-sacrificial element which permeates this house. It is only in recent years that expectant women are becoming aware of how they can regain active control over this critical time in their and their children's lives.

All those with whom your sensitized mother communicates carry profound influences upon your psyche, especially the hidden elements. These include her family, friends, medical advisors, midwife and even hospital staff, so it is essential to identify from whom these influences derive and what they imply to you, so that you can decipher the hidden components of your psyche. In traditional astrology the ten degrees immediately above the Ascendant represent hidden parts of your personality. In the time scale these ten degrees cover the seven weeks before birth and planets registering within this zone are integral to your personality. These influences precede your birth and their ramifications precede every assertion of your personality throughout life. This is often responsible for the unconscious tension we all feel just before important meetings, tests, introductions to new people, performances or events which place focus upon our personality. The importance of the awareness of expectant women during this time cannot be underestimated. Her various responses may determine the difference between a difficult or a sublime personality in her offspring.

In *Horoscope 10* the Saturn/Pluto conjunction indicates hard labour and isolation coming from the father by the square to the Sun, producing great inhibition and physical discomfort by simply being around others. This is further sensitized by the sextile from Neptune. The resultant configuration produces a person who fears others, but also fears solitude, the only outlet being through the imaginative fantasy of Neptune. The more recognition, the greater the feelings of tension. This is an extreme case of pressure being placed upon the mother by the

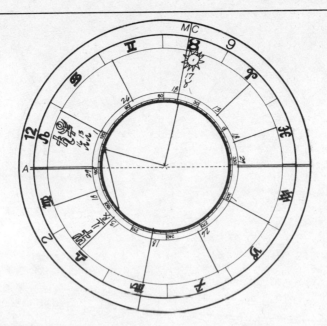

Horoscope 10: The 12th House

withdrawal of attention by the father.

As birth approaches, the mother becomes aware of the many possible birth circumstances. The best monitor of the pre-birth situation is the mother's conscious and unconscious perceptions. She should be naturally directed to eat the correct foods, to exercise at the proper times and in the right way, and to begin to orient herself to the daily cycles which eventually determine the time of birth.

When birth is approached naturally, there are either the supportive Sun, Moon, Mercury, Venus or Jupiter just before (above) the Ascendant or an absence of planets. Mars or Saturn registering just before birth usually show a doctor or midwife responsible for the delivery, the influence upon the delivery and the effect upon your personality. The implication is that force (Mars) or constriction (Saturn) are elements in delivery technique. The use of force would make the mother resist; and the use of constriction, as in the stirrups in common use in hospitals, would make her tighten. These influences are transmitted directly to your personality.

In *Horoscope 11*, the conjunction of Sun in the last degree of the critical Virgo is conjunct Saturn in the first degree of Libra in

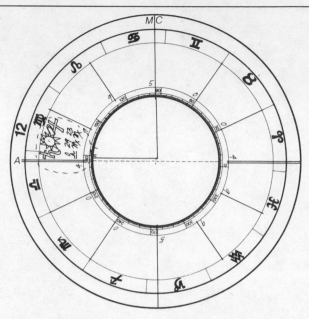

Horoscope 11: The 12th House

the horoscope of a child adopted at birth, where the Saturn/Sun conjunction is the recognition by the mother and father that they would be forever separated from their child, something they knew since the acceptance of pregnancy (square MC). The doctor temporarily became the father just before and during birth itself.

The registration of Uranus and Pluto, or aspects from them, signal drastic changes in attitude or physical circumstances just before birth. Since both planets are usually generational, the changes are from all the people present at birth; for example, hospital staff, friends, family or midwife taken as a whole.

Neptune in the 12th House indicates the degree of sensitivity of your mother right before birth. The traditional interpretation of Neptune/ASC is impressionability, illusions, sensory deception or drugs and it accompanies induced births or those where anaesthetics are administered. The use of drugs at birth are substitutes for your mother's natural sensitivities and are attempts to dull or eliminate her reactions to the birth process. Neptune indicates detachment and extreme sensitivity in the personality resulting from such a birth.

The Node in the 12th House describes your mother's associations leading up to your birth as a substratum of your eventual personality. The feeling of belonging to or being separate from a group of sympathetic friends, associates or hospital staff mirrors your personal attitude towards such groups and their ideas.

The Ascendant

Birth

The Ascendant registers at the moment you take your first breath and is the transition point between gestation and childhood. The description of birth as a *'process'* parallels the development of your personality as a process. Personality is not a 'thing' but a pattern of actions and acts which repeat themselves in a seemingly infinite number of variants during life.

Birth circumstances include everything that happens before, during and afterwards and the personality, which registers at birth, is a combination of those many influences patterned in time. Personality is a mechanism by which you act out instinctive and unconscious contents, and is strongly influenced by the atmosphere around your mother at birth. The zodiac sign on your Ascendant symbolizes this synchronistic relationship. Table 12 is a list of Ascendant signs and their associated environments and characters. The planets which rule each sign qualify the general qualities of the signs themselves.

The range of interpretations describe personalities derived from the nature of the birth environment. The choices as to which words are most apt are made in relation to the planets around the Ascendant, the circumstances described in gestation as leading up to the birth, and the planets which are in aspect to the Ascendant.

Planets conjunct your Ascendant show people and influences directly affecting your birth and personality. When a conjunction is *before* (above) the exact ASC, external influences affect the initiative part of your personality, and when *after* your ASC the influence is strongest after birth and is an aftereffect of your personality. The closeness to the Ascendant shows the strength

Table 12: Ascendant Birth Interpretation

Aries = Restless; energetic; self-assertive; rash; aggressive; selfish; impatient; and from Mars ruling, surgery and surgeons; aggressive doctors or midwives; impatient people; forceps injuries; hospitals.

Taurus = Stability; quiet; secure; domestic; sensual; beautiful; attractive; homely; and from Venus ruling, women; midwives; attractive people; artists; loving, attentive people; children.

Gemini = Changeable; ambiguous; adaptable; superficial; mobile; talkative; observative; dualistic; nervous; and from Mercury ruling, children; crowds; thinkers; gossips; hurriers; talkers; conversationalists.

Cancer = Moodiness; homeliness; simplicity; maternity; passivity; warmth; conservatism; reliance on others; sensitivity; and from the Moon ruling, feeling people; the instinctive; midwives; women; mothers; nurses; breast feeders; feminists.

Leo = Authoritative; confident; open-minded; joyous; self-confident; open; active; proud; prominent; game-playing; and from Sun ruling, warm; domineering; purposeful; boldness; extrovert.

Virgo = Naive; virginal; stable; critical; nervous; hospitals; reserve; clean; hygienic; sterile; cautious; attentive; pedantic; and from Mercury ruling, intellectual; medical students; doctors; nurses; observers; critics; digestive problems; collaborations; teams.

Libra = Balanced; harmonious; homely; lively; authoritarian; easy; vain; attentive; chatty; moody; obliging; social; and from Venus ruling, youths; women; nurses; midwives; woman doctors; beauties; friends.

Scorpio = Disharmonious; humid; hotheaded; cautious; industrious; passionate; separative; violent; surgical; impulsive; dangerous; brutal; forceful; and from Mars, surviving; surgeons and surgery; Caesareans; technicians; forceps; brutality; danger; force; and from Pluto ruling, tragic events; endurance; large hospitals; forceful deliveries; violent public events; circumcision.

Sagittarius = Enthusiastic; athletic; joyous; good humoured; expansive; foreign; natural; scattered; social; messy; lively; adventurous; talkative; religious; and from Jupiter ruling, expansive; doctors; grandparents and relatives; religious hospitals; nuns; nurses; foreign hospitals and countries; tolerance.

Capricorn = Concentration; seriousness; practicality; long labour; inhibition; hard work; goals; reserve; pragmatism; anxiety; physicality; and from Saturn ruling, will; restraint; doctors and surgeons; older people; strictness; paternalism; masculinity; slowness; methodicality repression; unemotional; materialistic; expensive.

Aquarius = Communal; abstract; friendly; detached; sociable;
            progressive; sympathetic; inventive; eccentric; idealistic;
            Utopian; planned; and from Saturn ruling, realised plans;
            seriousness; older doctors or grandparents; and from Uranus
            ruling, inventive, technological, instrumentative; original;
            unorthodox; mechanical; rebellious; scientific; changeable;
            rhythmic.

Pisces   = Self-sacrificial; lacking confidence; externally influenced;
            anaesthetic; depressed; vague; lazy; comfortable; peculiar;
            passive; asleep; weak; drugged; induced; gentle; simple; and
            from Jupiter ruling, institutional; isolated; contented;
            visionary; wasteful; religious; and from Neptune ruling,
            psychic; dreamy, drugged; idealistic; Utopian reserved;
            sensitive; mystical; escapist; overemotional; vague.

Table 13: ASC/Planet Interpretation

Aspect	*Personifications*
Sun/ASC	Father, men, doctor, grandfather
Moon/ASC	Mother, grandmother, midwife, nurse, women
Mercury/ASC	Friends, talkers, nurses, young children, gossips
Venus/ASC	Women, sisters, nurses, girls, attractive people, lovers, midwife
Mars/ASC	Surgeon, doctor, midwife, men, fighters, aggressors, male children
Jupiter/ASC	Doctor, midwife, uncle, aunt, grandparents, team, positivists, priests
Saturn/ASC	Doctor, hospital staff, grandparents, serious people, inhibitors, lonely people
Uranus/ASC	Excitable people, innovators, originals, technicians, orderlies
Neptune/ASC	Anaesthetists, nurses, psychics, sensitives, druggists, mediums
Pluto/ASC	Doctors, staff, powerful people, authorities, fascinating people, those in control
Node/ASC	Family, friends, nurses, colleagues, fellows, social workers

Influences

Relationships to men, recognition, popularity, personal attitudes to others, self-confidence, physical relations, the public, masculinity

Personal feelings about others, feminine influence, maternity, protection, breast feeding, sensitivity, receptivity, adaptability (alkaloids, induction, anaesthetics, drugs, watery birth)

Thoughts at birth, definition, talking, changing views, ideas, criticism, (sense stimuli, nerves)

Harmonious personality, loving atmosphere, art, adornment, beautiful surroundings, easy birth, pleasure, even tempered (good complexion, general appearance, proportions)

Fighting, teamwork, forceful success, physical strength, restlessness, decision (surgery, force, circumcision, violence, episiotomy, forceps, facial scar, accidents, Caesareans, birth apparatus)

Easy birth, pleasant experiences, agreeable manner, compromise, generosity, correct acts, successful operations (large baby, jaundice, difficult breast feeding)

Isolation, restriction, inhibition, seriousness, experience, hindrance, depression, seclusion, (separation, isolation, long labour, birth apparatus, skin trouble, blockages, tension, amputation, sensory disfunction, facial mark, premature birth, stillbirth, lack of attention)

Excitement, originality, scientific birth, movement, rhythmic, incidents, disquiet, sudden events, unexpected circumstances (quick birth, short labour induction, machines, monitors, headaches, forceps, accidents, sensitive skin, responsive nervous system, circumcision)

Impressionable, sensitive, insecure, peculiar contacts, disillusionment, sympathetic, exploitation, (inducement, anaesthetics, alcohol, drugs, peculiar birth, dreaming, water birth, sensory deception, malformations, incubators)

Fascinating personality, ambition, psychic forces, unusual influences, readjustment, dramatic changes, radical alterations (force, Caesarean, forceps, brutal birth, forced birth, physical transformation, surgery, accidents, circumcision)

Collective contacts, personal relations, family influences, social contact, teamwork, relating, (respiration, metabolism, hospital birth, anti-social behaviour)

of a planetary connection. The closer the orb, the more direct and integral the influence on your personality.

To understand personality through an analysis of birth requires a description of a sequence of influences before, during and after the birth. The sequence shows how your personality reveals itself in action and development over long periods of life and in short-term situations. Great attention to the mother in the pre-birth stage of labour followed by the child's removal immediately afterwards signifies a focus upon gaining the energy to assert the personality, followed by a rapid decrease in attention following its assertion. The sequence of events at birth is crucial to the description of the process of your personality. Planets conjunct or in aspect to your Ascendant show people present at birth, the influence they convey and their effect upon your personality. When the Ascendant or any planet is in one of the double signs (Gemini, Cancer, Libra, Sagittarius, Aquarius or Pisces) the personifications and effects are doubled and show more than one person and influence. Table 13 shows the planets and their effects as influences at birth. Each person/planet shows as an aspect or sub-personality of your whole personality. The planets in this situation are like traditional planet/Ascendant aspects.

When the planets are combined, they mutually affect each other. When Mars and Saturn are both involved, it is a difficult labour (Saturn) requiring the assistance or intervention of a doctor (Mars). If the difficulty of Saturn were complemented by a positive Jupiter aspect, it would mean that the labour was long and hard, but that there were no complications. If Mars and Saturn are in sextile or trine to the Ascendant, the surgeon performs a supportive role. A trine from Saturn can be an older person who lends support; a square from the Moon is a woman or grandmother exerting a tensioning influence.

Your birth is described by combining who was there (as determined by the planets) with the atmosphere at the birth (from the Ascendant sign). In *Horoscope 12*, the Libra Ascendant is bracketed by Mars and then Neptune. The doctor (Mars) administered an injection and gas at birth, but the Sun square indicates detachment from the father and/or doctor. Afterwards the anaesthetic was deemed unnecessary (reflected in Mars/Neptune = square Sun). The individual suffered for many years from insomnia as a result of the suffocation at his birth, and received unnecessary drug treatment again!

Horoscope 13 is a straightforward forceps birth, indicated by

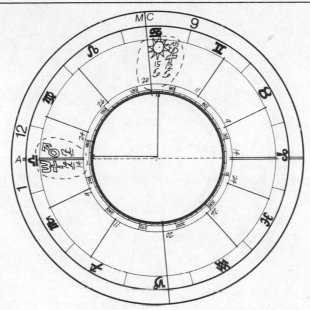

Horoscope 12: The Ascendant

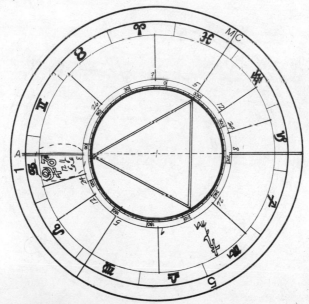

Horoscope 13: The Ascendant

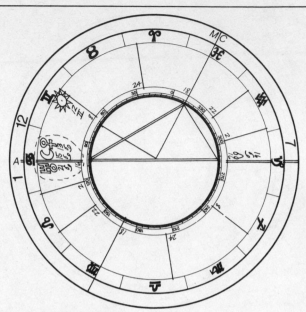

Horoscope 14: The Ascendant

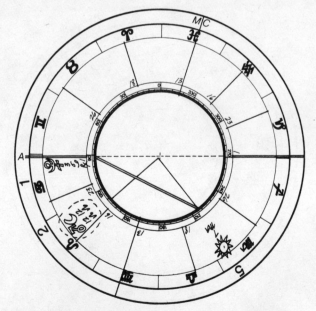

Horoscope 15: The Ascendant

the Mars/Pluto conjunction with the Ascendant. The aftereffect is exaggerated by the restriction of the birth canal (trine Saturn), but is caused because the doctor induces the birth (trine to the Pisces MC, ruled by Neptunian drugs). The resultant personality is homely and maternal, but behind the stable Cancerian appearance is stress, force and aggression concentrated upon emotional matters.

Horoscope 14 is the horoscope of the firstborn of twins, indicated by the Pisces MC and justified by the Moon, Ascendant and Uranus all in the double sign Cancer and opposed to the associative Node in Capricorn. The twins are female and this, the elder twin, has the opposition Node, indicating fellowship and family contact opposed in the 1st House of her personality, instead of in the 12th House as does her younger sister. The 1st House is an intense urge to associate and the 12th House is an intense urge to be alone. In reality, these are the primary characteristics defining the differences between the twins.

Horoscope 15 shows a birth where the father is very important (trine Sun), but absent (Sun in Scorpio), so a local doctor (Pluto) takes over and delivers the child successfully. The personality carries much strength derived from the doctor and as a result shows a woman who has a strong public identity of her own, but also a powerful and inaccessible husband.

During gestation your mother is the primary perceptive intermediary and many birth aspects are qualified by the way she perceived the situation and reacted. Now, you have drawn your first breath and all circumstances from now register directly upon you.

Octave of Childhood

At birth you enter the Octave of Childhood, which extends to the age of about seven years old, during which time you create and adapt the personality which registered at birth. Because influences during childhood are received through the medium of the family, it is necessary to understand your childhood home and relationship to your family in order to understand the nature of your personality. These houses are below the horizon in the horoscope, so their influences are subjective, unconscious and accountable to influences beyond your immediate control.

Your personality develops against the already existing structure of your parents' relationship to each other and to others within your family. Your own development during childhood is rapid compared to the more static framework of your family. You must continually contrast your instinctive grasp of relationships to the attitudes your parents project onto you as rules of behaviour. This interchange creates a value system by which you live your life.

Planets in childhood and their aspects from the other two octaves represent people around you and those upon whom you base your personality. They are models of behaviour to be accepted, rejected, excluded or integrated. Since most childhood influences are carried by those within and accessible to your family circle, your attitudes are highly conditioned by the prevailing familial reality. You may or may not be free to adopt your own opinions and ways of behaviour; this depends upon what is acceptable to your family. One of your primary tasks during this time is to understand what the family is and what its attitudes are.

Freud believed that a child recapitulates the development of all mankind during childhood. The four houses of childhood describe a collective development (we all must enact it), which is also individually unique. The early developments of mankind are mythological, and childhood events carry a mythological and fantastic atmosphere – even your parents' stories play their part in defining your personality.

The Sun during childhood is the vital relationship to your father. His influence during gestation is indirect, but during childhood you gradually realize his relative importance within the family. This is often because most fathers have little direct contact until their children begin to speak or even later. When the Sun registers at this time your father exerts a strong influence upon your personality. Due to natural contact with grandfathers and uncles during childhood, there is a likelihood that they also participate in the solar qualities. Aspects from the Sun to planets in childhood show indirect paternal qualities. As in Horoscope 15, the father is missing at birth, but later in childhood, at one year old, the Moon and Mars are square to the Sun indicating a permanent separation.

The Moon during childhood is your early feelings about your mother and feminine continuity from gestation, where it was of primary significance. As in gestation maternal qualities are the medium within which you are physically created, in childhood mother is more a protector and guide to personality development. Immediately after birth, you cannot differentiate yourself from your mother because of necessary and natural survival instincts; you are bonded to her. Only gradually do you begin to separate from her and her influence. By the end of childhood you have distinguished yourself from her and from other women, but early on she can be interchangeable with nannies, grandmothers, aunts, surrogate mothers and even older sisters.

Mercury during childhood is communication, as even in the womb you receive and evaluate sounds and words. The primary manifestation of Mercury is other children and the effect they have on you, unless Mercury is in aspect to either the Sun or Moon, when the main communication is with one of your parents. Mercury indicates children at home, while aspects from Mercury to planets in childhood are children outside your immediate family. Other planets aspecting Mercury qualify its personifications. For example, when Mercury and Saturn are in aspect to a planet in childhood, the communication may come from a talkative grandparent.

Venus during childhood represents adaptation to or relationship with young women or children who affect your love or aesthetic sense. In aspect to the Moon, Venus can be the aesthetic quality of your mother. Venus is people and objects you accept readily and to whom you are willing to accommodate yourself. Drawing, painting, music, taste in clothes and the general look of your family's world either clashes with (for square or opposition aspects) or supports your outlook.

Mars during childhood is the desire to go beyond parents or to react against your family. Mars is active, wilful and can be destructive, yet mobile and intense, as its function is to activate and break up static situations in order that creativity may issue from them. Mars also governs accidents and feverish childhood diseases caused by or restricting active mobility.

Jupiter during childhood denotes expansion or support from family friends or those outside the family, and religious attitudes prevalent at home. Generosity and optimism keynote the events and people described by Jupiter and transmitted by them.

Saturn during childhood shows restrictions defining and limiting your development. It is the tendency to isolate yourself, withdraw and concentrate upon your own way, and is carried by those whom you observe doing this themselves. The influences are serious, concentrated, pessimistic or negative and may derive from financial situations and locale as well as individuals. The family doctor is often indicated here.

Uranus during childhood is eccentric, unusual, disruptive or independent tendencies which do not conform to your family's rules or perspectives. Restless, highly strung, erratic and rhythmic influences predominate as vehicles for Uranus' pattern-breaking effects.

Neptune during childhood is sensitivity, receptivity and psychic links in feelings of your family and others. Fantasies, imaginary friends, toys or animals which generate their own identities, dreams, and the world of make-believe are defined by Neptune. Often Neptune is not equivalent to a real person or animal, but is accumulated among many imaginary figures or counterparts of family members. The connection to these fancies is exaggerated during illness or times of weakness.

Pluto during childhood is association with and relation to the public outside your family, often conveyed by propaganda in the media. Contact with news and famous individuals through television exposes you to accepted opinion and the rules of the world at large. Pluto also carries prevailing attitudes towards child-raising, from popular viewpoints to rejection as shown by violence and abuse.

The Node during childhood is the ability to adapt to your family and associated relatives, neighbours and friends as an overall unit.

A predominance of planets in this octave indicates that the ability to create your personality within the family situation is central to and a governing factor in the formation of your world view.

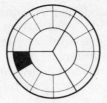

The 1st House   *(Aries)*

Birth until seven months old

In the first seven months after birth you are totally reliant upon your mother for food and support, and she becomes an extension of your will. The demands you make upon her are instinctive and require immediate gratification, and she responds instinctively to meet your demands. The quality of this interchange is defined by the sign or signs occupying the first house. Fire signs show immediate assertion; Earth signs are physical links; Air signs are communications; and Water signs are emotional attachments. As each house is usually intersected by more than one sign (and element), the mother/child relationship goes through a change at some point amidst this house.

In *Horoscope 16* the time from birth until seven months old is

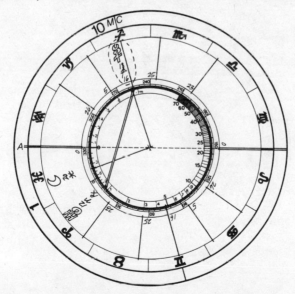

Horoscope 16: The 1st House

in the isolated Pisces, and the remaining nine months of the 1st House is occupied by the self-assertive Aries. A dramatic change occurs at this time, implying that the child's character is obscure initially, but suddenly clarifies itself and becomes assertive. This change refers to the mother, indicated by the Pisces Moon square Mercury and the MC, and shows that feminine dominance over personality is prominent. Planets near the Ascendant in the 1st House signify treatment immediately after birth. Such influences could be separation from the mother in Scorpio or Pisces, or the planets Saturn, Neptune or Node. These planets show those in addition to your mother who influence you; surrogates who assist her, substitutes for her in necessity, or even replacements when difficulties occur. In Horoscope 16 the Pisces Moon could be a nurse or fantasy of mother, either as substitutes for actual attention of the mother.

In *Horoscope 17* a child is adopted at ten weeks old by a surrogate mother, indicated by the Moon and Jupiter in the double sign Aquarius in trine to Mars in the 8th House of separation. The following Venus is a young woman (sister) who resists his self-assertion and is fanatically threatened by (opposed Pluto) yet sensitive to him (trine Neptune). This introduces surrogate

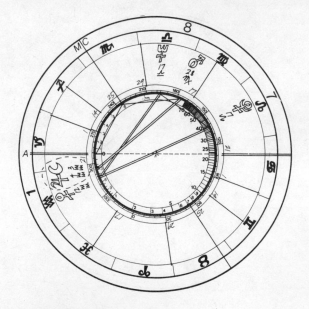

Horoscope 17: The 1st House

emotional attitudes into his personality through attraction and subservience to group morals and collective sexual customs (Venus/Pluto). The example is of a homosexual male whose detachment from the maternal bond and reliance upon the feelings and support of others is simultaneously idealistic, dreamy and violent.

For many decades it was standard practice to separate newborn children from their mothers directly after delivery. The detached and brutal practices include being handled by rubber gloved hands, being powdered with various chemicals, held upside down and spanked, circumcised, umbilical cords cut before natural separation time, being wrapped in sterile tight sheets, incubated, and many others. All these practices were considered the standard and thought to be essential to antenatal health. It is now clear that most of these practices are as harmful as they are unnecessary. The traumatic act of separation for hours after birth interrupts the natural bonding of child and mother. The effects of a generation of these practices upon the western world shows in the widespread violence and alienation in world youth.

The women's movement has been responsible for the recognition and alteration of these unnatural practices, and a return to natural childbirth practices is well under way. The education of women during pregnancy, exercises to promote natural delivery without anaesthetics, support from other women, monitoring by midwives instead of doctors, delivery at home in positive surroundings and conditions, close physical connections with the mother even before the umbilical cord is naturally severed, and an encouragement of breastfeeding are all integral to public knowledge. In fact, the return to natural birthing practices is called 'alternative' birth!

The manner of antenatal treatment is often indicated in the horoscope. A square or opposition from or to the Moon is separation from mother. Saturn near or in aspect to the ASC is separation, inhibition or restraint caused by a doctor or others. Mars is brutality or aggressive treatment, surgery or rough handling, as well as force in delivery itself. Uranus shows technology, erratic behaviour, accidents, abrupt transition, changes in rhythm or the unexpected. Neptune is drug treatment, the use of and response to anaesthetics, induction, substances administered through breast milk or bottle, or gasses. Pluto is a threat to life, alteration caused by other children or influences from the hospital or the outside world. The Node is adaptation to the family in addition to the mother's exclusive control. Jupiter governs dietary matters and general hygiene.

The first five degrees are influences related to the post-natal period of one month. The remaining degrees of the 1st House describe bonding to those who tend you, those with whom you have close personal contact, and those who represent extensions of your personality. The archetypal Aries qualities of this house create a world as a contiguous whole surrounding your centre, an attitude which those with Aries Sun or Moon retain forever. The variety of people present during the 1st House time determines the multiplicity of assertive subpersonalities, as distinct from your personality itself. The primary criteria are that your appetites are gratified, your nappies dry and your demands for attention met. At this stage positive influences cannot be differentiated from negative influences as they are all integrated into your world.

In *Horoscope 18* Pluto registers at five weeks old, as a dramatic change after the extrovert Leo birth. The square of Scorpio Sun to the ASC and the trine from Mars is traumatic surgery performed by a doctor, possibly unnecessarily (square Sun). The effects of this do not register until Pluto produces a forceful separation (Sun square Pluto), inner shocks and blood disease (Ebertin's indications of Moon/Pluto), brutal treatment resulting from surgery (Mars/Pluto) and mysterious circumstances (Neptune sextile to Pluto). It has been proven recently that an immediate cutting of the umbilical cord and the resultant interruption of blood flow from the placenta influences digestion afterwards. (See Laing, *The Facts of Life*) In this case the child almost died from faulty digestive processes. At the sensitive opposition to Pluto at 16 Aquarius at twenty-seven years old, the subject was threatened with death from the digestive aftereffects of extensive and self-destructive drug use.

In *Horoscope 19* there was a mysterious near death (Neptune square Venus sextile Pluto) at three months old, the cause of which was never discovered. In both these examples the individuals are fearful that, when they present their personality, they will be threatened with physical harm, even in situations when there is no apparent cause for such concern.

The elements of the signs in the 1st House define your assertive direction. Fire requires energy from others; Earth, physical contact; Air, verbal and audial response; and Water requires emotional feedback. Cardinal, Fixed and Mutable modes of the elements determine whether your environment is initiatory,

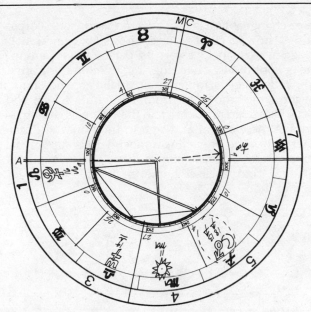

Horoscope 18: The 1st House

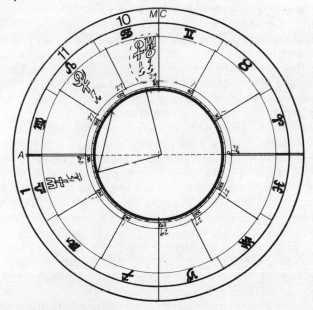

Horoscope 19: The 1st House

stable or changeable. Having a fixed water sign Scorpio in the 1st House shows a child who requires stable emotional attachment against which to assert its personality. Gemini would require a continually changing, highly communicative atmosphere, reflecting its mutable air qualities. The signs in this house show the kind of environment within which you assert yourself. Planets in residence and their aspects combine with or undermine the element and sign in the house and determine whether or not the prevailing atmosphere is supportive or obstructive. The 1st House shows those individuals who were essential in your earliest home environment and how you adapted to them.

The 2nd House   (Taurus)

Seven months until one year and eight months old
The 2nd House is your emergence into the physical world as a separate object among other objects. Generally, you are weaned from mother's milk and begin eating solid food at about this time. You contact the physical world and learn to utilize natural resources including objects, sounds, people and behaviour. Your level of access determines your later attitudes towards material and the physical world.

Planets in the 2nd House show people and influences which determine and qualify your physical reality. The Sun or Moon indicate that parents are primarily identified as being object-like, or that they are the bearers or custodians of objects. Venus is accommodation to the physical world and Mars is the desire to change it. Mercury is thought about objects or their use in communication; Jupiter is the will to obtain more; and Saturn is a limitation with their presence. Often planets here symbolize family members and reflect a tendency to adopt or resist physicality depending upon prevailing family attitudes and circumstances, like the improvement or disintegration of your father's business and material attitudes.

The signs in this house define your attitude towards material matters and your body. Earth signs are natural here; Air signs reflect the physical world as an abstract idea, as words or as the material for communication; Fire signs use the physical world as the background for self-expression; and Water signs relate to their feelings about things. Emotions concentrated upon parents are similar to feelings about objects, such as an obsession with teddy bears, rugs, blankets and thumbs. The object is the only respite from a threatening world.

In *Horoscope 20* the Sun is in Sagittarius, indicating that a girl's father was away travelling in a foreign country, yet was central to her. As she was born in December 1940, it is clear that this intervention was due to the war, and in fact her father was killed at this time. The Sun is almost unaspected, and yet loosely connects with a trine from Pluto, indicating a transformation of the father image, forced separation and a drastic change. The woman possessing this horoscope seeks an evasive material security through men which inevitably leads to their departure, and her changes of relationship echo dramatic alterations of physical circumstances in her life.

In *Horoscope 21*, a one year one month old girl is presented with twin sisters (the Libra influence as a double sign). Saturn conjunct Neptune is a restriction producing weakness,

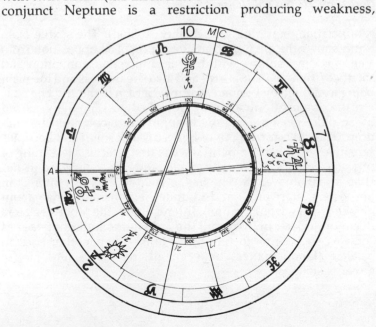

Horoscope 20: The 2nd House

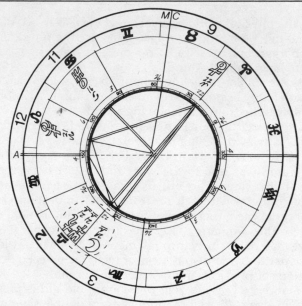

Horoscope 21: The 2nd House

renunciation, suffering and duality (twins!). The sextile from
Pluto shows the ensuing transformation. The opposition from
Venus is the resulting withdrawal of affection, inhibition and
sacrifice (from Venus/Saturn) and also dreaminess and idealism
being tensioned by Venus/Neptune. Saturn in the 2nd House is
a restriction in attention and parental contact, possibly caused
by an older person or nanny brought in to look after the children. The girl is forced out of her central position and becomes
sensitive about her competition. The first effect is a lessening of
physical contact, eventually manifesting as a decrease in her
share of family wealth. She has to yield to the great interest in
her sisters afterwards, and is quite nervous and tense about
herself (square from Uranus). Interestingly, the Moon registers
five months later in Libra and the 3rd House, indicating that as
soon as she begins to talk (3rd House), her mother tries to
balance (Libra) matters between all the sisters (3rd House
governs siblings).

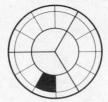

The 3rd House   (Gemini)

One year and eight months until three years and six months old
In the 3rd House you learn to walk, talk and communicate in other ways. These extensions in movement amplify your range of influence and the variety of experiences you encounter. As language is primarily imitative, it is critical to identify who influenced you at this time, how you learned to communicate and what influences were transmitted to you. Your world is unbound from the obsession with objects of the 2nd House and directed to people, primarily children like brothers and sisters.

Planets in the 3rd House show the nature of communication as symbolized by people within your home and family. Luminaries show parents as primary models of communication. Mercury, Venus and Mars are almost always other children with whom you identify or spend time. Jupiter and Saturn represent aunts, uncles, grandparents, housekeepers or nannies who either expand or limit self-expression. Although Jupiter and Saturn are usually identifiable as specific people, sometimes Jupiter is the expansive side of all relatives and Saturn the limiting side of them, or they may symbolize the expansive and limiting parental sides of your family structure. Uranus and Pluto show dominant changes in your environment coming from the world, as through the media, or from the inside. Neptune is sensitivity or insecurity about movement, change and communication. The Node shows collective values where no individual is a primary model, but rather the whole family or group.

As there is a powerful fantasy element during this time, most of your family carry prominent inner images within you sometimes related to, but often a distortion of, an objective reality. Nicknames, family jokes and special characteristics imagined or real fall into this category. The more planets in this house, the more complex and potentially dualistic your communication, as there are more models with whom you connect. Sometimes imaginary figures seem real, just as real people seem obscure. Planets in the 3rd House with aspects to or from many planets

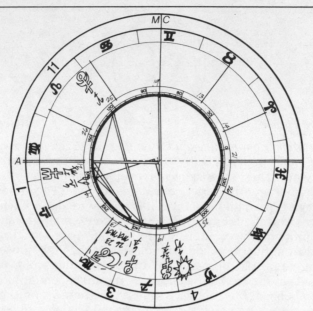

Horoscope 22: The 3rd House

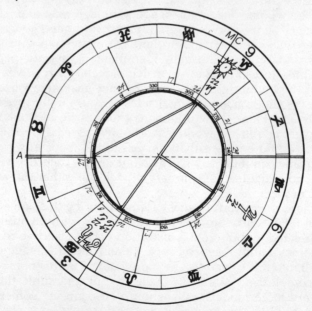

Horoscope 23: The 3rd House

outside the house indicate that most models are from outside the immediate family system, or that the family transmits ways of behaviour deriving from the world outside.

The Gemini archetype of the twins doubles personifications in this house. The Sun produces double father images literally or as the working father vs. the homebody father, while Jupiter produces doubled sets of grandparents.

An absence of planets in the 3rd House indicates a lack of specific models for communication, which can result from being an only child. As usual, the signs occupying the house determine the type of adaptation and diversity of communicative power. Fire signs communicate intuitively through energy exchange; Earth signs with physical means like drawing, building, toy manipulation or touch; the natural Air signs are verbal and use movement; and Water signs seek to express feelings through gestures and words.

In *Horoscope 22* the birth and early life as indicated by the Virgo ASC followed by Neptune and the square Node shows isolation caused by a lack of attention, particularly from the father. The child makes up by attentively learning the witty, biting, sarcastic and pugnacious verbal style of his mother through her arguments and fights to control the family. This aggressive Scorpionic manifestation of the 3rd House then changes to the beneficent Venus in the warm and loving Sagittarius, showing an ability to adapt to other after the fact (Venus/Node) and an aptitude for making his manner an attraction. All this is perfect in the horoscope of a journalist!

In *Horoscope 23* an incident occurred when a one year and five month old child, just as he was learning to talk and express himself, was nearly strangled by his older brother. The severe danger is indicated by the Saturn/Mars conjunction (the death axis in Ebertin) and the opposition to the Sun shows that the father was aloof to the situation, even indirectly encouraging the elder child. This produces a deep inhibition connected with talking and self-expression. Whenever he tries to express himself, he finds his throat so constricted that the pain forces him to abandon all attempts.

The 4th House   (Cancer)

Three years and six months until seven years old

During the 4th House you realize that you produce effects in others and responses in yourself due to your communicative abilities. The range and nature of these responses defines your emotional reaction to the family: the way you feel about them is a reflection of how you feel about yourself. You begin to try out the range of contents and question the beliefs and behaviour of your family, especially your parents. The nature of this informal yet critical inquest determines the firmness of your own family circumstances later in life.

Planets in this house show emotional models and the tenor of your feelings. Although the 4th House is traditionally associated with the parent of the same sex (the father for a male and the mother for a female), there are other criteria which determine the general emotional slant. One factor is the gender of the sign on the cusp of the house. If the sign on the cusp is a water or earth sign, then the emotional dominance is feminine, while if a fire or air sign, the dominance is masculine. The other factor is the planets in the house. Obviously, when either the Sun or Moon are here, the equivalent parent is the emotional prototype, as is the case when the Sun or Moon aspect any planets here. When the Sun is in a feminine sign or the Moon in a masculine sign, the identification is blended. When either luminary is in one of the dual signs (see page 11), the identification is dualistic, which generates a tendency for multiple relationships later in life as a response to multiple parental attitudes here. Mercury shows changeable thoughts and the necessity to think about the way you feel. Venus and Mars are usually sisters and brothers or other children who provide physical, non-parental influences. Jupiter and Saturn are the grandparents, aunts or uncles, surrogates, relatives, priests and doctors who determine emotional family values despite being outside the immediate family. Uranus is the urge to break away from the home and family, or eccentric behaviour within the family. Neptune is extreme sensitivity and psychic contact within the family as a whole, or instability when not recognized. Pluto is restlessness, revolutionary influences, a need for isolation, and often changes in residence or alterations of the family situation, such as those caused by world affairs. The Node indicates very close contact with the family, including grandparents and the parental home and homeland. An empty 4th House shows an undifferentiated home life where the influence is unconscious and instinctive. When there are only one or few planets in this house, but many aspects from planets elsewhere, you seek family organization and its equivalent feelings from outside sources.

In *Horoscope 24*, at the registration of Pluto in the 4th House, the father left, never to return until the sensitive sextile of the Sun into the 6th House at nineteen years old. The fact that Pluto is trined by the Moon and Venus and in sextile to the Node (family) and Neptune (mystery and imagination) implies that this youngster was left with an immediate family of mother and sister by her father after lengthy and severe restrictions, caused by the earlier registration of Saturn opposed by the Sun/father. This principle manifests as a fear that as soon as she opens herself up to someone, they will leave her immediately.

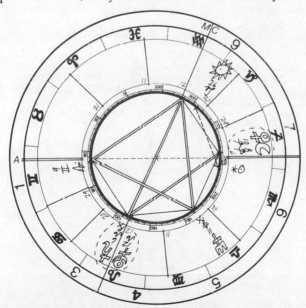

Horoscope 24: The 4th House

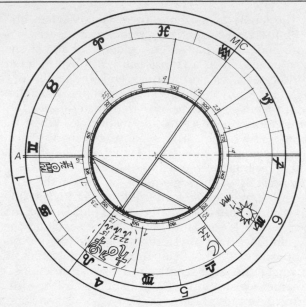

Horoscope 25: The 4th House

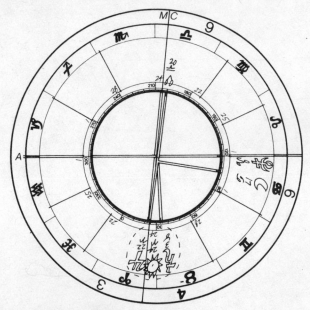

Horoscope 26: The 4th House

Horoscope 25 shows violence at home through Pluto, Mars and Saturn in the domineering Leo in the 4th House, in sextile to the victimized mother (Moon in Libra) and caused by the very separative father (square from Scorpio Sun). That these three are opposed to the MC may even mean that the pentup tension felt by the father at the moment conception was realized broke out suddenly at this later time. Not only was this motif repeated in his own marital relationship, but the subject is a social worker and psychologist helping battered children, even though he did not remember the incident until brought to his attention.

Horoscope 26 shows a paternally dominated family where the Sun/father is always preceded by his Jupiter/brother, while their Saturn/father always has the last word as family head. Although the Aquarius ASC is an apparently idealistic and humanitarian environment, the reality is very arrogant and separative by the square from Pluto. This is a very strong and forceful family oriented configuration, but there is danger from the self-obsession and power struggle between the three masculine parental figures.

Fire signs in the 4th House are active, individualistic and intuitive attitude towards family and home; Earth signs value physical security and visual contact; with Air signs the spoken parental views count more heavily than the reality; while for the natural Water signs the feeling of home and family are optimal.

As this house is the summation and termination of the Childhood Octave, it also determines the emotional response to your ability to create a personality within the home and family, the root of your emotional set and tone for life.

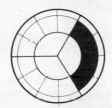

Octave of Maturity

By the end of the 4th House you have received a body during gestation and a personality during childhood. During maturity, you must combine body with personality and project the resultant combination into the outside world. You gradually leave the influence of parents and family and adapt to increasingly greater and broader contexts. The early stages of this octave occur during school years: the 5th House being primary education and the 6th House being secondary education and/or early working life. The 7th House from twenty-three years five months until about forty-two is the time of partnerships and most important contact with the world, and the 8th House is the gradual withdrawal from life leading up to death. The first two houses of this octave are unconscious, being below the horizon, while the last two are conscious, being above the horizon. This reflects an increasing control over life and the gradual creation of objectivity with age.

As in gestation you create a body and in childhood a personality, the function of maturity is to contact and accept your soul. Your soul actually enters its physical vehicle at the registration of the MC, just after conception, but remains latent until you synthesize attitudes in life to its command. *Soul* is the ability to see and understand life as a whole in time, as reflected by the entire horoscope circle of life. This corresponds to modern concepts of "holistic health" - seeing the body, personality and soul as integral components of a meaningful whole. This also involves understanding life as a process instead of as a series of insular present moments strung together like beads on a necklace.

There are hypotheses current in the medical profession which ascribe to time perception the major cause of stress-related diseases such as heart disease, hypertension and cancer. (See Dossey, *Space,|Time|and Medicine*) Revolutionary cures for these killers are related to the new perception of time inherent in the Log Time Scale presented in this book. Development in gestation is primarily physical; development in childhood is primarily emotional; and development in maturity is primarily mental. Your state of mind determines your health, welfare and the quality of all relationships. The ability to see yourself as a whole being in time is essential for a healthy, holistic life.

You must understand the part you play in life. The events, characters and settings of the first two life stages of gestation and childhood teach you certain ground rules and ways of acting. In maturity you must acccept your part and play it out with maximum comprehension, feeling, joy and, above all, life.

The planets registering in maturity are particularly important because they describe higher manifestations of each planetary quality. Your entire previous life is the background for this third stage of development and planets have a particularly potent effect. Whereas in the earlier stages the planets are primarily other people in your life, in maturity the planets are distinctly you and events are determined and acted out by you. One object of maturity is to transcend personal models, to integrate them all into your whole, and to transpersonalize life. You must go beyond environment, heredity, parents and friends into the sacred and timeless realm of wholeness.

The Sun during maturity is the conscious paternal focus of your vitality. During maturity the influence of your father declines as you take over the fatherly reality in your own creative life. The gradients of this transition are from a protective father at the end of childhood, to the teacher in the 5th and 6th Houses, to the father in you in the 7th and 8th Houses. The Sun during this time represents the drive towards recognition, acknowledgement, personal focus and strength. The goal involves individuality and self-esteem as well as the ability to meet the practical goals in life of success, health and the creation of a family life.

The Moon during maturity is the transference of the maternal image from your mother to those with whom you have the deepest feeling connections. Your mother's influence is strongest and deepest in gestation, protective during childhood at home, and during maturity begins to reconstruct itself in your own homing instinct and choice of partner. As you detach from your mother, you find and accept the soul. The motherly influence becomes integrated into your whole as you bring feelings into line with the will to exist in the world. The Moon is feelings and protective instinct, and on the higher level the Moon is emotional reality as a whole and the summation of your hereditary disposition.

Mercury during maturity is communication with friends, students, workers, associates, salesmen, agents, mediators, intellectual leaders, organizers, friends and their effect upon your mental reality. The context for communication you create around yourself is echoed in the people with whom you express your thoughts. The intermediary function of getting your ideas out into the world may be delegated to others or may be an integral part of your own reality. After your daily life is structured, you quest for higher ideals which reflect a transcendent view beyond ordinary life. Mercury can also refer to the passing of life structures onto children, or through intellectual products like books or other creative acts.

Venus during maturity is relationship to your loves, those you find and who find you attractive, mistresses, artists, musicians and sexual partners. Venus is also the milieu of these contacts in social life, entertainment, cultural venue and friendly relationships. Venus is also children.

Mars during maturity is the desire to change your world with athletic, sexual, mechanical, skilful and aggressive activities. Initially Mars energies are projected onto physical fitness, athletic competition and sexual investigation, which later transforms into the desire to focus energy within business, marriage and associations. Doctors, surgeons, craftsmen or soldiers fall under Mars' jurisdiction. When energy is blocked during these houses it becomes rechannelled into physical therapies, sexual relations outside marriage or, if it is not redirected, it is forced inwards until it creates the physical afflictions which affect many people towards the end of their lives.

Jupiter during maturity shows your life philosophy and those from whom and with whom it is formed and used. The influence can be religious, psychological, philosophical or financial, and promotes expansion and optimism. The expansion first takes the form of being able to feel a part of groups and schools, and later is the possibility of growing beyond the institutions of life. Jupiter may be officials, religious people, gurus, psychologists, psychiatrists, those of high character, wealth and esteem, speculators, healers and all people who carry fortunate connections.

Saturn during maturity describes life systems which define your responsibilities, sense of security and community, and ability to establish and fit into collective patterns in your home and society. Saturn is those who maintain these organizational systems like doctors, bank managers, employers, partners and associates, as well as those who are serious, older, strict, conservative, hard-working and mature. Towards the 8th House, you possibly become a grandparent or older person and represent the existing or declining order.

Uranus during maturity represents sudden changes, inventions, independence, erratic drives and all influences which serve to break up rigidity and patterns in your life. The carriers of these influences are reformers, eccentrics, inventors, unusual teachers, therapists and unusual associations or partners. The impact of Uranus ranges from submission to teachers or gurus to exerting a transformative influence upon your own life and that of others.

Neptune during maturity is the gradual transformation of

youthful fantasies and ideals into sensitivity followed by detachment. Concern for society is envisioned by romantics,
sensitives, mediums, spiritual people and rejected by alcoholics, mediators, hypochondriacs and seducers. Drug
experiences and mystical reveries, confusion and wondering,
all contribute to Neptune's influence.

Pluto during maturity is your relationship to collective values
and changes in society. The influence is carried by those people
in personal and public life who understand or force collective
values. You may either be altered by a changing civilization or
be a transformer yourself. Pluto symbolizes revolutionaries,
transformers, those who exert psychic or magical influence over
the masses, the media, politicians, gurus, domineering partners or employers and those who force change. Pluto's
registration often generates changes in job, residence, partnership and overall view of life.

The Node during maturity indicates teamwork, your family,
and the alliances, collaborations, marriages and partnerships
you form. Professional associations, political parties, labour
unions and groups all show Node influences.

A predominance of planets in maturity shows that the focus
of life is to become stronger and more important.

The 5th House   (Leo)

Seven years until thirteen years old
The 5th House is a higher level of the 1st House where you
asserted yourself, and you now exteriorize yourself into the
world outside the family and become conscious of who you are.
The primary device in this understanding is game-playing:
organized ways of exchanging energy, feelings, ideas and
intuitions. The random and self-centred play of childhood
becomes more involved and the choices of friends, school subjects, sports and diversions all describe and are affected by the
games you play. Giving, taking, winning and losing are all part
of personal relationships; ultimately the object is to enjoy and
receive fulfilment from games rather than placing paramount

importance upon winning, although many people would contest this interpretation.

Civilization rests upon playing by the rules adopted by ancestors. During primary education you learn these rules, their history and application. Your approach to game-playing in school and at home determines the kind and quality of relationships you form in the world.

Planets in the 5th House are those with whom you play and after whom you pattern your own games. Positive signs show an active and extrovert approach to games, while negative signs show a passive and introvert approach. The luminaries include not only parents, but new prototypes such as teachers, heroes in books and media, and older children. The Sun asserts the importance of game-playing and is a person after whom this trait is patterned. The Moon denotes imaginative, emotional and romantic motivations in play and is carried by those who feel this is important. Mercury loves change and nurtures the idea of the game as central. Venus focuses upon creative activities and the entertainment value of games and their rules, but Mars is aggressive, physical, competitive and unruly. Jupiter wishes to extend the importance of play and promotes a broad range of activities, while Saturn concentrates upon specialties, suppresses creativity through conservatism, wishes for security and associates with older children. Uranus creates original games which diverge from accepted rules. Neptune dreams and fantasizes more readily than it acts, expects ideal situations and tires easily of the reality of games and rules. Pluto dominates, rules and forces others to join and play games to which they might not otherwise be exposed, or popular games. The Node tends to play and accept rules adopted by everyone else without dissent. If you have no planets in the 5th House, it shows a lack of importance of schooling and games in your life.

Fire signs in the 5th House indicate an intuitive, instinctive and active approach to games; Earth signs rely upon physical stability and might, or may be the child who owns the ball and knows he will be included in the game; Air signs discuss and treat games as ideas and continually alter the rules to suit their needs; and Water signs take the results of games emotionally and value the role of the participants seriously.

In *Horoscope 27*, at eleven years four months a young girl is sent off to a very strict boarding school (Saturn), where she is cut off from her mother (Moon sextile Saturn). This inhibits her

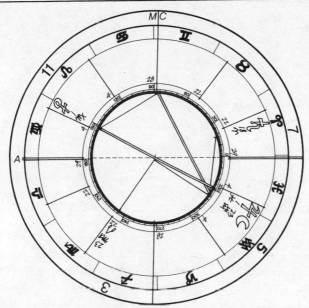

Horoscope 27: The 5th House

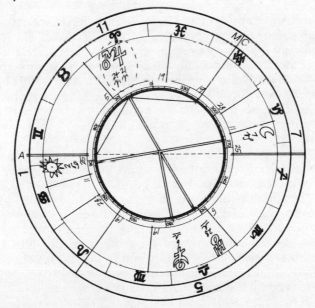

Horoscope 28: The 5th House

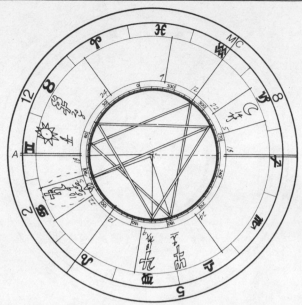

Horoscope 29: The 5th House

and results in anti-social behaviour and a resistance to school (Moon square Scorpio Node).

Horoscope 28 shows a dramatic change in parental relationship (Pluto in Libra), especially since Pluto is in square to both Sun/father and Moon/mother, implying that he is the object of a dispute between his parents. This conflict on a higher level implies that he must choose between his father's personal strength and his mother's emotional strength in public situations.

Horoscope 29 is a change in residence to a foreign country at the registration of Jupiter in Virgo in the 5th House. It is interesting that the 5th House begins at the early age of two years ten months old, implying that this child begins playing games at a very early age and expands through his move away from home (square Gemini ASC). Moon trine Jupiter is travel, happiness and religion, and the trine from the 12th House Mercury is constructive, literate and isolated. This shows that the individual benefits from changes of residence as isolation increases communicative and speculative ventures.

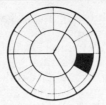

The 6th House   (Virgo)

Thirteen years until twenty-three years and five months old

At the beginning of the 6th House puberty is at its height and the body comes into focus. Suddenly sexuality is a central factor in the game-playing of the previous house and the rules of the games change dramatically. The choices you make and the way you make them become binding, as during the time of secondary education you determine your future direction and work relationships. The general tenor of your choices are physical as you select diet, clothing, activities and work disciplines, and systematically regain control from your parents, who formerly made such decisions for you.

Planets in the 6th House determine attitudes towards school and work, teachers and employers who guide you and friends whose choices affect your own. The Sun here promotes paternal ambition which is either a reflection of or reaction against father, which may be competitive or supportive. The Moon stresses feelings over practicality, serving, the functional aspects of life and changeable moods which affect logical decisions. Mercury appreciates detail but does not see the whole clearly, producing nervousness when choices must be made. Venus shows reliance upon school and work relationships and an ability to adapt easily, while Mars focuses upon efficiency, vitality, hard work and a desire to succeed. Jupiter is opportunistic, philosophical and loyal. Saturn is conscientious, selfish, serious, reponsible and concentrates on security. Uranus institutes original methods in school and work, new techniques, and implies changes in focus. Neptune drifts idealistically, makes sacrifices to causes and is influenced by prevailing situations, especially when under the influence of drugs or alcohol. Pluto is attraction to large scale occupations, large universities and mass movements in education or technology. The Node is association with others for guidance and protection.

Fire signs in the 6th House indicate that choices are intuitive and based on the energy they carry; Earth signs show decisions based on tangible values, financial gain or possessions; Air signs value the ideas behind work more than its rewards; and Water signs feel their way into certain types of school or work where fine valuations are essential.

Horoscope 30 belongs to an eighty-nine year old doctor whose parents were told by an astrologer shortly after birth that he would not survive! At the age of twenty-three years old (Saturn in Libra), he became a medical doctor following the tradition (Saturn) of his father (Saturn squared by the Sun). As Saturn was the doctor who delivered him successfully, and who was criticized by his observing father (again, Sun square both Saturn and the ASC), the subject practised medicine but remained critical of his own profession, eventually espousing the most modern spiritual healing techniques (Saturn/science trine Neptune/psychic, Moon/helping and Pluto/affecting the masses).

Horoscope 31 shows concentrated development in the 6th House beginning with the Sun/Jupiter conjunction in Virgo, as recognition for hard work by teachers and father (both indicated by the Sun), and from the school itself (Jupiter). The sextile of Sun/Jupiter to Saturn shows concentration on work, and

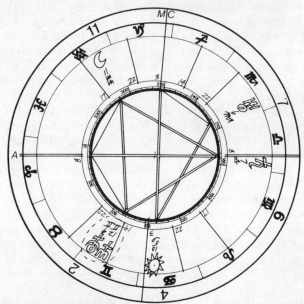

Horoscope 30: The 6th House

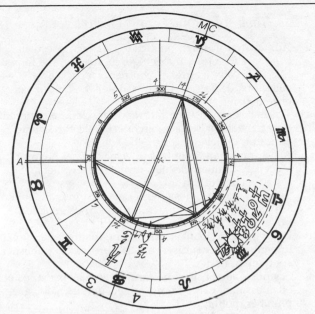

Horoscope 31: The 6th House

to the Venus-ruled Taurus Ascendant, involves artistic work. At nine years and five months, he is criticised verbally (Mercury in Virgo) by his family (sextile Node), and goes off by himself (Mercury trine MC). At Venus the artistic occupation is prominent and indicates a desire (Mars) to be known by the public (Libra) for creativity (Venus conjunct Mars), which is increasingly focused on fantasy subjects and rock/drug culture (all from Neptune). He utilizes the positive Mars/Neptune aspect of inspiration and its surrogate in the drug culture of the 1960's as a pop-rock-fantasy artist.

As the 6th House governs your school training and occupation, Table 14 describes briefly the occupations congenial to planets here:

Table 14: *Planets and Occupations*

Sun	Administrator, stars, politicians, leaders, speculators, company directors, public figures, royalty, the famous.
Moon	Midwife, cook, gardener, vintner, sailor, brewers, collectors, dealers, domestics, hoteliers, landowner, obstetricians.
Mercury	Teacher, journalist, writer, reporter, clerk, accountant, agent, mediator, artisan, architect, solicitor, cabbie, educator, optician.
Venus	Artist, musician, entertainer, actor, nurse, broker, associate, clothier, cashier, furnisher, jewellers, restaurateur, treasurer.
Mars	Surgeon, builder, designer, engineer, fireman, adventurer, athlete, butcher, manufacturer, machinist, soldier, physiotherapist, police.
Jupiter	Lawyer, judge, banker, physician, insurer, clergyman, foreigner, merchandiser, official, professor, publisher, sportsman, trader.
Saturn	Scientist, doctor, banker, farmer, archaeologist, osteopath, businessman, cattle-raiser, miner, dentist, geologist, plumber, potter.
Uranus	Astrologer, radio-TV, musician, technologist, electrician, healer, fliers, cartoonist, electronics, feminist, mechanic, physicist.
Neptune	Chemist, anaesthetist, astronaut, dancer, distiller, medium, psychic, navy, oiler, photographer, poet, psychologist, wizard.
Pluto	Revolutionary, undertaker, taxman, atomic scientist, insurer, outlaw, prostitute.

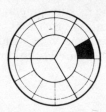

The 7th House   **(Libra)**

Twenty-three years and five months until forty-two years old
As you approach the cusp of the 7th House, exactly opposite
the Ascendant/personality, a more objective attitude towards
life begins as you complete the lower, subjective half of the

horoscope of childhood and the first half of maturity. The domination of parents, family and birth circumstances must be recognized, worked through and resolved through partnerships. Partnerships sublimate the self-oriented first 23 years of life by requiring you to give away to others as much energy, emotion, material and ideas as you have received; all in order to balance out life:

Planets in the 7th House show those with whom you have emotional or work partnerships, new people encountered once you enter the world, and attitudes to such contacts and realities. The Sun represents a strong capable, close and conscious relationship and the person with whom you form this relationship. When in double signs, you can expect to have more than one partner. The Moon stresses domestic and emotional sides of partnership, and can indicate an instinctive partnership. Mercury is changeable and indicates more than one partner, often a choice of one younger, more intellectual or nervous, and describes those who mediate between you and the world. Venus shows deep physical attachment in relations where affection, love and aesthetics dominate. Mars is independent, selfish, aggressively sexual and impulsive in making and breaking relationships. Jupiter values social status and financial advantages in relationships, often prospers in more than one relationship as a way of expanding a world view. Saturn is responsible, conscientious and concentrated yet limiting relationships to older and more inhibited partners. Uranus is a wish to remain independent despite rapid attraction, and a romantic attitude which produces unexpected situations which form and dissipate quickly. Neptune is a dream of ideal partnership and attracts those admired from afar, often with ensuing disillusionment; or platonic unions where sacrifice is required. Pluto indicates relationships as a bridge to public affairs; mass values often determine the degree of cooperation, thereby producing great changes of attitude. The Node represents special aptitude for groups, circles of friends, communal circumstances, clubs and politics as outlets or substitutes for collective expression of views. No planets in the 7th House shows partnerships and partners as a continuation of earlier attitudes, people, events or identifications.

For most adults, the 7th House time after twenty-three years and five months old is the region of the horoscope in which they are most interested. This house is the collection of the entire planetary pattern from previous ages all the way back to conception, and your last chance to affect or become aware of your destiny. By the time of your entrance into the 8th House, you will not possess enough energy to rectify laziness here. In many cases, the actual positions of planets in the horoscope are such that there are no planets in the 7th or 8th Houses (which cover only 17% of the entire horoscope wheel), in which case the sensitive points are essential for describing the process of maturity and for prediction beyond your current age. Sensitive points are harmonic registrations at the exact aspect points of planets in the horoscope projected into an area you wish to study more closely. Even when there are already planets in the 7th House, it is important to identify and interpret sensitive points.

To fill this area with as many sensitive points as possible, you should use the minor aspects of 30 and 150 degrees, and possibly even those of 45 and 135 degrees.

In *Horoscope 32* a highly creative person enters the initiatory Aries on the 7th House cusp, indicating a new beginning and creativity until forty-two years old. The benefic planets Venus and Jupiter register at twenty-four years ten months and twenty-seven years five months, and the malefic planets Saturn and Mars register at thirty-nine years one month and forty years eight months, but we want to discover what happened in the intervening time. The planets themselves describe the transformation of a creative man (Venus conjunct Jupiter) with innovative powers (Aries) to a condition of inhibition and a separation from these powers as a result of excessive sexuality (Mars sextiled from the Sun and MC, and squared by Pluto), increased flirtations with danger (Mars square Pluto) and restraint (Mars conjunct Saturn). He is surrounded by beneficial and helpful people early on (Venus and Jupiter), but increasingly attracted aggressive and binding people (Mars and Saturn).

The sensitive points in this horoscope are the semisextile (30 degrees) to the Moon at 9 Aries at twenty-eight years five months; the semisextile Uranus at 18 Aries at thirty-three years five months; the opposition Node at 23 Aries at thirty-six years eleven months; and the sextile from the Sun at 25 Aries at thirty-eight years six months. Even though there are no planets at these points, the sensitive points are treated as though there were. The sequence of planets and sensitive points is shown in Table 15, with the intervals between planets interpreted as aspects between the two limiting planets.

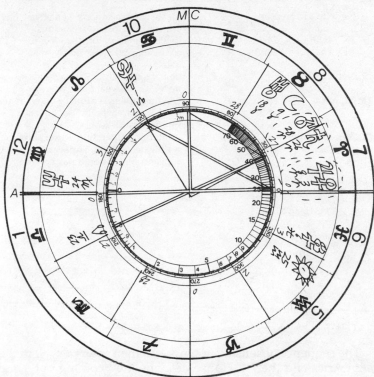

Horoscope 32: The 7th House

Table 15: Sensitive Point Sequence

1. Natal Jupiter   08 Aries 46
                at 27 yr 05 mo
Magnaminity, a philosophy of independence, expansion, of self.

2. Jupiter to 30 Moon
Happiness, social conscience, travel, negligent emotions.

3. 30 Moon   09 Aries 54
                at 28 yr 05 mo
Impulsive partnership, acting without thinking, strong personality.

4. Moon to 30 Uranus
Emotional tensions, instinct, sudden events in partnership, strain.

5. 30 Uranus   18 Aries 08
                at 33 yr 05 mo
Restlessness, reforms, blinding zeal, violence, dreamy enthusiasts, eccentric partnerships.

6. Uranus to 180 Node
Shared experiences, incidents, upsets with others in partnerships, activity, restlessness.

7. 180 Node   23 Aries 10
                at 36 yr 11 mo
Ruling others, submission, striving to lead others (groups), teamwork is difficult.

8. Node to 150 Neptune		Idealistic associations, sensitive groups, antisocial, deceptions.
9. 150 Neptune	24 Aries 55 at 38 yr 03 mo	Realised inspiration, rich feelings, confusion, no aims, insane-mad ideals.
10. Neptune to 60 Sun		Sensitivity, delicacy, imagination, uncertainty, weakness, diseases.
11. 60 Sun	25 Aries 20 at 38 yr 06 mo	Leading others, enthusiasm, courage, lust for power, boldness, advance through ruthlessness.
12. Sun to natal Saturn		Inhibition, separation, absorption, seriousness, work, suppression, concentration upon a partnership.

The sequence of sensitive points and their intervals, all in the sign Aries and the 7th House describe the "coming out" into active homosexuality in Horoscope 32. The process starts creatively, becomes highly emotional with the Moon, then erratic and unusual with Uranus. The registration of the 180 Node sees a transference into a gay community, which exaggerated the idealistic content (Node to Neptune), culminating in the registration of the Sun (literally, a man in his life), and then the final link into the Saturn/Mars conjunction astride the 8th House cusp, showing physical threats and violence in relationships. Any zone of the horoscope, but especially the 7th and 8th Houses can be analyzed as this sequence has been.

Horoscope 33 shows the registration of Mars and Mercury in Pisces, the sign of isolation and subjection to external forces. Since Mars is in square to the Node, the influence involves family and the public in a difficult collaboration, a lack of team spirit, tense unions and quarrelling. When this individual was thirty-two years two months old, a middle-eastern revolution unseated her powerful family, forced a retreat to Europe and effectively terminated a long-term marriage. The impulsive

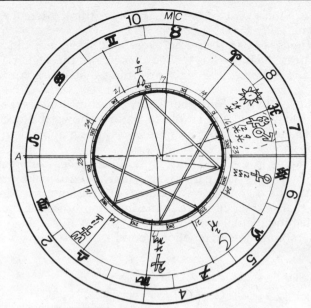

Horoscope 33: The 7th House

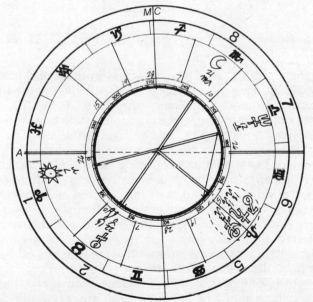

Horoscope 34: The 7th House

nature of this event led to the necessity to think (Mercury) more diplomatically.

In *Horoscope 34* a thirty-one year and six month old young woman is diagnosed as having diabetes at the registration of Neptune in Libra (the sign governing diabetes according to Cornell, *The Encyclopedia of Medical Astrology*, p. 159.). Neptune is opposed by the Sun (the vitality), and indicates separation from a man; and the sextile to Saturn shows the necessary renunciation, suffering, sacrifice and caution applied after the diagnosis.

Fire signs in the 7th House indicate creative, dominant and ardent partners and partnerships; Earth signs make practical unions where cumulative resources are paramount; Air signs think that partnerships are primarily communicative means of establishing mental and social ideas; and Water signs feel that partnership is a deep emotional bond.

The 8th House   (Scorpio)

Forty-two years old until death

After the drive for security and success in the world has been sublimated during the 7th House, the 8th House is the time of withdrawal from and meditation upon life. As you gradually release control over affairs, the favourable direction is towards a metaphysical reality, a broader and less materialistic perspective of life. During this time there is a natural decline of the senses which were manifested during the opposite 2nd House: energy lessens, physical problems become central, senses weaken, mind is more and more internalized and private, and finally even your emotional grasp is eliminated. Your time sense is such that events which in early life would have come, manifested themselves and left in weeks now take years. Injuries and illnesses which formerly were brushed off become major liabilities. Financial shortcomings become critical problems which only get worse. You lose family and life-long friends who cannot be replaced and are even difficult to remember. The most important guide to this time is to relinquish control gracefully, as it is inevitable. The 8th House is the time of separation and death.

Planets in the 8th House indicate attitudes to metaphysical reality, to the physical situation during the last phase of life and, when indicated, the manner of death. The Sun in the 8th House shows that the centre remains hidden until the latter stages of life and a gain in strength, insight, and inner emotional stability with advanced age. Additionally, an interest in metaphysical arts and a deep will which survives all physical danger is symbolized by the Sun. The Moon denotes extreme sensitivity and striving for truth beyond physical circumstances, financial dependence upon women or protecting family, as well as an emotional old age. Mercury shows a mind specifically interested in metaphysical ideas, pursuits, secrecy and ideas derived from others and a lively old age. Venus indicates relationships which produce gain, the importance of art, and intense feelings towards the loss of physical appearance. Mars indicates a sex drive into late life, persistence in retaining energy, aggressive independence until the end and a tendency to die quickly. Jupiter is hopeful, confident and philosophical about life and death while indicating a natural death. Saturn resists relinquishing physical energy and property, and is hampered by these matters, yet is so disciplined and rigid that a long life can be indicated. Uranus is more eccentric and independent with age, shows psychic values and telepathic phenomena, possibly a deep vision into the mysteries amidst changeable physical conditions and points towards a sudden end. Neptune increases sensitivity and also vulnerability, physically and financially; its nervous component increases the likelihood of death by wasting away, undiagnosed or psychosomatic disease, in drug therapy or in hospital. Pluto shows an attitude which accepts the necessity of death and regeneration manifest in an interest in occult subjects and arts, and can expect a great change in attitude and feeling late in life. The Node shows increasing attraction to communes, monastic situations, withdrawal from the world, groups, societies or larger communities of people with similar views. No planets in the 8th House shows that the last house in life is almost entirely affected by events and circumstances which have resulted from earlier acts or attitudes, as karmic repercussions of past life deeds.

Fire signs in the 8th House exhibit great energy and vitality once life's business is finished, reaching a peak while others decline; Earth signs concentrate upon physical fitness and financial resources; Air signs are withdrawn into the thoughts and memories of life; and the Water signs have strong and deep emotional reponses to the ability to contact the soul and complete life.

Horoscope 35 shows a woman who, late in life, abandoned a relationship with her older husband (Saturn in the 7th) and began a love relationship, indicated by Venus in Sagittarius (a foreign relation), trine Neptune (dreaminess, sensitivity and idealism), and in a positive square to Jupiter and Uranus in Aries (the configuration of a new beginning). The marriage produces opulence and popularity (Venus/Jupiter) and arousal, impulsive acts and eccentricity (Venus/Uranus). The registration of Mars at fifty-one years old indicates the coming of menapause (Mars in Capricorn being physical matters) and a male grandchild, possibly evoking a fantasy earlier in life at the 4th House registration of Neptune.

In *Horoscope 36* the student of a great mystic resolved upon his teacher's death, the idealistic Mars in Aquarius, to carry on his work, to realize plans and to resolve problems as an effect of the death (Mars sextile Saturn). The awareness of death, the '*last*

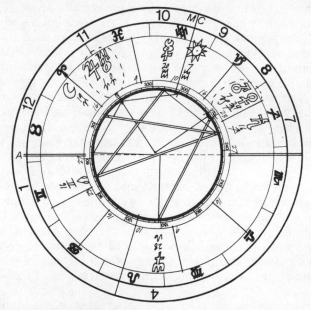

Horoscope 35: The 8th House

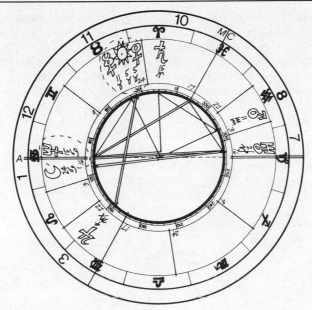

Horoscope 36: The 8th House

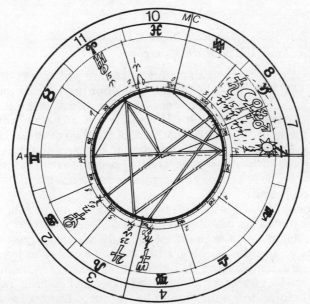

Horoscope 37: The 8th House

judgement', and the right way to die is central to our subject and his master, Ouspensky.

Horoscope 37 is a famous modern guru who suddenly, after achieving enormous popularity, wealth, following and recognition, left his Indian base and sought refuge in the US under threat to his life from illness and political resistance. His popularity is indicated by the succession of Mars, Mercury, Venus and Moon in Capricorn, the sign of recognition and fame. The Venus and Moon conjunction is the essence of love and devotion liberating tensions, sexual inhibitions, eccentricities and musical energies by the square of both planets to Uranus (license). The prominent material undercurrent is shown by the Capricornian sign quality. At the registration of Saturn opposed Pluto the great change occurs at forty-nine years two months, and the hardening-up process has critical effects upon his health. This is the configuration of a magician and adept, but also of a martyr.

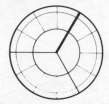

The 9th House Cusp/Death Moment

As life is a process, so all events in life are processes within a process. Conception, birth, the transition from childhood to maturity, and death are changes in state which every human being experiences. The 9th House cusp is archetypically the death moment. Due to the mathematics of the Placidèan House division system, it is possible and often happens that this cusp registers as early as forty years old, or past the age of a hundred years old. The 9th cusp is the symbolic death point and is not to be taken literally!

In some horoscopes there are many points at which life may be threatened or possibly terminated. Determination of the exact time of death is the most difficult analytical question in astrology, and the astrologer has a responsibility to leave an open mind on this issue. Unless circumstances are exceptional and knowledge about the manner and time of death is necessary or helpful, this issue should be left open. Dangerous times should be identified, but not stated as possible death.

When the 9th cusp registers in life, as in *Horoscope 7*, it must be understood as a great transition. The transition is either a revelation which terminates existing life values and patterns, an insight into a different and higher level of reality, or a negative step away from life into a more mechanistic reality. This cusp can coincide with retirement, the onset of senility, a radical change in life like moving into a rest home, the death of a long-time partner, a change in residence after a long and stable home life or a physical disability which forever alters one's life style as in the case of heart attacks, diagnosed cancers and other crises. On the more positive side, it can indicate a new awareness of life's mysteries, an involvement with communal organizations which relieve isolation or even being taken into the care of others. In earlier Eastern societies, this would mark the time when a man, after having completed his life as a husband, father and householder, gives up his possessions and leaves to wander the high Himalayas as a wandering monk until death. This is the time of stepping beyond the world, exemplified by the 9th House values of higher mind, religion, psychology and philosophy.

In our Horoscope 7, the 9th cusp registers at the age of forty-five years nine months, and the houses are so compacted that he even passes the MC/10th House cusp at sixty-six years three months old. As the MC is ego-consciousness and the sense of life's objectives, individuation and spiritualization, this point provides an opportunity for passing and transforming the highest level of the ego during life. Usually the MC/ego is a goal toward which we spend our lives moving, yet never quite reaching. Not only does he have the opportunity to pass the MC, but he may also reach the Sun in Aquarius a second time around at the age of eighty-five years. This is a true completion and the person has a unique opportunity to close and resolve the circle of life.

Horoscope 38 is of the current American president who passed the 9th cusp at fifty-one years old in 1962, the year that he switched from the Democratic to Republican parties, a major decision. At the registration of the Aquarius Sun at the age of fifty-six years old he was Governor of California, certainly a strong position. At the sensitive trine to Pluto he became President, an event that constituted a great change and brought power over the masses.

Sometimes the 7th and 8th Houses are expanded instead of compacted, and there are planets which register past the age of

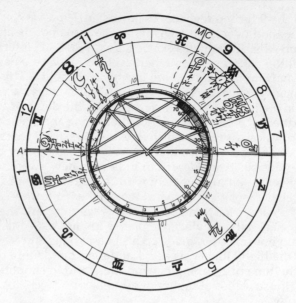

Horoscope 38: The 9th House – Ronald Reagan

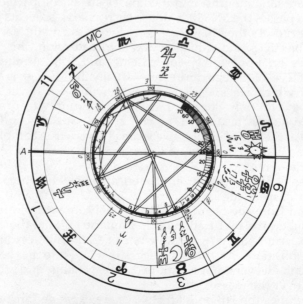

Horoscope 39: The 9th House – Carl Jung

a hundred years old, yet are still within the 8th House. This implies an influence which carries on after death either in the world or within the family. *Horoscope 39* belongs to Carl Jung, the great psychologist, whose Jupiter in Libra registers at the equivalent of a hundred and eighteen years old! The implications of Jung's work remain many years beyond his physical life. In fact, Jung was interested in alchemy in his later years, especially the *'mysterium coniunctionis'* or mystery of the conjunction of the King/Sun and the Queen/Moon, described clearly by Jupiter (a philosophy, psychology or religion) of the conjunction (Libra).

Planets that register after death indicate posthumous recognition or a lasting effect upon those who survive the individual. This is often the case when people die early in life, yet have planets registering afterwards. Their emotional, spiritual or even mental existence remains to have an influence upon family or society.

Transcending Your Story

A majority of people occupy life simply surviving. Their lives are significant only to themselves; they never attempt to extend the focus of life beyond the immediate situation. It is possible to extend your reality beyond the 'mortal coil' and transcend the story of your life. To do so it is necessary to remain awake to the positive and negative events, people and processes of life, and to integrate them all into a complete whole.

Most people, when asked to remember and date the important events of their lives can only locate graduation from school, marriage, births of their children, the date of divorce and others of like kind as being critical. The times in between simply drop out of the whole. Their lives are shallow and bleak, and events are only the outer manifestation of a missing inner life. All meaning has disappeared from life, leaving a series of legal transactions instead.

Humanistic psychology regards the process of personal growth as the focus of life. The manifestation of a full, active, successful life is paramount, and the individual resulting satisfies his or her social, personal and hereditary conditions totally. While these goals are elusive to all but a few people, there are lessons learned in life through the horoscope which point to higher levels of awareness and understanding. Once life is mapped out and its events and personifications defined, you can see that it is continually alive within and is being relived and re-experienced daily. Past events and dead parents remain with you throughout life as lessons and guides. The basic information of life – the dates, places, people and times – and the meaning of the whole is brought into every subsequent life situation. If you remember nothing, you learn nothing. Only by recognizing the past in your present and future can you move beyond the mundane. You are trapped by the past until you understand it clearly enough to recognize and transcend its games. Every event, problem, difficult person or relationship, every recalcitrant child you raise, creates possibilities for transcendence. Often, the greater the difficulties, the more you must try to remain awake and find the higher value of experiences. All difficulties in life reflect problems within which have yet to be resolved and identify parts of the whole of which you are not yet aware. Wholeness requires the identification of those missing parts.

The only way to move beyond life into the transcendent realm is to make use of what you know about yourself to help others to a clearer understanding of themselves. The best way to communicate unity to others is by example. If you live life accepting adverse conditions in the same manner as beneficial circumstances and learn and grow from everyone around, you set such an example. When you can maintain equilibrium in spite of difficulties, you do not avoid confrontation nor become complacent amidst plenty: you can live life consciously.

When awareness exists, events indicated in the future lose their terror. Often people try to make what appear to be difficult combinations of planets in their future go away because they wish to avoid problems. But, you cannot make difficulties go away. If a Saturn registration, indicating restriction, limitation and concentration, is due at a certain time, the nature of Saturn determines the correct attitude. To try to throw a party or to expand socially is contrary to the message of Saturn. If you throw a party, people will have prior arrangements or will feel inhibited while there. If you try to go out, the car will have a flat tyre. The restriction will operate whatever you do. If you approach the situation creatively, you realize that if you stay at home alone and confront those problems which you have avoided, then the concentration of Saturn can work for you. If you do not use the concentrating energy of Saturn on your own terms, then its effect registers against your will. It is better to use the difficult influences of the planets rather than leave yourself open to their influence when you least expect or want it. If a difficult Venus aspect is about to operate, indicating a confrontation with a woman, the confrontation cannot be avoided, but the woman with whom you have the confrontation can be chosen, including the woman within you. It can be the woman associate at work with whose work you are dissatisfied, or your wife. You can choose to use the influence to confront the situation in a creative way, but if not it will rebound back at you. This principle operates with all the planets and in all events in your life. You must try to understand the demands of life and use all situations maximally.

Ordinary people believe that they are living creative and fulfilling lives, but often they repeat their past ad infinitum. The only way to move past early childish patterns, determined by parents, is to observe your reactions and actions. Only then can you rectify life patterns by using them consciously. This is the object of Your Story, to transcend your role, the other characters and the entire situation of life.

★Chapter Eight★
Complete Interpretation

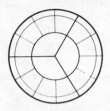

The last chapter described how to interpret your astrological Life★Time house by house around the horoscope, starting from before conception. It would be very helpful at this point to outline the procedure for the complete analysis of the horoscope from the beginning. The second part of this chapter is a complete analysis.

The interpretation can be divided into three discrete sections: The Computation and Drawing of the Horoscope, the Determination of the Sequence of Dates in Life, and the Interpretation from Tables. The following is an outline for interpretation.

I. Computing and Drawing the Horoscope

1. *Birth Data*

   Correct birth data is the first requirement for accurate interpretation. You require the exact day, month, year, place and time of birth. Even when hospitals record exact birth times they are often inaccurate by five minutes or more. It is necessary to use birth data as given, even though you know it is estimated. Once interpretation has been done, it is possible to adjust the ASC to its correct position. Be especially careful of birth times given on the even hour or half-hour.

2. *Horoscope Computation*

   The horoscope must be calculated from ephemerides and tables of houses, or by computer as suggested in the introduction (and Appendix C). The computation should yield the degree and zodiac sign of the twelve houses including the ASC and MC, the ten planets and the node. Some computer horoscopes calculate and list all aspects, and the Life★Time Service printout dates all planets and sensitive points as well.

3. *Create Horoscope Diagram*

On the frontispiece of this book is a blank horoscope form on which you should draw your horoscope. For the first try you should photocopy this page in case of error. The procedure is to first draw in the radiating lines for the twelve house cusps; then to enter the positions of the ten planets and the node in their correct signs and houses; then draw in the aspect lines which connect planets to the ASC, MC and to each other. The final form should look like the example horoscopes in this book.

II. Determining the Sequence of Dates

4. *Date House and Sign Cusps*

Using the small disk photocopied from the frontispiece or the table in Appendix A, read off the dates in years and months of all house cusps in the horoscope, starting with conception point at the 9th House cusp. (See Chapter Three, pp. 55-61.)

5. *Date Planets and the Node*

Read off the dates of the planets and the node from conception to the age of ninety-nine years. (See Chapter Four, p. 78-79.)

6. *Determine and Date Sensitive Points*

Determine the sensitive points for any part of the horoscope you wish to study in depth. Usually this is from the age of twenty-three (the descendant) up to and beyond your present age, although it may be any time. The sensitive point locations also determine the dating of aspect combinations, as described in Chapter Five on p. 93-98.

The Life★Time Astrology print-out, described in Appendix C lists all house cusps, planets and sensitive points throughout life.

III. Individual Analysis (of each planet, personal and sensitive point)

7. *Planet by Sign*

   Each planet, personal point (MC and ASC) and sensitive point is first considered by its zodiac sign, describing its quality and mode of action. (See the left side of the Interpretation Tables in Chapter Six, pp. 108-132.)

8. *Planet by House*

   Each planet, personal and sensitive point is considered by house position (as demonstrated in Chapter Seven) and its age of registration is determined. The house location qualifies judgements such as conscious/ unconscious according to whether they are above or below the horizon; selfish/selfless according to whether the planet is in the left or right halves. (See the right side of the Interpretation Tables in Chapter Six, pp. 109-133, and Chapter Seven.)

9. *Planet Rulership, Exaltation or Element*

   Each planet is evaluated in strength according to whether it is in the sign or house it rules or is in detriment; within which it is exalted or in fall; or in an element which is congenial or uncongenial. (See Chapter Four, p. 66.)

10. *Planetary Personifications*

    Determine who the planet represents, and the characteristics this implies, qualified by the above factors. (See Chapter Seven throughout.)

11. *Aspect Constellations*

    For each planet or personal point, determine all planets and personal points which aspect them within permissible orbs of influence (Chapter Five, pp. 81-101.)

12. *Aspect Sequence*

    Determine the aspecting planets which register before, at and after the planet or personal point in question, date their sensitive points (See Chapter Five, p. 93-96), and determine the sequence of influences and the span of time covered by the constellation.

13. *Aspect Time Connections*

    Determine the dates of the initial registrations of the aspecting planets or personal points, whether they are back towards conception or ahead towards death.(See

Chapter Five, p. 96-98.)

14. *Aspect Personifications*
Determine the other personifications created by aspecting planets or personal points from the Aspect Interpretation Table in Chapter Six.

15. *Aspect Interpretation*
Look up the suggested interpretation of the aspect combination leading up to the planet and then away from the planet, all the time keeping the above information in mind.

IV. *Interpretation of the Life ★ Time*

16. *Before Conception*
Find the luminary, Sun or Moon, closest to the 9th House cusp in a clockwise direction as an indicator of the parent responsible for the impulse to conceive you, and evaluate as above in (III) and in Chapter Seven, pp. 151-156. Then analyze the other luminary according to the same rules.

17. *Conception Point*
Evaluate the conception point/9th House cusp by element, sign and aspect. (See Chapter Seven, p. 156.)

18. *9th House*
Interpret planets in the 9th House according to the procedure in steps 7-16 above.

19. *The Midheaven (MC)*
Evaluate the MC by element, sign and the very important sequence of aspect sensitive points around its registration.

20. *The 10th House*
21. *The 11th House*
22. *The 12th House*
23. *The Ascendant (ASC)*
Evaluate the birth moment by interpreting the sign on the ASC as the environment into which the birth occurred; the sequence of aspect sensitive points describe the events before, during and after birth and those people who were present or who affected the birth; and then the total blend of influences describe the personality. (See Chapter Seven, pp. 179-187.) The birth conditions and personifications are shown in the table in Chapter Seven, on p. 180-183.

24. *The 1st House*
25. *The 2nd House*
26. *The 3rd House*
27. *The 4th House*
28. *The 5th House*
29. *The 6th House*
30. *The 7th House/Descendant*

The 7th House cusp begins the objective, conscious half of the horoscope, being directly opposite the birth moment and registration of the personality. This cusp may be valued by taking the qualities of the sign on the cusp and whatever planets or sensitive points fall near the cusp. These will usually be planets which also aspect the Ascendant. From this time on, all sensitive points should be evaluated in the way prescribed in steps 7-15, with the following alterations:

– To interpret a sensitive point, first take the planet or sensitive point which immediately precedes it and interpret the aspect combination from the tables. This describes the circumstances leading into the event in question.

– The sensitive point itself is valued by the quality of the planet, its sign position, its house position, and the quality of its aspect (See Chapter Five, page 93.)

– The personification(s) of the sensitive point are determined by sign, house and aspect positions, as in the tables.

– The situation is described by the combination of the sensitive point with the next following planet or sensitive point.

31. *The 8th House*
32. *The 9th House/Death and Transcendent Point*

The 9th House cusp is sometimes passed during life and shows a great transition. The archetypal age is seventy-seven, although it can register as early as the forties or well past a hundred. This transition and its implications are described in Chapter Seven, pp. 226-231.

Interpretation of the horoscope involves many complicated steps, but with experience the entire process becomes very clear and easy, and the analysis becomes more and more accurate. The interpretation begins with a written listing of the planetary positions, house cusps, personal and sensitive points, and their various interpretations from the Interpretation Tables in Chapter Six. You should then take all the information and try to turn it into a life story. Follow the format and style of Chapter Seven and you will develop an understanding of interpretation.

When you identify characters in gestation, carry them through the rest of life by following the aspects lines. Events in early life are repeated and embellished at those times when their aspects or sensitive points register later in life. People's lives are more consistent, when seen from this viewpoint, than they often appear on the surface. In the beginning you will produce much more information than seems necessary, but this is edited to make a more concise interpretation. With time, you will discover the nature of the profound process of Life★Time Astrology and its implications.

The Horoscope Interpretation of John Lennon

The best way to illustrate Life★Time Astrology is with a complete horoscope analysis. The examples given in Chapter Seven show how individual planets and their constellations may be interpreted house by house, but the entire sequence of planets and aspects is vital to the interpretation of a whole life. Planets registering early in the horoscope provide a context within which later events may be seen, allowing us to understand life holistically.

The choice of an individual for this type of analysis is difficult, due to the many demands of the material which should be presented. It would not be fair to do such an analysis of an individual who is still alive, as it would be an infringement upon his or her future life. Yet, it should be a contemporary figure because our time is changing so rapidly, and historical figures would be much less relevant. Therefore, it must be someone who is contemporary but who has died in the recent past. The person must be important enough for his/her life to be in the common domain, and so that there is information available against which to compare the astrological analysis. Preferably he/she should have a creative life which expresses an inner reality apart from outer events, because Life★Time Astrology describes such psychic facts as an integral part of life. The primary criticism of many astrological proofs is that the events described are past and that the analysis takes advantage of retrospection. It is very difficult to resist the thought that events are fitted to the astrology, but I have tried not to bend astrological facts to fit the person. Most of the interpretation is, therefore, derived from the tables in this book, and includes aspects of John Lennon's reality which are not usually available to the public.

For all the above-noted reasons, I feel that the horoscope of John Lennon (Figure 24) is particularly relevant for our purpose. Lennon is symbolic of the generation born during the Second World War: his life and death carried the ambiguities and complexities of our present world. Although he was a leader of the most famous band the world has ever known, The Beatles, he was isolated, lonely and probably never met anyone who understood him, apart from Yoko Ono. He claimed to be more popular than Jesus; known to millions, but never really known at all. Many of his inner feelings came out in his songs, but he still remains controversial and unknowable. His music disturbed both critics and admirers, who variously attributed his inspiration to LSD-induced hallucinations, random choices from Alice in Wonderland, political commentary, eschatological literature or just trashy lyricism. None of these provides us with a cohesive, consistent picture, but his horoscope does.

With Life★Time Astrology we may describe the inner life of John Lennon which counterbalances and complements what we know of his outer public life. One of his most controversial songs, "I Am The Walrus" states his astrological character very clearly: "I am he as you are he as you are me as we are all together". As we shall see through the analysis, this phrase echoes the story of John Lennon's inner and outer life.

We must remember that everything about John Lennon's mother, father, relatives, wives, children and associates is reflected in his own mechanisms. Influences derived from his mother during gestation are very strong, deep and describe attitudes typical of the latter part of his strange life.

John Winston Lennon was born on 9 October 1940, at 06:30 p.m. (18:30) British Summer Time in Liverpool (For sources, see Appendix F).

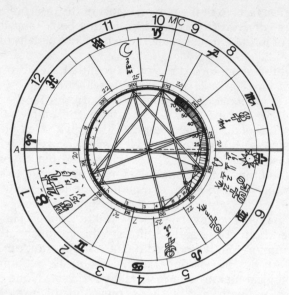

Figure 24: John Lennon's Horoscope

Before Conception

First we want to find which of John's parents is responsible for
his conception, as a metaphor for the initiating part of his
creative nature. To move in a clockwise direction from the
conception point at 20 Sagittarius, we come first to the Sun in
Libra in the 6th House. John's father is responsible for the
impulse to conceive a child, but as the Sun is below the horizon,
he is unconscious of this impulse. John's masculine side is
instinctively initiatory. The Sun in Libra shows an attempt to
balance a marriage relationship by providing a child as an
intermediary. The Sun in the 6th is absorption in work, as well
as a naive, remote and critical manner. (*Fred Lennon was a seaman
and was often away from his wife for months at a time.*)

As there is no direct aspect relationship between the Sun and
Moon, one must conclude that the parental relationship is
slight. Both Sun and Moon are in double air signs, so both
parents are ambiguous and idealistic.

The Moon in Aquarius follows the Sun in a clockwise
direction from conception point. The Aquarian qualities of
detachment, abstraction and the love of company are

dominant, especially as the 11th House is the natural house of Aquarius. This shows a friendly relationship, numerous friends, mainly women, but of superficial quality and short duration. (*Julia Lennon lived with her parents and was a cinema usherette.*)

Conception Point/9th House Cusp

The conception point registers at 20 Sagittarius, and the father's role is amplified by the sextile from the Sun (father). Sagittarius is sensual and materialistic on the lower level, but philosophical and independent on the higher level. The physical act of conception is pleasurable, yet both parents remain aloof. (*The contrast between sensual and philosophical describes John's spontaneous creative drive which was often silly, but carried a serious life view.*)

MC in Capricorn

(*35 weeks before birth = early February 1940*)
Capricorn MC shows John's mother concentrating upon herself, being forced to deal with practical matters. Conception is sensed physically, as Capricorn is an earth sign and shows emotional restraint.

The sextile of Mercury in Scorpio (7th) to the MC indicates that mother thinks (Mercury) about separating (Scorpio) from her relationship (7th House), and that her friends and family encourage this. Mercury in Scorpio is disruptive and sceptical.

The square of the Node in Libra produces joint difficulties and inconstancy in a relationship. The mother favours her own interests (MC) above those of her marriage. As the Node is family, the mother also differs with her own family about her marriage. (*Julia's sisters and family disapproved of her marriage and tried to convince her to leave.*)

Saturn and Jupiter in Taurus are in trine to the MC, the combination showing both restriction and optimism carried by doctor and parents, and probably manifest as morning sickness. Mother is ambiguous, as Saturn/Jupiter is manic-depressive. The combination is alternately materialistic and religious. (*Julia relied financially upon her parents and she did not want a child. Liverpool was being bombed at the time.*)

Venus in Virgo in trine to the MC is friends with whom she shares her taste in music and films, a great release to her.
(Note: The two major constellations in John Lennon's horoscope have Mercury in common. (See Figures 15 and 16 on p. 88-89.) Constellation B includes MC, Venus, Mercury, Jupiter, Saturn and Node while Constellation C includes Moon, Uranus, Mercury, Pluto, Neptune and Mars. The two constellations interweave throughout his life, but do not join up until the registration of Mercury at thirty-four years old. Constellation A is the Ascendant opposition Sun. In early life, the three major groups of planets must be treated as being separate from each other. Thus John has three parts of himself which are difficult to join together. His personality (Ascendant) and Sun (public face) are dualistic and are probably never resolved. Every horoscope must be broken down in this way.)

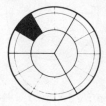

Moon in Aquarius and 11th House

(*31 weeks before birth = early March 1940*)
Because gestation is interpreted from his mother's viewpoint, the Moon refers to Julia's detachment and independence from her mother. There is much tension, due to the opposition, square and Mars aspects to the Moon.

The trine from Mars indicates tension, emotional intensity and impulsive acts, possibly effects from the war atmosphere of 1940 Liverpool. (*Fred was away at war, increasing Julia's concern for herself and her child.*)

The opposition from Pluto in Leo is directly due to the war. Mother's emotions (Moon) are abstracted and infiltrated by extreme emotion and fanaticism, generating maximum tension. (*Shocking the masses was inherent in John's musical career.*)

The square from Mercury in Scorpio is indecision when friends press his mother to decide about her relationship. (*Julia's mother opposed her relationship, and when Mercury registered at thirty-four years old John left Yoko and ran off with his secretary (Mercury)*).

The trine from Neptune shows uncertainty and inner vision, making his mother open to unconscious fantasy and unreality in her pregnancy.

The trine from Uranus is also tensely unpredictable and refers to physical safety (Taurus). The stress of carrying a child amidst such violent chaos pushed his mother's emotions to their limit.

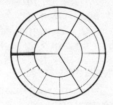

Ascendant Aries

(*Birth moment* = *October 1940*)
John Winston Lennon was born during a heavy bombing raid which jeopardised the entire hospital. Aries Ascendant is restless, assertive, impatient and easily derives from the warlike atmosphere.

The only aspect to the Ascendant is an opposition from the Libra Sun, indicating a separation from the father. As Libra is a double sign, the Sun also refers to a delivering doctor as a surrogate father image. Both ASC and Sun are in masculine signs, but unaspected to any other planets. (*Fred was away in the Navy when John was born, and his grandfather became a temporary father. John's involvement with the Beatles and his paternal surrogates – producer George Martin, manager Brian Epstein, the Maharishi Mahesh Yogi and, later the psychologist Arthur Janov reflect this theme. These men carried the missing father because from birth Fred gradually departed from John's life. The solar energy can do nothing but be projected onto the father and come back again – it has no other possible route.*)

Saturn and Jupiter in Taurus in the 1st House

(6 months old = April 1941)
Saturn and Jupiter refer to grandparents and show restriction followed by expansion, and isolation in spite of support. (*Fred sent little money and Julia abandoned John to her parents.*)

The opposition from Mercury is a separation notification by letter. (*When John was three months old Fred was supposed to return to be drafted, but missed the boat and found himself imprisoned on Ellis Island, New York − the immigration processing centre for the US − for desertion. At the exact registration of Saturn and Jupiter, Fred was in jail again in North Africa, which signalled the end of the marriage, even though he sent support for a further eighteen months. It is ironic that thirty-four years later John was denied citizenship to the US by the same immigration authorities!*)

The trine from the MC in Capricorn shows that John's grandparents' aims are material and practical. (*His late songs "Born in a Prison" and "Isolation" both reflect his insular early life. The isolation was a foretaste of John's isolation when, years later, he was a millionaire, yet alone.*)

Uranus in Taurus in the 1st House

(10 months old = August 1941)
Uranus in Taurus shows tension, restlessness and financial instability affecting John's personality, which is original and wilful.

The trine from the Moon shows mother creating great emotional tension through sudden unconscious changes of mind, expressed as attention to John alternating with resistance. (*This characterized his relations with women and described his creative process.*)

The trine from Neptune in Virgo is confused, unstable and again unconscious, but generates a vivid inner fantasy life in John at this very early age.

(*At this time Julia's sister Mary, called by John Aunt Mimi, gradually began taking care of John while at his grandparents house.*

Aunt Mimi performed the maternal role that neither Julia nor her parents could. John carried a duality about both parental roles in his life.)

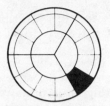

Pluto in Leo in the 5th House

(5 years old = October 1945)
Pluto in Leo indicates extraordinary achievements at school and dramatic self expression, creativity and talent. The 5th House is dynamic, self aware, forceful, creative and is the time of primary school education.

The sextile from Mars in Libra shows activity and ruthlessness channelled into speculative 5th House directions through partnerships with other boys. (*John was rebellious at the Dovedale Primary School and tried to run away continually.*)

The opposition from the Moon in Aquarius represents extreme emotional expression which produces shocks from what initially appear to be a games (5th House). Also involved in this T-square is the square from Mercury in Scorpio in the 7th House, where again there are thoughts of separation in a relationship related to John's parents, and the expression of excessive opposition and crudeness. (*Fred returned and took John on holiday to Blackpool, planning vaguely to take him away to New Zealand and applied persuasive emotional threats to this end. This would have been amplified by the generational Plutonian wartime influences in the air.*)

Venus in Virgo in the 6th House

(9 years and 2 months old = December 1949)
At seven years three months old John entered the large 6th

House of school and work. Venus indicates art, music and friends, but the sign Virgo is critical, perfectionist and cold. The 6th House is the entrance into puberty and a Virgoan naive expression of sexuality.

The trine from the Capricorn MC shows individuality and tangibility to his artistic creative drive, yet vanity and conceit also.

The sextile from Mercury in Scorpio again indicates cleverness, but the omnipresent sense of separation. Success with girls, with writing and other aesthetic interests are qualified by the innate cruelty of Scorpio. (*John was an entertainer at school, wrote his own books in his own fantasy language, and illustrated them as well.*)

Neptune in Virgo in the 6th House

(*14 years and 7 months old = May 1955*)
Neptune in Virgo indicates great sensitivity directed towards criticism of others, almost a defence mechanism against others.

The trine from Uranus is inspired, mystical, artistic and unstable, and refers back to the 1st House when parental security was least stable. (*John was shocked by the death of his Uncle George amidst his increasing creative drive.*)

The trine from the Moon in Aquarius is refined, imaginative and inspired feelings which attach themselves to women. (*John began to be involved with girls and friends, and reestablished contact with his mother, occasionally singing with her during visits.*)

Libra Time in the 6th House

(*16 years old = October 1956*)
At sixteen years old John enters the sign of partnership and sublimation, through which he storms until twenty-eight years six months old (1969).

Mars in Libra in the 6th House

(*16 years and 8 months old = June 1957*)
The distance between Neptune and Mars is too great to be a conjunction, but can be interpreted as a Mars/Neptune aspect, showing the shift from the sensitivity and dreaminess of Neptune to the aggression and strong desire of Mars. Mars in Libra is very social, involved in leading public events and

idealism, while in the 6th House it is hard work, endurance and a method applied skilfully. (*The Mars personification was probably the effect of rock'n'rollers Elvis Presley and Jerry Lee Lewis upon John's self-image, as well as his competition and friendship with Paul McCartney.*)

The trine from the Moon in Aquarius is a close but abstract relationship with his mother which is interrupted. Aquarius also shows a duplication of the feminine image at this time. (*John's mother was killed in an automobile accident, which shocked him deeply. At about the same time he met and won Cynthia Powell, who later became his first wife.*)

The sextile from Pluto indicates great effort, strength and ambition in a creative (Leo) way, manifest in a work relationship with others with the aim of recognition. (*John and Paul met George Harrison in mid-1957 and they formed the Quarrymen who played aggressive and intensely rhythmical music.*)

The square from the MC is the intense competition within the group and the need for John to establish his personality as dominant and resolute. (*There was a power struggle between John and Paul which communicated itself through their music.*)

Node in Libra in the 6th House

(19 years and 7 months old = May 1960)
The Node in Libra is a formal business partnership (6th House) that receives criticism, but is adaptable and has an aptitude for public affairs. The square from the MC shows group objectives that are very strong and which rely upon individual differences being sublimated by the collective. (*The Beatles were fiercely individualistic as they played and lived together in the red-light district of Hamburg.*)

Sun in Libra in the 6th House

(21 years and 11 months old = September 1962)
The Sun in Libra registers in September 1962, which indicates contact with the public, success, consistency and through the 6th House a methodical improvement in working circumstances, all made possible by surrogate father images, as Libra is a double sign. (*Brian Epstein took over their management. George Martin of the record company EMI auditioned the Beatles and in August 1962 John became a father. In September 1962, the Beatles recorded "Love Me Do", a classic Libran concept, and by the following*

year Beatlemania had swept the world.)

The only aspect is the opposition from the Ascendant in Aries which registers also at the Descendant at the age of twenty-three years five months old, in April 1964. (*John's public persona was already at odds with an inner tension to be independent and self-assertive. He was quoted at this time, "I knew what we were doing, and I knew the game. So I let it happen. We were selling out all right, right from the moment we began to get really big". At this exact time the Beatles appeared on the Ed Sullivan Show and at Carnegie Hall in New York, played the Palladium in London and generated an estimated fifty million dollars of commerce. In May 1966, John said that the Beatles were more popular than Jesus. By then he was totally disenchanted with his popularity and within months the Beatles played their last live performance together.*)

Note: From this time on, the sensitive points are interpreted as well as the planets.

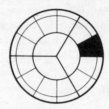

Sensitive Inconjunct Uranus at 25 Libra in the 7th House

(26 years and 4 months old = February 1967)
The sensitive inconjunct aspect of 150 degrees from Uranus is treated as a tensioned Uranus in Libra and the 7th House. This indicates new relationships, divorce, irritability, affairs in quick association, eccentric relations and rebelliousness. (*John experienced disillusionment with suburban success, began to break away and wrote "Strawberry Fields Forever', a reference to a children's home near where he lived in Liverpool. His music evoked the stream of consciousness typical of the earlier registration of Uranus in his childhood.*)

Sensitive Semisextile Neptune at 26 Libra in the 7th House

(26 years and 7 months old = May 1967)
The time between Uranus and Neptune is treated as Uranus/Neptune aspect indicating unconsciousness, drugs, inner vision, inspiration with mysticism and journeys of importance. (*During early 1967 John took many LSD trips which*

changed both his life and music.)

Neptune is an uncertain relation indicating receptivity, high ideals, drug abuse, impulsive acts and seductiveness. (*The Beatles met the Maharishi Yogi and felt misled. John wrote the song "Sexy Sadie" and discovered that his mentor Brian Epstein had died of a drug overdose. John then meets and sponsors an exhibition by an avant-garde artist, Yoko Ono, his future wife.*)

Scorpio Time in the 7th House

(28 years and 6 months old = April 1969)
At this time John enters the Scorpio time which takes him until the end of his life. Scorpio shows withdrawal, separation, occultism and reliance upon others' emotions, intuition and energies. (*John divorced Cynthia and joined with Yoko Ono. They spent interminable time in bed, in bags, in the nude, in court for drugs and in conflict with everyone. This was their way of campaigning for Peace. The film "Let It Be" portrayed the estrangement and isolation, which led to John (and Yoko) doing Janov's Primal Scream Therapy as an antidote for his self-obsession. He declared in the song "God" that denial of mother, father, magic, religion and all else culminates only in his belief in himself and Yoko. . .'That's reality!'*)

Sensitive Sextile Venus Square Moon at 3 Scorpio in the 7th House

(30 years and 7 months old = April 1971)
This contact is feminine and qualified by the Scorpionic element of, separation. Moon/Venus produces love, devotion, conception and graceful involvement, but the square aspect creates great tension and difficulties. (*John and Yoko were devoted to each other and to art. They left for the USA and unsuccessfully tried to have a child, as Yoko had many miscarriages. John did his solo album "Imagine".*)

Sensitive Square Pluto at 4 Scorpio in the 7th House

(31 years and 2 months old = December 1971)
This is the destruction of existing behaviour patterns affecting relationships (7th House). (*John's marriage to Yoko was very tense amidst their life in New York.*)

Mercury at 8 Scorpio in the 7th House

(34 years old = October 1974)
Mercury indicates verbal criticism in a relationship (7th House), sarcasm, arguments and separation. All previous registrations of Mercury in Scorpio produce traumatic events with women. The aspects to Mercury range from the sextile from Venus three and a half years earlier to the oppositions from Jupiter and Saturn which register four years later. The Mercury registration thus covers almost eight years of John's life.

The square from the Moon and the sextile from Venus show a deterioration of his marriage, with another woman or artistic endeavour replacing her. The square from Pluto shows great persuasion and understanding, but also cunning secrecy behind the scenes. The sextile from the MC just before Mercury is John's attempt to analyze and know himself, but he only succeeded in finding himself more confused than before. Mercury is an intermediary who allows John to separate himself from his relationship. (*In 1974 John left Yoko for her secretary and entered a time of alcoholism, promiscuity and excess which lasted for 18 months.*)

Sensitive Semisextile Node at 11 Scorpio in the 7th House

(35 years and 4 months old = February 1976)
This shows association through force of circumstances, cooperation and teamwork in relation to the public. The Node being in Scorpio paradoxically means that he withdraws from associations as well as entering others. (*John and Yoko were reconciled at a party.*)

Sensitive Semisquare Neptune at 11 Scorpio in the 7th House

(35 years and 8 months old = June 1976)
The Neptune/Node contact is an idealistic association evoking spiritual contact, but the tensioning aspect produces antisocial behaviour and disturbances in John's inner life. (*At this time Yoko became pregnant, and Sean was born on John's birthday in 1976. John was devoted to his son and exchanged roles with Yoko, becoming a househusband to Sean.*)

Sensitive Opposition Saturn and Jupiter at 13 Scorpio in the 7th House

(37 years and 3 months = January 1978)
This is patient waiting for the resolution of practical matters, being diplomatic and developing real estate. There are two very different tendencies in operation, from the spiritual and metaphysical philosophy of Jupiter to the overtly materialistic indulgence of Saturn. *(John and Yoko split responsibilities; John became mother and Yoko the father, dealing with and resolving John's longstanding financial problems. Their immigration struggle was won, evoking father Fred's dilemma earlier when Jupiter and Saturn initially registered. They purchased property all over the US, planes and boats, using John's estimated 150 million dollar worth.)*

Sensitive Semisextile Sun at 16 Scorpio in the 7th House

(39 years and 7 months old = May 1980)
Sun in Scorpio is wilful, forceful, dynamic, imperturbable and again wishes to enter the world of new associations and recognition. *(It evoked the earlier time when the Beatles come into public view. John emerged from isolation and made an album "Double Fantasy" with Yoko. They both developed an interest in astrology and shared responsibilities equally.)*

Death at 17 Scorpio

(40 years and 2 months old = December 1980)
Having been a recluse for five years, John became more and more visible. After mixing a song "Walking On Thin Ice", John was shot dead in front of his home in New York City at 22:50 EST on the 8th of December, 1980. The sensitive semisquare from Mars shows, when combined with the Sun, strained relations, violence, daring and contention.

John Lennon's assassin Mark Chapman also has Sun opposition Ascendant, but in the signs Taurus and Scorpio. The most significant connection was that Chapman's Venus is at 19 Aries 45, a mere minute of arc from John's Ascendant. Chapman identified so closely with John that he thought he was John. Chapman felt he looked like Lennon and even signed his name. A further connection is that the Uranus (shock, change) in Yoko's horoscope is within one degree of this connection, at 20 Aries.

Conclusion

We can understand from this Life★Time analysis of John Lennon's horoscope that his life was far from the pleasant idyll many believed. His music and life emerged from intense emotional pain, largely created by his young and irresponsible mother and his father who was never there. Throughout his life he repeated the patterns set out by those parents: his progress through the sixties reflected his mother and her dreamy existence, while he disappeared from his own first son for long periods of time. The essential drive for separation of his parents also characterizes the incredible strain John Lennon brought to bear on his own marriages. And, although he found surrogate fathers throughout his life, most of them exited awkwardly from his life's stage. Through his later music and his lifelong inner search he attempted to transcend his fate, primarily through his feminine nature as reflected in his wife.

The overall process of John Lennon's life and horoscope is revealing as a device for understanding and confronting life itself. Lennon used the experiences and feelings behind appearances in his difficult life as subject matter for profound messages to his entire generation. The pain and silliness, the joy of love and the torture of abandonment, the belief in God and the nihilism of the twentieth century, the espousal of "Give Peace a Chance" to the cruel assassination. All these components are described in John Lennon's horoscope.

★ Chapter Nine ★
Future Tense

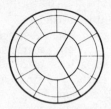

Once the story of our life is reconstructed, we must act upon it. The difficult events of life, their causes and the people who caused them, are as important a part of us as the glorious achievements we attribute to ourselves. Everything in our life is our responsibility and comes into play every day. Every successive perception of the rest of our life will be compared to the total of all previous days we have lived, in accordance with Life★Time Astrology.

The role we have been chosen to play in life is ordained before we are born. Our parents, siblings, relatives, location, race, religion and many other factors are determined absolutely at birth. We cannot alter even the smallest detail. We must understand the implications of our own life and its known and unknown factors. We must use them rather than spend life fighting them – they will not change! We can change appearance, name, location and act, but the essence within remains. We must see ourself and our life just as it is before we can transform and transcend the whole.

Many people at present want to change themselves – they want to change their lives around and be someone other than who they are; they want their current life and the problems inherent in that life to disappear overnight, and to wake up one morning and find themselves resurrected in perfect form. Yet, who would they be, if not themselves donning another disguise? Would you like to have no past? It is just not possible to change who we are, only how we are.

Dramatic parts are preset. The individual words, the gestures and the conclusion of a role are identical for every actor or actress who plays the role. Some actors and actresses cannot handle the part because they do not fit or cannot develop the character: they cannot bring it to life. Other actors and actresses not only play a role but transform it into a reflection of all humanity and all life. Every individual carries meaning communicable to an entire audience.

True understanding of the essence beneath or behind appearances is the key to being a transcendental being rather than a machine. Great actors and actresses bring out the essence of even minor parts. To bring truth to life is the task we must perform in being ourself. First we must understand our life and its roles, and then learn how to transcend the part. Every act and circumstance of life can carry understanding and power.

The difficulties of character and life are positive advantages because they give us the opportunity to overcome them. Every life is interesting, as much a result of difficult aspects as of positive points of character. Our life is the source of our creativity.

Prediction

In the framework of traditional astrology prediction is considered a separate function from character analysis. Many, if not most, astrologers provide extremely accurate and perceptive character analysis, but are unwilling to make predictions. Part of the reason for this unlikely situation is that without the Life★Time Scale it is very difficult to make accurate predictions. Existing techniques are quite unreliable, to the extent that even the best professionals resist prediction. The mainstream in astrology is moving towards a psychological approach and most modern literature is oriented in this direction. Prediction, which is what most people think of as the mainstay of astrology is dismissed.

The great advantage of Life★Time Astrology is that psychology and prediction are integral and natural parts of the process of life. Predictions are made in exactly the same way and with the same vocabulary as the past is analysed. A virtue of the time scale is that most future events are manifestations of earlier events, and as such may be described in relation to these earlier events. An example is the horoscope of John Lennon, in which the conjunction of Saturn and Jupiter registered when he was 6 months old. On the basis of the sign and house location of Saturn and Jupiter, and the planets in aspect to them, we can determine what happened to the child John and who participated in the events described. At that time John was a child and had no control over what occurred when his mother and father both abandoned him. He was left with surrogate parents; his grandparents and aunt. The time of the opposition is thirty- seven years three months old, when we would expect a situation opposite to the earlier event, except that now John would be the father and his own son the child! When the opposition registered in 1978, John took responsibility for his son. John won his struggle with American immigration authorities and was allowed to stay in the USA, reflecting his father's immigration struggle at the original registration. John compensated for his lack of a parent by devoting himself to his own child, thus making a positive turnaround of the earlier difficult situation.

Predictions are made at the registration of natal planets in the future and at the sensitive points of planets which have already registered in our past. Each time a sensitive point comes up, we have an opportunity to see the equivalent part of ourself. If Saturn and Jupiter represent grandparents early in life and the conjunction means the combination of optimism/philosophy and pessimism/materialism, when the sensitive points register in late life, we have the chance to rectify or transform the way our grandparents acted towards us. In life the basic patterns of behaviour remain the same, only our attitude towards these patterns may change. We can either remain unconscious and unaware of the patterns, or try to stay awake, see them clearly and transform them.

When we reconstruct our life using Life★Time Astrology, the fact that we can date every event in the past accurately means that we can investigate these events astrologically and experientially. By collaging together the astrological pattern and the tapestry of our memory, we can discover the correspondences between the two. The combination is a bit like the knots of memories interweaving the design of a life pattern to make a beautiful Persian carpet. Once we know what behaviour patterns are typical of the previous registrations of the serious Saturn and who acted the patterns out in our life, we can understand the implications of Saturn sensitive points which register ahead in the time scale, in our future. To know our past is a prerequisite to knowing our future.

Even when we do not have natal planets registering after our present age in the horoscope, we can determine and date the future pattern of sensitive points as far ahead as we wish. By combining the procedures explained in Chapters Three, Four and Five for finding the location and date of the house cusps, planets and sensitive points, we have a picture of our future, and can interpret it as in Chapter Seven. The use of the Life ★ Time printouts described in the appendix allows such an analysis without any calculations at all.

```
 90  VENUS        JAN  1982  23.26  TAU...
135  SUN          SEP  1982  24.18  TAU...
150  MARS         OCT  1983  25.46  TAU...
120  JUPITER      DEC  1984  27.16  TAU...
 60  MOON         JAN  1985  27.21  TAU...
***0 CUSP 8       MAR  1985  27.30  TAU...
150  ASCENDANT    MAY  1987   0.14  GEM...
 45  NODE         JUN  1990   3.51  GEM...
120  NEPTUNE      OCT  1992   6.25  GEM...
 30  SATURN       JUN  1993   7.09  GEM...
150  SUN          JUL  1995   9.18  GEM...
 60  PLUTO        DEC  1995   9.45  GEM...
***0 URANUS       MAR  1996  10.00  GEM...
 60  M.C.         FEB  1997  10.51  GEM...
 45  MOON         AUG  1998  12.21  GEM...
```

Figure 25: Life ★ Time Computer Printout
The printout lists the MC, ASC, Node and the planets in their order from conception. Each position is dated by month and year and located by zodiacal position. The sensitive points are preceded by the number of aspect degrees they are away from their natal position. Natal positions are preceded by three stars.

Figure 25 is a computer printout of a series of planets, house cusps and sensitive points with their dates and zodiacal locations. The interpretation follows the same structure as we have seen described in detail. The salient points in such a predictive analysis would be as follows for the brief span shown in the illustration:

1. The only planet registering is Uranus in March 1996 in the sign Gemini and the 8th House.
2. There is a transition from Taurus to Gemini in May 1987.

3. The first five sensitive points are in the 7th House, and in March 1985 the 8th House is entered.
4. Each sensitive point, for example 120 Neptune, is treated as an event occurring at the indicated time of October 1992. This event is interpreted as Neptune in Gemini and Neptune in the 8th House, positively aspected.
5. The circumstances leading up to 120 Neptune are indicated by the transition from 45 Node to 120 Neptune and is treated as a Node/Neptune aspect covering the time from June 1990 to October 1992.
6. The affects of this event are indicated by the transition from 120 Neptune to 30 Saturn, which is interpreted as a Neptune/Saturn aspect.
7. The future is described as a process just as the past is described as a process. There is no disturbance in this continuous process.

Our Future

The question always asked about astrology is: If there is 'free will' or is the universe a clockwork in which everything down to the smallest detail is totally predictable? Are the events in our lives destined to happen whatever we do to prevent or alter them? Are we a pawn of a higher power which predetermines all mechanisms in the universe?

Life★Time Astrology defines a universe which is very similar to that of the new physics. The static Euclidean-Newtonian universe has given way to a vibrant, relativistic Einsteinian universe where flux reigns. Science no longer believes that there are basic building blocks of which the universe is made, but only webs of event relationships. The interactions between particles are more important than the particles themselves. (See Capra, *The Tao of Physics* and Zukav, *The Dancing Wu Li Masters*) Everything in the universe is related to everything else because everything is composed of waves of energy, and because of this the patterns of events may be predicted, but only by using probability. The physicist takes the initial state of an observed system and determines what the possible pasts and later states of the same system will be within certain probabilities. With Life★Time Astrology we take an observed system (our life) at an initial point (birth) and predict a sequence of earlier (gestation and childhood) and later states (our future). Using accumulated astrological observations of the behaviour of the planets in relation to each other the cycles of our probable future pattern can be dated and interpreted.

The movements of the planets round the horoscope are similar to the standing waves physicists use to make predictions. In astrology there is a probability that a certain event is to happen at a particular time. As we can see from Figure 26, a planet in the horoscope makes a standing wave pattern round the circle of our lifetime. At the peaks and troughs, events of the character of the planet are more probable than at the intermediate points, where there is the least likelihood of an event carrying the planetary influence. When all the peaks and troughs are dated by the time scale (the peaks and troughs are sensitive points), we have a picture of our probable life in time, showing the times when planetary influences will affect us. When the waves of all the planets are superimposed, as in the Life★Time printouts, the resulting pattern of interference shows an accurate probabilistic pattern for the most critical events in our life. Our free will is concerned

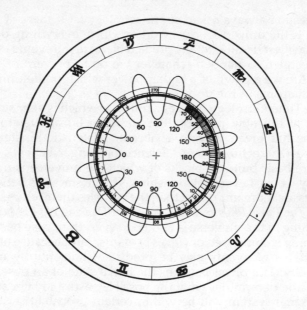

Figure 26: Harmonics
A planet at 0 Aries generates harmonics around the entire circle at 30 (and also 45) degree increments. At each of these harmonic positions a vibration of the quality of the original event would function, and each position can be dated throughout life.

with the way in which we interpret and use the events and their patterns in our life.

The psychologist Carl Jung stated that maximum free will is equivalent to maximum consciousness. We are not free to change most components of our being such as our physical appearance, innate intelligence, genetic background or national origin, but we can opt to be aware or unaware of ourself. The less aware we are of our characteristics and life, the more mechanical and predictable we are. The true object of Life★Time Astrology is to present us with our life pattern, past, present and future, with which we can compare and organize our memories and attitudes. Only by knowing our life script thoroughly can we perform our role in life effectively, interpret events faithfully and convey as much meaning as possible. The more self-aware we are, the less we resist being ourself. Many people do not understand who they are and, as a result, are their own worst enemy and greatest barrier to living a whole life. We must use both the easy and difficult components of our character to achieve wholeness. We could say that maximum consciousness is equivalent to maximum wholeness.

The Astrological Memory System

Apart from its use as a way of determining character and life events, astrology also functions as a method for organising the mind. (Cf. Frances Yates, *The Art of Memory*). The qualities of the planets, signs, houses and aspects are categories of existence by which life events may be described and stored. Once we know that Sun/Moon contacts refer to male/female relationships, all data about our own and others' relationships are unconsciously filed in that category. All we must then do to recall what we know of relationships or to compare our knowledge of relationships to someone else's is to explore the mental category 'Sun/Moon'. When we read of such relationships, observe them in life or the cinema, or wish to understand them, we place such perceptions in their appropriate field. Eventually we order our entire field of life perceptions in this way. As it is organically based on geometrical patterns as described in this book, the relations between categories and the distribution of the categories are clear and natural. Our memory improves, the quality of our experience improves and we benefit from our experience, rather than throwing it away.

An advantage of ordering our memory astrologically is that we are participating in an organizational system which has been in operation for many thousands of years and which has the benefit of all humankind's experience, back to the roots of life. Carl Jung believed that knowledge of the stars involved retrieving information projected there by people for untold millennia. The planet Jupiter thus carries all philosophical or religious concepts of all men and women, and to understand Jupiter is to tap into its essence and to gain access to this unparalleled reservoir of our collective heritage. We identify and assimilate the ancient gods and goddesses into our present identity as integral parts of a whole which reflects the entire history of our universe.

Life★Time Astrology is a key which we may use to unlock our own life, and in understanding ourself obtain a more profound understanding of all beings and all life.

★ Bibliography ★

Sourcebooks

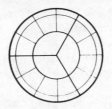

Beard, Ruth M., *An Outline of Piaget's Developmental Psychology*, 1969, Routledge & Kegan Paul, London.

Bohm, David, *Wholeness and the Implicate Order*, 1980, Routledge & Kegan Paul, London.

Capra, Fritjof, *The Tao of Physics*, 1975, Wildwood House, London.

Collin, Rodney, *The Theory of Celestial Influence*, 1954, Robinson and Watkins, London.

Cornell, Dr. H. L., *Encyclopedia of Medical Astrology* (Revised Edition), 1972, Llewellyn Publications and Samuel Weiser, New York.

Davison, Ron, *Astrology*, 1963, Arco Publishing Company, New York.

Dossey, Dr. Larry, *Space, Time & Medicine*, 1982, Shambala, Boulder.

Du Nouy, Lecomte, *Biological Time*, 1936, Methuen, London.

Ebertin, Reinhold, *The Combination of Stellar Influences*, 1981, The American Federation of Astrologers, Tempe, Arizona.

Erlewine, Michael, *Manual of Computer Programming for Astrologers*, 1980, Matrix, Big Rapids, Michigan.

Flanagan, Geraldine Lux, *The First Nine Months*, 1970, Heinemann, London.

Fraser, J. T. (Editor), *The Voices of Time*, 1968, Allen Lane, London.

Hone, Margaret, *The Modern Textbook of Astrology*, 1951, L. N. Fowler, London.

Huber, Bruno & Louise, *Man and His World*, 1978, Weiser, New York.

Jung, Carl, *Psychological Types*, 1923, Routledge & Kegan Paul, London.

Laing, R. D., *The Facts of Life*, 1976, Allen Lane, London.

Mann, A. T., *The Phenomenon Book of Calendars 1979-1980*, 1979, Simon & Schuster, New York and Dragon's World, London.

......, *The Round Art*, 1979, Dragon's World, London and Mayflower, New York.

Mayo, Jeff, *Astrology*, 1964, Hodder and Stoughton, London.

Rudyhar, Dane, *The Astrology of Personality*, 1963, Doubleday, Garden City.

Sheldrake, Rupert, *A New Science of Life*, 1981, Blond & Briggs, London.

Watson, James, *The Double Helix*, 1968, Weidenfeld and Nicolson, London.

Yates, Frances, *The Art of Memory*, 1966, Routledge & Kegan Paul, London.

Zukav, Gary, *The Dancing Wu Li Masters*, 1979, Rider and Hutchinson, London.

Appendix A

Table for Converting Age in Years into Degrees from the ASC

To find the number of degrees from the ASC equivalent to a certain age, we take the degrees opposite the age below in the table and add them to the ASC. Use the degree equivalents from 0 to 360 as in the inner ring at the left. When the sum is greater than 360, we must subtract 360 for the correct result.

Example: An ASC of 19 Leo = 139°   true longitude, at 57 years old

$$\begin{array}{r} 139° \\ +\ 225° \\ \hline 364° \\ -360 \\ \hline 004° \end{array}$$

004° true longitude is 4° Aries

Age	Degrees from Ascendant	Age	Degrees from Ascendant	Age	Degrees from Ascendant
01	043.29	34	198.46	67	233.33
02	066.52	35	200.15	68	234.19
03	082.57	36	201.41	69	235.04
04	095.13	37	203.05	70	235.48
05	105.08	38	204.27	71	236.32
06	113.28	39	205.46	72	237.16
07	120.39	40	207.04	73	237.58
08	126.58	41	208.20	74	238.40
09	132.36	42	209.34	75	239.22
10	137.41	43	210.46	76	240.03
11	142.18	44	211.57	77	240.43
12	146.33	45	213.06	78	241.23
13	150.29	46	214.13	79	242.03
14	154.09	47	215.19	80	242.42
15	157.33	48	216.24	81	243.20
16	160.46	49	217.28	82	243.58
17	163.47	50	218.30	83	244.36
18	166.38	51	219.31	84	245.13
19	169.20	52	220.30	85	245.50
20	171.55	53	221.29	86	246.26
21	174.22	54	222.27	87	247.02
22	176.42	55	223.24	88	247.37
23	178.57	56	224.19	89	248.12
24	181.06	57	225.14	90	248.47
25	183.09	58	226.07	91	249.21
26	185.08	59	227.00	92	249.55
27	187.03	60	227.52	93	250.28
28	188.54	61	228.43	94	251.02
29	190.41	62	229.33	95	251.34
30	192.24	63	230.23	96	252.07
31	194.04	64	231.11	97	252.39
32	195.41	65	231.59	98	253.11
33	197.15	66	232.46	99	253.42
				100	254.14

Appendix B

Conversion Formulae for Pocket Calculators

In addition to using the calculation tables on page 000 in this book, the position of any planet at a given date may be determined by a simple formula with a pocket calculator. We can calculate degrees from the ASC into years of age, or vice versa.

Degrees from the ASC into Years Decimal

Years Decimal = $((x + 120)/120)$ *INV LOG* − 10) * .0766

Where x = *number of degrees from the ASC in true longitude*
Where * = *multiply*

The answer is given in Years Decimal as 25.75 years would be twenty-five years and .75 of a year, or 9 months. To find the month during the year multiply the decimal times 12 months. (.75 year times 12 months = 9 months)

Years Decimal into Degrees from the ASC

Degrees from the ASC = $((y/.0766) + 10)$ *LOG* * 120 − 120 + *ASC*

Where y = *Age in Years Decimal*
Where * = *multiply*
Where *ASC* = *Ascendant in true longitude (degrees from 0 Aries)*

The answer is given in true longitude in the horoscope. To find degrees from the ASC, do not add the ASC at the end of the formula.

The author thanks Ad Strack van Schijndel of Holland for these formulae.

Your personal Life★Time dates may be ordered from

Astro Computing Services
P.O. Box 16430
San Diego, CA 92116
(619) 297-9203

or call toll free 800-826-1085 to order by using MasterCard or Visa. Please specify the date, time, and place of birth when ordering either a natal horoscope or a report of your Life★Time dates.

Further Studies and Uses for Life★Time Astrology

Once the periphery of your horoscope is graded with dates according to Life★Time Astrology, many other systems may also be added. The Midpoints of the planets are points at which the influence of pairs of planets join. The 156 direct midpoints may all be dated accurately around your horoscope. The aspects to these direct midpoints, called 'indirect midpoints' may also be dated.

Transiting planets are the actual present-time positions of the planets in the sky. The transits may be dated in the time scale also. As they move around your horoscope, they evoke the times in your life where they fall or other planets which they aspect. When a planet transits your natal 3rd House, it keys off whatever events happened when you were 2 to 4 years old.

The standard directional systems of astrology are Progressions, Solar Arc Directions and Primary Directions. The positions of all planets in any of these directional systems may be dated with the Life★Time Scale.

The Solar Return is another predictive system which interfaces with Life★Time Astrology. The Solar Return is the horoscope of the moment when the Sun returns to the exact position each year as it was at your birth. The resultant horoscope describes one year, from birthday to birthday, and its events key off various combinations of natal planets and their original registration times. This allows you to consider the present in light of the past and future of your life.

Life★Time Astrology provides the ground against which all other systems of astrology may be accurately compared. A sequel to this book, Life★Time Prediction, will explore these predictive systems in great detail.

John Lennon's Birth Information

The birth time of 06:30 p.m. British Summer Time was given to Roger Elliott by John Lennon, and used by Ray Connolly in *"John Lennon 1940-1980, A Biography"* (1980) and by Hunter Davie in *"The Beatles"* (1968, reissued 1981). The same time is given in Fowler's *"Compendium"*, but is incorrectly calculated for 06:30 p.m. GMT instead of British Summer Time, a time difference of one hour. A further verification of this time is that John Lennon's Aunt Mimi believed it to be the correct, which is in turn verified by Fred Lennon's second wife, the astrologer Pauline Stone of Brighton.

An incorrect variant 08:30 a.m. BST is given by Sybil Leek in *"Astrology"* (1972), by Pauline Hayward of the Moore School of Astrology, and by Lois Rodden in *"The American Book of Charts"* (1978). A further incorrect version is given in *"Transit"* Journal, Issue No. 35, where a time of 07:00 p.m. BST is erroneously attributed to Davies.

★ *Index* ★

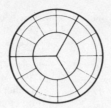